Romans
Galatians

ABOUT THE AUTHORS

General Editor

Clinton E. Arnold (PhD, University of Aberdeen), professor and chairman, department of New Testament, Talbot School of Theology, Biola University, Los Angeles, California

Romans:

Douglas J. Moo (PhD, University of St. Andrews), Blanchard professor of New Testament, Wheaton College Graduate School, Wheaton, Illinois

Galatians:

Ralph P. Martin (PhD, University of London, King's College), distinguished scholar in residence, Fuller Theological Seminary, Haggard School of Theology, Azusa Pacific University, Logos Evangelical Seminary, El Monte, California; *Julie L. Wu* (PhD, Fuller Theological Seminary), vice president and professor of New Testament, China Bible Seminary, Hong Kong, China.

Zondervan Illustrated Bible Backgrounds Commentary

Romans
Galatians

Douglas J. Moo
Ralph P. Martin
Julie L. Wu

Clinton E. Arnold   *general editor*

ZONDERVAN®

ZONDERVAN.com/
AUTHORTRACKER
follow your favorite authors

Zondervan Illustrated Bible Backgrounds Commentary: Romans, Galatians
    Romans—Copyright © 2002 by Douglas J. Moo
    Galatians—Copyright © 2002 by Ralph P. Martin and Julie Wu

Requests for information should be addressed to:

Zondervan, *Grand Rapids, Michigan 49530*

Library of Congress Cataloging-in-Publication Data
    Zondervan illustrated Bible backgrounds commentary / Clinton E. Arnold, general editor.
      p.cm.
    Includes bibliographical references.
    ISBN-10: 0-310-27833-3
    ISBN-13: 978-0-310-27833-7
    1. Bible. N.T.—Commentaries. I. Arnold, Clinton E.
    BS2341.52.Z66 2001
    225.7—dc21   2001046801
                                            CIP

Printed in China

Interior design by Sherri L. Hoffman

08 09 10 11 12 13 • 12 11 10 9 8 7 6 5 4 3 2

CONTENTS

INTRODUCTION

All readers of the Bible have a tendency to view what it says it through their own culture and life circumstances. This can happen almost subconsiously as we read the pages of the text.

When most people in the church read about the thief on the cross, for instance, they immediately think of a burglar that held up a store or broke into a home. They may be rather shocked to find out that the guy was actually a Jewish revolutionary figure who was part of a growing movement in Palestine eager to throw off Roman rule.

It also comes as something of a surprise to contemporary Christians that "cursing" in the New Testament era had little or nothing to do with cussing somebody out. It had far more to do with the invocation of spirits to cause someone harm.

No doubt there is a need in the church for learning more about the world of the New Testament to avoid erroneous interpretations of the text of Scripture. But relevant historical and cultural insights also provide an added dimension of perspective to the words of the Bible. This kind of information often functions in the same way as watching a movie in color rather than in black and white. Finding out, for instance, how Paul compared Christ's victory on the cross to a joyous celebration parade in honor of a Roman general after winning an extraordinary battle brings does indeed magnify the profundity and implications of Jesus' work on the cross. Discovering that the factions at Corinth ("I follow Paul . . . I follow Apollos . . .") had plenty of precedent in the local cults ("I follow Aphrodite; I follow Apollo . . .") helps us understand the "why" of a particular problem. Learning about the water supply from the springs of Hierapolis that flowed into Laodicea as "lukewarm" water enables us to appreciate the relevance of the metaphor Jesus used when he addressed the spiritual laxity of this church.

My sense is that most Christians are eager to learn more about the real life setting of the New Testament. In the preaching and teaching of the Bible in the church, congregants are always grateful when they learn something of the background and historical context of the text. It not only helps them understand the text more accurately, but often enables them to identify with the people and circumstances of the Bible. I have been asked on countless occasions by Christians, "Where can I get access to good historical background information about this passage?" Earnest Christians are hungry for information that makes their Bibles come alive.

The stimulus for this commentary came from the church and the aim is to serve the church. The contributors to this series have sought to provide illuminating and interesting historical/cultural background information. The intent was to draw upon relevant papyri, inscriptions, archaeological discoveries, and the numerous studies of Judaism, Roman culture, Hellenism, and other features of the world of the New Testament and to make the results accessible to people in the church. We recognize that some readers of the commentary will want to go further, and so the sources of the information have been carefully documented in endnotes.

The written information has been supplemented with hundreds of photographs, maps, charts, artwork, and other graphics that help the reader better understand the world of the New Testament. Each of the writers was given an opportunity to dream up a "wish list" of illustrations that he thought would help to illustrate the passages in the New Testament book for which he was writing commentary. Although we were not able to obtain everything they were looking for, we came close.

The team of commentators are writing for the benefit of the broad array of Christians who simply want to better understand their Bibles from the vantage point of the historical context. This is an installment in a new genre of "Bible background" commentaries that was kicked off by Craig Keener's fine volume. Consequently, this is not an "exegetical" commentary that provides linguistic insight and background into Greek constructions and verb tenses. Neither is this work an "expository" commentary that provides a verse-by-verse exposition of the text; for

in-depth philological or theological insight, readers will need to have other more specialized or comprehensive commentaries available. Nor is this an "historical-critical" commentary, although the contributors are all scholars and have already made substantial academic contributions on the New Testament books they are writing on for this set. The team intentionally does not engage all of the issues that are discussed in the scholarly guild.

Rather, our goal is to offer a reading and interpretation of the text informed by what we regard as the most relevant historical information. For many in the church, this commentary will serve as an important entry point into the interpretation and appreciation of the text. For other more serious students of the Word, these volumes will provide an important supplement to many of the fine exegetical, expository, and critical available.

The contributors represent a group of scholars who embrace the Bible as the Word of God and believe that the message of its pages has life-changing relevance for faith and practice today. Accordingly, we offer "Reflections" on the relevance of the Scripture to life for every chapter of the New Testament.

I pray that this commentary brings you both delight and insight in digging deeper into the Word of God.

Clinton E. Arnold
General Editor

LIST OF SIDEBARS

Romans

Galatians

INDEX OF PHOTOS AND MAPS

ABBREVIATIONS

1. Books of the Bible and Apocrypha

1 Chron.	1 Chronicles
2 Chron.	2 Chronicles
1 Cor.	1 Corinthians
2 Cor.	2 Corinthians
1 Esd.	1 Esdras
2 Esd.	2 Esdras
1 John	1 John
2 John	2 John
3 John	3 John
1 Kings	1 Kings
2 Kings	2 Kings
1 Macc.	1 Maccabees
2 Macc.	2 Maccabees
1 Peter	1 Peter
2 Peter	2 Peter
1 Sam.	1 Samuel
2 Sam.	2 Samuel
1 Thess.	1 Thessalonians
2 Thess.	2 Thessalonians
1 Tim.	1 Timothy
2 Tim.	2 Timothy
Acts	Acts
Amos	Amos
Bar.	Baruch
Bel	Bel and the Dragon
Col.	Colossians
Dan.	Daniel
Deut.	Deuteronomy
Eccl.	Ecclesiastes
Ep. Jer.	Epistle of Jeremiah
Eph.	Ephesians
Est.	Esther
Ezek.	Ezekiel
Ex.	Exodus
Ezra	Ezra
Gal.	Galatians
Gen.	Genesis
Hab.	Habakkuk
Hag.	Haggai
Heb.	Hebrews
Hos.	Hosea
Isa.	Isaiah
James	James
Jer.	Jeremiah
Job	Job
Joel	Joel
John	John
Jonah	Jonah
Josh.	Joshua
Jude	Jude
Judg.	Judges
Judith	Judith
Lam.	Lamentations
Lev.	Leviticus
Luke	Luke
Mal.	Malachi
Mark	Mark
Matt.	Matthew
Mic.	Micah
Nah.	Nahum
Neh.	Nehemiah
Num.	Numbers
Obad.	Obadiah
Phil.	Philippians
Philem.	Philemon
Pr. Man.	Prayer of Manassah
Prov.	Proverbs
Ps.	Psalm
Rest. of Est.	The Rest of Esther
Rev.	Revelation
Rom.	Romans
Ruth	Ruth
S. of III Ch.	The Song of the Three Holy Children
Sir.	Sirach/Ecclesiasticus
Song	Song of Songs
Sus.	Susanna
Titus	Titus
Tobit	Tobit
Wisd. Sol.	The Wisdom of Solomon
Zech.	Zechariah
Zeph.	Zephaniah

2. Old and New Testament Pseudepigrapha and Rabbinic Literature

Individual tractates of rabbinic literature follow the abbreviations of the *SBL Handbook of Style*, pp. 79–80. Qumran documents follow standard Dead Sea Scroll conventions.

2 Bar.	*2 Baruch*
3 Bar.	*3 Baruch*
4 Bar.	*4 Baruch*
1 En.	*1 Enoch*
2 En.	*2 Enoch*
3 En.	*3 Enoch*
4 Ezra	*4 Ezra*

3 Macc.	3 Maccabees
4 Macc.	4 Maccabees
5 Macc.	5 Maccabees
Acts Phil.	Acts of Philip
Acts Pet.	Acts of Peter and the 12 Apostles
Apoc. Elijah	Apocalypse of Elijah
As. Mos.	Assumption of Moses
b.	Babylonian Talmud (+ tractate)
Gos. Thom.	Gospel of Thomas
Jos. Asen.	Joseph and Aseneth
Jub.	Jubilees
Let. Aris.	Letter of Aristeas
m.	Mishnah (+ tractate)
Mek.	Mekilta
Midr.	Midrash I (+ biblical book)
Odes Sol.	Odes of Solomon
Pesiq. Rab.	Pesiqta Rabbati
Pirqe. R. El.	Pirqe Rabbi Eliezer
Pss. Sol.	Psalms of Solomon
Rab.	Rabbah (+biblical book); (e.g., Gen. Rab.=Genesis Rabbah)
S. ʿOlam Rab.	Seder ʿOlam Rabbah
Sem.	Semahot
Sib. Or.	Sibylline Oracles
T. Ab.	Testament of Abraham
T. Adam	Testament of Adam
T. Ash.	Testament of Asher
T. Benj.	Testament of Benjamin
T. Dan	Testament of Dan
T. Gad	Testament of Gad
T. Hez.	Testament of Hezekiah
T. Isaac	Testament of Isaac
T. Iss.	Testament of Issachar
T. Jac.	Testament of Jacob
T. Job	Testament of Job
T. Jos.	Testament of Joseph
T. Jud.	Testament of Judah
T. Levi	Testament of Levi
T. Mos.	Testament of Moses
T. Naph.	Testament of Naphtali
T. Reu.	Testament of Reuben
T. Sim.	Testament of Simeon
T. Sol.	Testament of Solomon
T. Zeb.	Testament of Zebulum
Tanh.	Tanhuma
Tg. Isa.	Targum of Isaiah
Tg. Lam.	Targum of Lamentations
Tg. Neof.	Targum Neofiti
Tg. Onq.	Targum Onqelos
Tg. Ps.-J	Targum Pseudo-Jonathan
y.	Jerusalem Talmud (+ tractate)

3. Classical Historians

For an extended list of classical historians and church fathers, see *SBL Handbook of Style*, pp. 84–87. For many works of classical antiquity, the abbreviations have been subjected to the author's discretion; the names of these works should be obvious upon consulting entries of the classical writers in classical dictionaries or encyclopedias.

Eusebius

Eccl. Hist.	Ecclesiastical History

Josephus

Ag. Ap.	Against Apion
Ant.	Jewish Antiquities
J.W.	Jewish War
Life	The Life

Philo

Abraham	On the Life of Abraham
Agriculture	On Agriculture
Alleg. Interp	Allegorical Interpretation
Animals	Whether Animals Have Reason
Cherubim	On the Cherubim
Confusion	On the Confusion of Thomas
Contempl. Life	On the Contemplative Life
Creation	On the Creation of the World
Curses	On Curses
Decalogue	On the Decalogue
Dreams	On Dreams
Drunkenness	On Drunkenness
Embassy	On the Embassy to Gaius
Eternity	On the Eternity of the World
Flaccus	Against Flaccus
Flight	On Flight and Finding
Giants	On Giants
God	On God
Heir	Who Is the Heir?
Hypothetica	Hypothetica
Joseph	On the Life of Joseph
Migration	On the Migration of Abraham
Moses	On the Life of Moses
Names	On the Change of Names
Person	That Every Good Person Is Free
Planting	On Planting
Posterity	On the Posterity of Cain
Prelim. Studies	On the Preliminary Studies
Providence	On Providence
QE	Questions and Answers on Exodus
QG	Questions and Answers on Genesis
Rewards	On Rewards and Punishments
Sacrifices	On the Sacrifices of Cain and Abel
Sobriety	On Sobriety
Spec. Laws	On the Special Laws
Unchangeable	That God Is Unchangeable
Virtues	On the Virtues
Worse	That the Worse Attacks the Better

Apostolic Fathers

1 Clem.	First Letter of Clement
Barn.	Epistle of Barnabas
Clem. Hom.	Ancient Homily of Clement (also called 2 Clement)
Did.	Didache
Herm. Vis.; Sim.	Shepherd of Hermas, Visions; Similitudes
Ignatius	Epistles of Ignatius (followed by the letter's name)
Mart. Pol.	Martyrdom of Polycarp

4. Modern Abbreviations

AASOR	Annual of the American Schools of Oriental Research
AB	Anchor Bible
ABD	Anchor Bible Dictionary
ABRL	Anchor Bible Reference Library
AGJU	Arbeiten zur Geschichte des antiken Judentums und des Urchristentums
AH	Agricultural History
ALGHJ	Arbeiten zur Literatur und Geschichte des Hellenistischen Judentums
AnBib	Analecta biblica
ANRW	Aufstieg und Niedergang der römischen Welt
ANTC	Abingdon New Testament Commentaries
BAGD	Bauer, W., W. F. Arndt, F. W. Gingrich, and F. W. Danker. Greek-English Lexicon of the New Testament and Other Early Christina Literature (2d. ed.)
BA	Biblical Archaeologist
BAFCS	Book of Acts in Its First Century Setting
BAR	Biblical Archaeology Review
BASOR	Bulletin of the American Schools of Oriental Research
BBC	Bible Background Commentary
BBR	Bulletin for Biblical Research
BDB	Brown, F., S. R. Driver, and C. A. Briggs. A Hebrew and English Lexicon of the Old Testament
BDF	Blass, F., A. Debrunner, and R. W. Funk. A Greek Grammar of the New Testament and Other Early Christian Literature
BECNT	Baker Exegetical Commentary on the New Testament
BI	Biblical Illustrator
Bib	Biblica
BibSac	Bibliotheca Sacra
BLT	Brethren Life and Thought
BNTC	Black's New Testament Commentary

BRev	Bible Review
BSHJ	Baltimore Studies in the History of Judaism
BST	The Bible Speaks Today
BSV	Biblical Social Values
BT	The Bible Translator
BTB	Biblical Theology Bulletin
BZ	Biblische Zeitschrift
CBQ	Catholic Biblical Quarterly
CBTJ	Calvary Baptist Theological Journal
CGTC	Cambridge Greek Testament Commentary
CH	Church History
CIL	Corpus inscriptionum latinarum
CPJ	Corpus papyrorum judaicorum
CRINT	Compendia rerum iudaicarum ad Novum Testamentum
CTJ	Calvin Theological Journal
CTM	Concordia Theological Monthly
CTT	Contours of Christian Theology
DBI	Dictionary of Biblical Imagery
DCM	Dictionary of Classical Mythology.
DDD	Dictionary of Deities and Demons in the Bible
DJBP	Dictionary of Judaism in the Biblical Period
DJG	Dictionary of Jesus and the Gospels
DLNT	Dictionary of the Later New Testament and Its Developments
DNTB	Dictionary of New Testament Background
DPL	Dictionary of Paul and His Letters
EBC	Expositor's Bible Commentary
EDBT	Evangelical Dictionary of Biblical Theology
EDNT	Exegetical Dictionary of the New Testament
EJR	Encyclopedia of the Jewish Religion
EPRO	Études préliminaires aux religions orientales dans l'empire romain
EvQ	Evangelical Quarterly
ExpTim	Expository Times
FRLANT	Forschungen zur Religion und Literatur des Alten und Neuen Testament
GNC	Good News Commentary
GNS	Good News Studies
HCNT	Hellenistic Commentary to the New Testament
HDB	Hastings Dictionary of the Bible
HJP	History of the Jewish People in the Age of Jesus Christ, by E. Schürer
HTR	Harvard Theological Review
HTS	Harvard Theological Studies
HUCA	Hebrew Union College Annual

IBD	*Illustrated Bible Dictionary*	*New Docs*	*New Documents Illustrating Early Christianity*
IBS	*Irish Biblical Studies*		
ICC	International Critical Commentary	NIBC	New International Biblical Commentary
IDB	*The Interpreter's Dictionary of the Bible*	NICNT	New International Commentary on the New Testament
IEJ	*Israel Exploration Journal*	*NIDNTT*	*New International Dictionary of New Testament Theology*
IG	*Inscriptiones graecae*		
IGRR	*Inscriptiones graecae ad res romanas pertinentes*	NIGTC	New International Greek Testament Commentary
ILS	*Inscriptiones Latinae Selectae*	NIVAC	NIV Application Commentary
Imm	*Immanuel*	*NorTT*	*Norsk Teologisk Tidsskrift*
ISBE	International Standard Bible Encyclopedia	*NoT*	*Notes on Translation*
		NovT	*Novum Testamentum*
Int	*Interpretation*	NovTSup	Novum Testamentum Supplements
IvE	*Inschriften von Ephesos*		
IVPNTC	InterVarsity Press New Testament Commentary	NTAbh	Neutestamentliche Abhandlungen
JAC	*Jahrbuch fur Antike und Christentum*	*NTS*	*New Testament Studies*
		NTT	New Testament Theology
JBL	*Journal of Biblical Literature*	NTTS	New Testament Tools and Studies
JETS	*Journal of the Evangelical Theological Society*		
		OAG	*Oxford Archaeological Guides*
JHS	*Journal of Hellenic Studies*	OCCC	*Oxford Companion to Classical Civilization*
JJS	*Journal of Jewish Studies*		
JOAIW	*Jahreshefte des Osterreeichischen Archaologischen Instites in Wien*	OCD	*Oxford Classical Dictionary*
		ODCC	*The Oxford Dictionary of the Christian Church*
JSJ	*Journal for the Study of Judaism in the Persian, Hellenistic, and Roman Periods*	OGIS	*Orientis graeci inscriptiones selectae*
		OHCW	*The Oxford History of the Classical World*
JRS	*Journal of Roman Studies*		
JSNT	*Journal for the Study of the New Testament*	OHRW	*Oxford History of the Roman World*
JSNTSup	Journal for the Study of the New Testament: Supplement Series	OTP	*Old Testament Pseudepigrapha*, ed. by J. H. Charlesworth
JSOT	*Journal for the Study of the Old Testament*		
JSOTSup	Journal for the Study of the Old Testament: Supplement Series	PEQ	*Palestine Exploration Quarterly*
		PG	*Patrologia graeca*
JTS	*Journal of Theological Studies*	*PGM*	*Papyri graecae magicae: Die griechischen Zauberpapyri*
KTR	*Kings Theological Review*		
LCL	Loeb Classical Library	*PL*	*Patrologia latina*
LEC	Library of Early Christianity	PNTC	Pelican New Testament Commentaries
LSJ	Liddell, H. G., R. Scott, H. S. Jones. *A Greek-English Lexicon*		
		Rb	*Revista biblica*
MM	Moulton, J. H., and G. Milligan. *The Vocabulary of the Greek Testament*	*RB*	*Revue biblique*
		RivB	*Rivista biblica italiana*
		RTR	*Reformed Theological Review*
MNTC	Moffatt New Testament Commentary	SB	Sources bibliques
		SBL	Society of Biblical Literature
NBD	*New Bible Dictionary*	SBLDS	Society of Biblical Literature Dissertation Series
NC	Narrative Commentaries		
NCBC	New Century Bible Commentary Eerdmans	SBLMS	Society of Biblical Literature Monograph Series
NEAE	*New Encyclopedia of Archaeological Excavations in the Holy Land*	*SBLSP*	*Society of Biblical Literature Seminar Papers*
		SBS	Stuttgarter Bibelstudien
NEASB	*Near East Archaeological Society Bulletin*	SBT	Studies in Biblical Theology
		SCJ	*Stone-Campbell Journal*

Scr	*Scripture*
SE	*Studia Evangelica*
SEG	*Supplementum epigraphicum graecum*
SJLA	Studies in Judaism in Late Antiquity
SJT	*Scottish Journal of Theology*
SNTSMS	Society for New Testament Studies Monograph Series
SSC	Social Science Commentary
SSCSSG	Social-Science Commentary on the Synoptic Gospels
Str-B	Strack, H. L., and P. Billerbeck. *Kommentar zum Neuen Testament aus Talmud und Midrasch*
TC	Thornapple Commentaries
TDNT	*Theological Dictionary of the New Testament*
TDOT	*Theological Dictionary of the Old Testament*
TLNT	*Theological Lexicon of the New Testament*
TLZ	*Theologische Literaturzeitung*
TNTC	Tyndale New Testament Commentary
TrinJ	*Trinity Journal*
TS	*Theological Studies*
TSAJ	Texte und Studien zum antiken Judentum
TWNT	*Theologische Wörterbuch zum Neuen Testament*
TynBul	*Tyndale Bulletin*
WBC	Word Biblical Commentary Waco: Word, 1982
WMANT	Wissenschaftliche Monographien zum Alten und Neuen Testament
WUNT	Wissenschaftliche Untersuchungen zum Neuen Testament
YJS	Yale Judaica Series
ZNW	*Zeitschrift fur die neutestamentliche Wissenschaft und die Junde der alteren Kirche*
ZPE	*Zeischrift der Papyrolgie und Epigraphkik*
ZPEB	*Zondervan Pictorial Encyclopedia of the Bible*

5. General Abbreviations

ad. loc.	in the place cited
b.	born
c., ca.	circa
cf.	compare
d.	died
ed(s).	editors(s), edited by
e.g.	for example
ET	English translation
frg.	fragment
i.e.	that is
ibid.	in the same place
idem	the same (author)
lit.	literally
1(1)	line(s)
MSS	manuscripts
n.d.	no date
NS	New Series
par.	parallel
passim	here and there
repr.	reprint
ser.	series
s.v.	*sub verbo*, under the word
trans.	translator, translated by; transitive

Zondervan Illustrated Bible Backgrounds Commentary

ROMANS

by Douglas J. Moo

All kinds of issues would need to be tackled in a full-scale introduction to Paul's letter to the Romans: not least the questions about the letter's purpose and theme. But the introductory remarks that follow will concentrate on the background issues that are the focus of this commentary. Other issues will be ignored or touched on only briefly.

Events Leading up to Paul's Writing of Romans

Understanding Paul's own situation as he writes Romans helps us appreciate the purpose and theme of the letter. In 15:14–22, he looks back at a period of ministry just concluded. "From Jerusalem all the way around to Illyricum," Paul tells us, "I have fully proclaimed the gospel of

TIBER RIVER

▶ **Romans**
IMPORTANT FACTS:

- **AUTHOR:** Paul the apostle.
- **DATE:** A.D. 57.
- **OCCASION:** Paul writes toward the end of the third missionary journey to a church that is divided between Jewish and Gentile Christians.
- **PURPOSE:** To help the Roman Christians understand the gospel, especially in its implications for the relationship of Jew and Gentile in the church.

show how the gospel spread from the Jews to the Gentiles. Second, the city stands at one geographic extremity in his missionary travels. At the other extremity is Illyricum, the Roman province occupying what is today Albania and parts of Yugoslavia and Bosnia-Herzegovina. Only here does Paul refer to missionary work in this province, although such a ministry can be fit easily into the movements of Paul on his third missionary journey (see comments on Rom. 15:19). An "arc" drawn from Jerusalem to Illyricum, therefore, passes over, or nearby, the important churches that Paul has planted in south Galatia (Pisidian Antioch, Lystra, Iconium, Derbe), Asia (Ephesus), Macedonia (Philippi, Thessalonica, Berea), and Achaia (Corinth).

Christ" (15:19). This verse indicates that Paul's ministry has reached a significant geographical turning point. As Luke tells us in Acts, Paul first preached Christ in Damascus (and perhaps Arabia) after his conversion (Acts 9:19–22; cf. Gal. 1:17). Only after three years did he go to Jerusalem to preach, and then only briefly (Gal. 1:18; cf. Acts 9:28–29). Why, then, mention Jerusalem as the starting point for his ministry? For two reasons. First, the city represents the center of Judaism, and Paul is concerned to

But what does Paul mean when he claims that he has "fully proclaimed" the gospel in these areas? The Greek has simply the equivalent of our verb "fulfill" (*peplērōkenai*). To "fulfill" the gospel, therefore, probably means to preach it sufficiently such that viable churches are established. These churches can then carry on the task of evangelism in their own territories while Paul moves on to plant new churches in virgin gospel territory (cf. 15:20–21).

In pursuit of this calling, Paul is moving on to Spain (15:24). On the way, he hopes to stop off in Rome, evidently to enlist the Roman Christians' support for his new gospel outreach (see comments on 15:24). But before he can begin his trip to the western Mediterranean, he must first return to Jerusalem (15:25). Throughout the third missionary journey, Paul has collected money from the Gentile churches he planted to bring back to the impoverished Jerusalem believers. Now he is ready to embark on this trip, and he earnestly asks the Roman Christians to pray for it (15:30–33). The collection represents for Paul a key step in what he hopes will be the reconciliation of Jewish and Gentile Christians in the early church.

The Life-Situation of Paul and Why He Wrote

Four pieces of information from 15:23–33 are especially helpful in understanding the situation of Paul as he writes Romans. First, he is almost certainly writing the letter during his winter stay in Corinth at the end of the third missionary journey (Acts 20:2–3; cf. 2 Cor. 13:1). Not only does this place and time best fit the movements Paul describes in chapter 15; it also explains why he commends to the Romans' attention a prominent woman from the church in Cenchrea, the seaport of Corinth (16:1–2).

Second, Paul is conscious of having reached a significant turning point in his missionary career. He has "fulfilled" the gospel task in the eastern Mediterranean and is now ready for new, fresh fields, "white for the harvest." Such a turning point is a natural time for Paul to reflect

◀
___

ROMAN CATACOMB

The "Priscilla Catacomb" dates to the second or third century A.D. and contains hundreds of burial niches.

___

THE MEDITERRANEAN WORLD

Judea to Spain.

▼

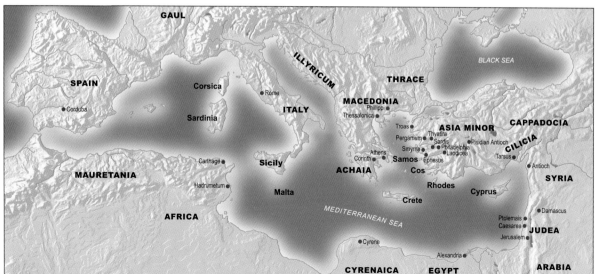

GAUL

ILLYRICUM

BLACK SEA

THRACE

SPAIN

Corsica

● Rome

MACEDONIA

Phillippi ●

● Corduba

ITALY

Thessalonica ●

Troas ●

ASIA MINOR

CAPPADOCIA

Sardinia

Thyatira ●

Pergamum ●

Sardis ●

● Pisidian Antioch

CILICIA

Smyrna ●

● Philadelphia

● Laodicea

Tarsus ●

Athens ●

Ephesus ●

Carthage ●

Corinth ●

Samos

● Antioch

Sicily

ACHAIA

Cos

SYRIA

MAURETANIA

Hadrumetum ●

Rhodes

Cyprus

● Damascus

Malta

Crete

MEDITERRANEAN SEA

Ptolemais ●

AFRICA

Caesarea ● JUDEA

Jerusalem ●

● Cyrene

Alexandria ●

CYRENAICA

EGYPT

ARABIA

on the gospel he has preached and the controversies he has come through.

Third, Paul is deeply concerned about the results of his impending trip to Jerusalem with all its implications for what is to him, and to many others, a central theological issue in the early church: the integration of Gentiles into the people of God. We should not be sur-

prised, then, that this issue plays such a large role in Romans.

Finally, Paul is seeking the support of the Roman Christians for his new ministry in Spain. Perhaps one of the reasons Paul writes this letter to the church in Rome is to introduce himself and explain his theology so that the church will feel comfortable in supporting him.

ROME

(top) The Forum.

(bottom right) The Arch of Titus, built by Domitian to celebrate his brother's military victory over Jerusalem and Judea.

(bottom left) The Via Appia.

Rome and Its Church

Some scholars surmise that Paul's own circumstances suffice to explain why he writes Romans. At a key transition point in his ministry, the apostle sets forth the gospel he preaches to the Roman Christians so that they can pray intelligently for his visit to Jerusalem and so that they will be willing to support his new evangelistic effort in Spain. But left out in all this is the Roman church itself. And what we know about that church provides further critical information about the nature and purpose of Romans.

We have no direct evidence about the origins of Christianity in Rome. The tradition that Peter (or Peter and Paul together) founded the church is almost certainly erroneous.[1] Not only is it difficult to place Peter in Rome at such an early date, but it is difficult to imagine Paul writing to a church founded by Peter in the way he does, considering his expressed principle not to build "on someone else's foundation" (15:20). No other tradition from the ancient church associates any other apostle with the founding of the church.

Thus, the assessment of the fourth-century Ambrosiaster is probably accurate: the Romans "embraced the faith of Christ, albeit according to the Jewish rite, without seeing any sign of mighty works

---

▶ The Disturbance of "Chrestus" and the Roman Church

One circumstance in the life of the Jews in Rome probably played a significant role in explaining why Paul writes Romans the way he does. The ancient historian Suetonius tells us that Emperor Claudius "expelled all the Jews from Rome because they were constantly rioting at the instigation of Chrestus" (*Life of Claudius* 25.2).

Most scholars are convinced that "Chrestus" is a corruption of the term "Christ" and that Suetonius is thereby hinting at disputes within the Jewish community over Jesus' claim to be the Christ. Modern historians are less certain over the date of this expulsion. But a fifth-century Christian writer, Orosius, puts the event in A.D. 49; and this date fits nicely with Acts 18:2, which tells us that Priscilla and Aquila ended up in Corinth during Paul's second missionary journey, "because Claudius had ordered all the Jews to leave Rome."[A-1]

One can imagine the catastrophic effect this would have had on the fledgling Christian community in Rome. Originating from the synagogue, the bulk of Christians would probably have been Jewish. Suddenly they are forced to leave (Claudius would not have distinguished Jews and Jewish-Christians). Left behind are Gentiles who had been converted over the years. Many, if not most, were probably from the class of "God-fearers," Gentiles who had an interest in Judaism and heard the message of Jesus in the synagogue. These Gentiles are the only Christians left in Rome, so the church naturally becomes less and less Jewish in orientation.

But by A.D. 54, the date of Claudius's death, Jews are beginning to return. As Jewish-Christians (like Priscilla and Aquila; cf. Rom. 16:3–5) filter back into the church, they find that they are now in a minority. The social tensions created by this history go a long way in explaining the tensions between Jews and Gentiles that the letter to the Romans abundantly attests (cf. 11:13, 25; 14:1–15:13).[A-2]

◀

CLAUDIUS

Roman emperor
A.D. 41–54.

or any of the apostles."[2] Luke tells us that "visitors from Rome" were present on the day of Pentecost (Acts 2:10). Some of them were probably converted as a result of Peter's powerful speech. They would have returned to their home city and begun preaching Jesus as the Messiah. We know that enough Jews had emigrated to Rome by the first century B.C. to make up a significant portion of the population.[3] The Jewish community was not apparently unified, with many synagogues independent of one another.[4] This circumstance may help explain why the Christians in Rome are also divided.

The Letter and Ancient Genre Considerations

Romans is, of course, a letter—but what kind of letter? Ancient authors used letters for many different purposes. Scholars have been eager to identify the particular persuasive, or "rhetorical," model that Romans belongs in. It has been labeled an "epideictic" letter,[5] an ambassadorial letter,[6] a "protreptic" letter,[7] and a "letter essay,"[8] to name just a few of the more prominent suggestions.

▶

ZENO

Father of Stoicism.

A good case can be made for several of these identifications. But, in the last analysis, Romans does not fit neatly into any specific genre. As James Dunn concludes, "the distinctiveness of the letter far outweighs the significance of its conformity with current literary or rhetorical custom."[9]

Other scholars have noted the similarities between sections of Romans and the diatribe. The diatribe was a style of argument popular with Cynic-Stoic philosophers (the best example being Epictetus's *Discourses* [1st–2d c. A.D.]). The diatribe features dialogues with fictional characters, rhetorical questions, and the use of the emphatic negation *mē genoito* ("may it never be!") to advance a line of argument. These are just the features Paul uses in passages such as 2:1–3:9; 3:27–31; 6:1–7:25; 9:14–23. Earlier scholars thought the diatribe had a polemical purpose and therefore tended to read Romans as a debate with an opponent (perhaps Jewish).[10] But scholars have recently come to realize that the diatribe was used more often as a means of clarifying truth for converts and disciples.[11] The dialogical "arguments" of Romans therefore have the purpose of helping the Christians in Rome better understand the gospel and its implications.

Address and Greeting (1:1–7)

People in Paul's day usually began their letters by identifying themselves and their addressee(s) and then adding a greeting. Acts 23:26 is a good example: "Claudius Lysias, To His Excellency, Governor Felix: Greetings." Paul follows this conventional structure but elaborates each element. He spends six verses identifying himself, probably because he needs to establish his credentials in a church that he did not found and has not visited. Paul claims to be an apostle, dedicated to the "gospel," the good news about Jesus, God's Son. This Jesus, a descendant of David in his earthly life, has now been invested with new power through his resurrection. It is this Jesus whom Paul serves by calling on Gentiles everywhere to trust God and to obey him. And since the Roman Christians are mainly Gentile, Paul has a perfect right to proclaim God's good news to them.

Servant of Christ Jesus (1:1). Great leaders in the Old Testament were also called "servants" of the Lord (see, e.g., Josh. 14:7: "I was forty years old when Moses the servant of the LORD sent me from Kadesh Barnea to explore the land"). The phrase therefore hints at Paul's own status and authority. "Christ" comes from the Greek word for "anointed" and is equivalent to the Hebrew-derived "Messiah." Placing "Christ" first focuses attention on the word as a title.

The gospel of God (1:1). "Gospel," or "good news," has backgrounds in both the Old Testament and the Roman world. The prophets used the word to depict God's saving intervention on behalf of his people: "You who bring good tidings to Zion, go up on a high mountain. You who bring good tidings to Jerusalem, lift up your voice with a shout, lift it up, do not be afraid; say to the towns of Judah, 'Here is your God!'" (Isa. 40:9). But the word was also applied by the Romans to the emperor, whose birth, life, and great deeds were "good news" for the world. A decree

ROME
▼

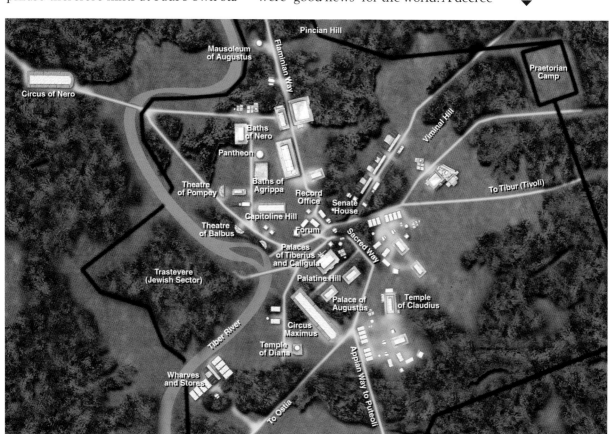

issued in 9 B.C. marking the birthday of Emperor Augustus, for instance, claims that his birth was "the beginning for the world of glad tidings."[12] The salvation and happiness that many Romans looked to the emperor to provide are available only, claims Paul, in Jesus Christ, the essence of the "good news of God."

A descendant of David (1:3). In the Old Testament, God promises that a descendant of David will have an eternal reign. Perhaps the most famous of such prophecies is found in 2 Samuel 7:12–14a, as the prophet Nathan addresses David: "When your days are over and you rest with your fathers, I will raise up your offspring to succeed you, who will come from your own body, and I will establish his kingdom. He is the one who will build a house for my Name, and I will establish the throne of his kingdom forever. I will be his father, and he will be my son." Paul is identifying Jesus as the one in whom the ultimate significance of this prophecy is fulfilled.

Declared with power to be the Son of God (1:4). The NIV suggests that the resurrection marked the time when God, as it were, "announced" to the world that Jesus was Son of God. But the verb Paul uses suggests rather that Jesus was appointed to a new role at the time of the resurrection. Since Jesus has always been Son of God (see 1:3), this new role must be "Son of God in power." Paul may again be alluding to Old Testament messianic passages—in this case, to ones that use language about the installment of a king to predict the coming of Messiah. Note, for instance, Psalm 2:7: "I will proclaim the decree of the LORD: He said to me, 'You are my Son; today I have become your Father.'"

And you also are among those who are called to belong to Jesus Christ (1:6). Or, better: "you also, called to belong to Jesus Christ, are among those [e.g., the Gentiles of 1:5]." Paul wants to claim the Roman Christians as Gentiles who belong within his sphere of ministry.

Thanksgiving and Occasion (1:8–15)

Paul continues to adapt the typical Greco-Roman letter form, which often had an expression of thanks at the beginning.[13] Paul is grateful to the Lord for the evidence of the Spirit's work in the Roman church and is hopeful that he will finally be able to pay them a visit and share his gospel with them.

That is, that you and I may be mutually encouraged by each other's faith (1:12). After expressing his desire to "impart . . . some spiritual gift" to the Romans, Paul immediately corrects himself by emphasizing the mutual spiritual benefit that he

▶

NEW TESTAMENT MANUSCRIPT

This papyrus fragment, known as 𝔭⁴⁶, dates to A.D. 200 and is the oldest surviving copy of the book of Romans.

hopes will follow from his visit. We need not doubt Paul's sincerity; but Paul is also using an ancient rhetorical convention, the *captatio benevolentiae*, to "capture the good will" of his audience. He does not want to come across as dictatorial or arrogant.

I planned many times to come to you (but have been prevented from doing so until now) (1:13). We cannot be certain what it was that kept Paul from visiting Rome earlier. But it was probably the need to minister to the churches that he had founded in the eastern Mediterranean. Paul is writing the letter from Corinth, a church that demanded a lot of his pastoral time and attention (see 1 and 2 Corinthians).

Greeks and non-Greeks (1:14). "Non-Greeks" translates the word *barbaros*, from which we get "barbarian." Greeks applied the word to people who could not speak Greek and who therefore used uncouth languages that sounded like nonsense ("bar-bar").

The Theme of the Letter (1:16–17)

These verses are the transition between the letter's introduction and its body. In them Paul announces the theme of the letter: the gospel. Paul proudly proclaims the gospel because he knows it unleashes God's power to rescue human beings— both Jews and Gentiles—from sin and death. The gospel has this power because God reveals his righteousness in it, which can only be experienced through faith.

First for the Jew, then for the Gentile (1:16). Running like a golden thread through Romans is the insistence that the gospel has overcome the distinction between Jew and Gentile. We find it difficult to appreciate just how deep the divide between Jew and Gentile was for first-century Jews. Jews believed that God had chosen them, from among all the nations of the earth, to be his very own people.

Two developments during the two centuries before Christ made it more important than ever for Jews to insist on their distinctiveness. First, the Seleucid ruler Antiochus Epiphanes tried to eradicate the Jewish religion. Pious Jews rose up in revolt and prevented the Seleucids from carrying out their intention (see the apocryphal books 1 and 2 Maccabees). But the experience strengthened Jewish resolve to maintain their distinctive culture. The second development leading to this same emphasis was the diaspora. By Jesus' time, many more Jews were living outside of Palestine than in it. Jews living as a minority in a hostile culture naturally focused on those lifestyle issues that maintained their separateness from the surrounding culture.

A righteousness from God (1:17). The NIV translation is interpretive; a more literal rendering would be simply "righteousness of God." The NIV assumes that Paul is speaking about righteousness as the "right status" that God gives to the sinner who believes. But the Old Testament background suggests a different way of understanding the phrase. Occurring over fifty times in the Old Testament, the phrase "his [e.g., God's] righteousness" sometimes refers to God's activity of "making things right" in the last days. Isaiah 46:13 is an excellent example: "I am bringing my righteousness near, it is not far away; and my salvation will not be delayed. I will grant salvation to Zion, my splendor to Israel." As a parallel to "salvation," God's "righteousness" is his activity of establishing "right" in a world that has gone terribly wrong. But it is important to note that this "rightness" is not moral but legal. Paul is not referring to God's activity of turning sinners into people who live "right" but to his act of proclaiming that sinners are "right" before him—innocent in the divine court of justice.[14]

"The righteous will live by faith" (1:17). We can also translate this, "the one who is righteous by faith will live" (see RSV; TEV). The words come from Habakkuk 2:4, which enjoin God's people, the "righteous," to look at the strange and perplexing work of God in Habakkuk's day with the eyes of faith. Paul finds in the language a key Old Testament insistence that faith is essential to establish true righteousness and life (see also Gal. 3:11; Heb. 10:38).

Gentiles Justly Stand Under God's Wrath (1:18–32)

Paul has introduced the theme of the letter: In the preaching of the gospel, God acts to put people in right relationship with himself. Any person, Gentile as well as Jew, who exercises trust in God can therefore be saved. But Paul postpones further explanation of this "good news" until 3:21 and following. First must come the "bad news." Paul knows that we will not appreciate the solution until we understand the problem. So, in 1:18–3:20 he explains that all human beings are locked up under sin's power and justly stand under the sentence of God's wrath. Both Gentiles (1:18–32) and Jews (2:1–29) have been given knowledge about God's will for human beings. But

they have all turned away from that knowledge and are therefore "without excuse" (1:20; cf. 2:1) before the righteous judgment of God.

In 1:18–32, Paul focuses on the way that human beings have turned from God's revelation in nature and fallen into idolatry (1:22–23, 25), illegitimate sexual behavior (1:24, 26–27), and all kinds of other sins (1:28–31). The passage is structured around the threefold repetition of human "exchange"/divine "giving over" (1:23–24, 25–26a, 26b–28). God has sentenced people to the consequences of the sin they have chosen for themselves.

The wrath of God (1:18). The "wrath of the gods" is a common theme in Greco-Roman literature. When other gods offend them, or human beings fail to give a god his or her due (e.g., by failing to offer sacrifices), the god reacts with "wrath." In keeping with the human qualities of the traditional Greek pantheon, this wrath could be selfish in its motivation and capricious in its effects. For this reason, some of the Greek philosophers urged people to avoid "wrath," since it manifested a lack of self-control. Some modern theologians echo this critique, claiming that the biblical teaching about God's wrath must be understood as a kind of mechanistic process within history.

But the God of the Bible is a personal God, and his wrath, while just and measured, is no impersonal force. The Old Testament frequently refers to God's wrath in precisely this way, as he inflicts punishment on human sin (e.g., Ex. 32:10–12; Num. 11:1; Jer. 21:3–7). But it also predicts a climactic outpouring of God's wrath in the last day (e.g., Isa. 63:3–6; Zeph. 1:15). Since Paul speaks similarly in this very context (Rom. 2:5), he may also think of the "revealing" of God's wrath in this verse as taking place on the Day of Judgment. But the present tense of the verb "being revealed" suggests rather that he is alluding to the many ways in which God manifests his wrath against sin in history.

Exchanged the glory of the immortal God for images made to look like mortal man and birds and animals and reptiles (1:23). Once people turned from knowledge of the true God (1:20–21), they "became fools" (1:22) and worshiped gods of their own making. Idolatry is the basic sin, and it was almost universal in the ancient world. Israel fell into the worship of false gods again and again, and God eventually sent the people into exile for their misplaced worship. But the Exile and various crises of the intertestamental period cured Israel of idolatry. In fact, Jewish writings from this period frequently mock the Gentiles for their foolish worship of gods fashioned by their own hands. One of the most important of these texts is found in the apocryphal book Wisdom of Solomon. Note, for instance 13:1–2:

For all people who were ignorant of God were foolish by nature; and they were unable from the good things that are seen to know the one who exists, nor did they recognize the artisan while paying heed to his works; but they supposed that either fire or wind or swift air, or the circle of the stars, or turbulent water, or the luminaries of heaven were the gods that rule the world.

Paul also alludes to two Old Testament texts. The threefold description of the animal world is reminiscent of the creation account: "And God said, 'Let the land produce living creatures according to their kinds: livestock, creatures that

move along the ground, and wild animals, each according to its kind.' And it was so" (Gen. 1:24). The language of "exchanging the glory" seems to reflect the psalmist's commentary on Israel's sin in fashioning and worshiping the golden

CANAANITE IDOLS
(left) Baal.
(right) Astarte.

calf (Ex. 32): "They exchanged their Glory for an image of a bull, which eats grass" (Ps. 106:20). By his choice of words, therefore, Paul brands idolatry as a tragic departure from the intention of God in creation, a departure that Israel herself has not escaped.

Because of this, God gave them over to shameful lusts (1:26). The move from idolatry to sexual sin again echoes typical Jewish diatribes against the Gentiles. Jews were relatively free from this sin, but it was rampant in the ancient Greco-Roman world.

They not only continue to do these very things but also approve of those who practice them (1:32). The suggestion that approval of the sin of others can be worse than one's own sin echoes Jewish teaching: "The two-faced are doubly punished because they both practice evil and approve of others who practice it; they imitate the spirits of error and join in the struggle against mankind" (*T. Asher* 6:2).

Jews Justly Stand Under God's Wrath (2:1–16)

After condemning Gentiles for turning from the knowledge of God that they were given in the created world, Paul now castigates Jews for failing to live up to the knowledge of God that they were given in the law. As a seasoned preacher of the gospel, Paul knows how Jews will react to his condemnation of the Gentiles in 1:18–32: They will be quite willing to join him in his denunciation. Thus, Paul denies that they have any right to assume they are superior to the Gentiles, for Jews do "the same things" as the Gentiles (2:1). They may not worship idols or engage in homosexuality; but they put their own law in the place of God and are just as guilty as Gentiles of "greed," "envy," "strife," and so on (see 1:29–31). As a result, Jews also "have no excuse" (2:1), storing up wrath for the day of wrath (2:5).

Paul justifies his critique of the Jews by arguing in the two following paragraphs that Jew and Gentile stand on the same footing before the judgment seat of God. God impartially judges every person—Jew and Gentile alike—on the basis of their works (2:6–11). The law, though a precious possession of the Jew, will make no difference in the outcome (2:12–16), for it is doing the law, not possessing it, that matters. Moreover, Gentiles, though not given the Mosaic law, also have some knowledge of God's law.

▶ Homosexuality

The Jewish viewpoint on sexual sin is well summarized in *Sybilline Oracles* 3.594–600: "Surpassing, indeed, all humans, they [Jewish men] are mindful of holy wedlock and do not engage in evil intercourse with male children, as do Phoenicians, Egyptians, and Romans, spacious Greece and many other nations, Persians, Galatians, and all Asia, transgressing the holy law of the immortal God." The Jews' condemnation of homosexuality is rooted, of course, in the Old Testament, which plainly and repeatedly denounces the practice (see, e.g., Gen. 19:1–28; Lev. 18:22; 20:13; Deut. 23:17–18). Many Greeks, however, not only tolerated homosexuality, but considered consensual sex between men to be a higher form of love than heterosexual relations. Contrary to revisionist interpretations, Paul follows the Old Testament and Jewish teaching in condemning homosexual practice as sinful.

▶ Paul and Rhetoric

When we use the word "rhetorical," we usually mean elaborate speech. But in the ancient world "rhetoric" was the art of persuasion and a prime subject of study.[A-3] The Greeks and Romans were fond of public speaking and developed sophisticated techniques to help a speaker to dazzle or persuade his audience. Paul occasionally uses some of the styles popular in the rhetorical schools (such as "diatribe"). But, as 1 Corinthians 2:1–5 reveals, he renounces many of the rhetorical "tricks" of his day, wanting his converts to be convinced by logic and the power of the Spirit rather than by superficial arguments. Preachers today would do well to follow Paul in turning their backs on any means of persuasion that do not rely on God's power and the working of the Spirit.

You, therefore, have no excuse (2:1). The "you" in Greek is singular. In 2:17 Paul identifies this person whom he is addressing as a Jew. Why does Paul point to a single Jew for his discussion? He is adopting an ancient literary style called the diatribe. Ancient Greeks used this style as a teaching device, letting their audience "listen in" to a discussion between two different viewpoints. Here Paul teaches the Roman church about his view of Judaism by describing for them the kind of argument he would make to the typical Jew about sin and salvation.

Do you show contempt for the riches of his kindness . . . not realizing that God's kindness leads you toward repentance? (2:4). With this question, Paul gets to the heart of the issue. Because of their covenant relationship with God, Jews frequently fell into the habit of thinking that they were immune from the judgment of God. The Old Testament prophets often critiqued this presumptuous attitude. But it remained as a basic attitude among the Jews in Paul's day.

Particularly informative of Paul's rhetorical move in this part of Romans is the sequence of thought in Wisdom of Solomon 11–15. As we noted in our comments on Romans 1:23, this book of the Apocrypha contains a long description of Gentile folly and sin (Wisd. Sol. 11–14). Paul echoes many of its points in Romans 1:18–32. Then, in Wisdom of Solomon 15, the author reflects on the situation of himself and other Jewish people: "But you, our God, are kind and true, patient, and ruling all things in mercy. For even if we sin we are yours, knowing your power; but we will not sin, because we know that you acknowledge us as yours. For to know you is complete righteousness, and to know your power is the root of immortality." The writer does just what Paul condemns: assumes that God's kindness guarantees escape from judgment for Jews.

God "will give to each person according to what he has done.". . . For God does not show favoritism (2:6–11). This paragraph is one of the clearest examples within the Bible of a popular way of arranging material in the ancient world that we call "chiasm." The word comes from the name of a Greek letter of the alphabet, chi, that looks like our "x." The literary form in question takes this name because it arranges material in an A-B-B'-A' pattern, as if each element were at the apex of the two lines of the "x." Romans 2:6–11 is a bit more complicated, following an A-B-C-C'-B'-A' arrangement:

A God "will give to each person according to what he has done." (v. 6)

  B To those who by persistence in doing good seek glory, honor and immortality, he will give eternal life. (v. 7)

    C But for those who are self-seeking and who reject the truth and follow evil, there will be wrath and anger. (v. 8)

    C' There will be trouble and distress for every human being who does evil: first for the Jew, then for the Gentile; (v. 9)

  B' but glory, honor and peace for everyone who does good: first for the Jew, then for the Gentile. (v. 10)

A' For God does not show favoritism. (v. 11)

The main point of a chiasm sometimes comes at its center, but in this case it comes at the "extremes" (point A/A'): God does not show favoritism in dispensing salvation and judgment to people.

All who sin apart from the law will also perish apart from the law, and all who sin under the law will be judged by the law (2:12). This is the first occurrence in Romans of the word "law" (*nomos*). The word occurs almost eighty times in the letter, and Paul's teaching on "law" runs right through all the topics he discusses. Yet the modern English reader can easily get the wrong impression about what Paul is talking about. We think of secular law or, if we are familiar with some theological traditions, of the commands of God for his people that are found throughout the Bible. But Paul's teaching is rooted in a more historical reading of the Bible. For him as a Jew, *nomos* is preeminently the law of Moses: the body of commands that God gave to his people Israel through his servant Moses.

Modern scholars often use the transliterated Hebrew word *torah* to denote this body of laws. In this verse, therefore, those "under the law" are Jews, placed under the jurisdiction of the Mosaic law by God himself. Those who sin "apart from the law" are then Gentiles. Not being Jews, they have not been made subject to the law of Moses. But Paul's point in this verse is that knowledge of that law makes no difference in the judgment: All people stand condemned. For, as Paul explains in 2:13, people can escape God's judgment only by doing the law—and the universal power of sin (see 3:9, 20) prevents people from ever fulfilling that law.

When Gentiles, who do not have the law, do by nature things required by the law, they are a law for themselves (2:14). Some commentators think that Paul is referring to Gentile Christians, who were not by "nature" or "birth" recipients of the law of Moses, but who now have that law "written on the heart," in accordance with the new covenant prophecy of Jeremiah 31:31–34.[15] But Paul's language appears rather to allude to a widespread Greco-Roman tradition about the "unwritten law." Stoic philosophers especially developed the notion of a universal moral standard rooted in nature. Hellenistic Jews, like the Alexandrian philosopher Philo, applied this notion to the Mosaic law: "All right reason is infallible law engraved not by this mortal or that, and thus perishable, nor on lifeless parchment or slabs, and therefore soulless as they, but immortal nature on the immortal mind, never to perish" (*Every Good Man Is Free* 46; see also *Special Laws* 1.36–54; *Abraham* 276).

Following this tradition, Paul claims that non-Christian Gentiles, even though they may never have heard of the law of Moses, have in their very natures, created by God, knowledge of the "rights and wrongs" that the law of Moses ultimately points to. They will therefore do things that the law of Moses itself demands, such as refraining from murder and adultery, honoring their parents, and so on. These universal moral absolutes reveal that all people have access to knowledge of God's moral will. Thus, he is just in condemning both Jew and Gentile (Rom. 2:15–16).

Judgment Despite the Law and Circumcision (2:17–29)

Now you, if you call yourself a Jew; if you rely on the law and brag about your relationship to God (2:17). With this verse Paul begins a long sentence in which he piles up description after description of the Jews' privileges and claims (2:17–20), only to show that these blessings mean little because Jews have not lived up to their privileges (2:21–24). As his address of a single Jew makes clear, Paul is again using the style of the diatribe (see 2:1–4). Ancient writers who used this style often criticized opponents for failing to "practice what they preached."[16] So Paul also claims that Jews, who take pride in their name because it means that they have been given the law with all its blessings, fail to do the law. As Paul has argued in 2:12–13, possession of the law without actually doing it does not count before God.

A guide for the blind, a light for those who are in the dark, an instructor of the foolish (2:19–20). These three descrip-tions of Israel's role as witness of God's power and grace to the world reflect both Old Testament and Jewish texts. According to Isaiah 42:6–7, God had destined Israel, his "servant," to be "a light for the Gentiles, to open eyes that are blind, to free captives from prison and to release from the dungeon those who sit in darkness" (see also 49:6). *Sibylline Oracles* 3.194–95 echoes this language: "The people of the great God will again be strong who will be guides in life for all mortals." Note also *1 Enoch* 105:1: "In those days, he says, 'The Lord will be patient and cause the children of the earth to hear. Reveal it to them with your wisdom, for you are their guides.'" This "evangelistic" mission to the world is one, however, that Israel has failed to accomplish. The Jews' preoccupation with the law and their failure to recognize Jesus as Messiah turned them, as Jesus himself claimed, into "blind guides" (Matt. 15:14). The servant's mission as "light to the Gentiles" has now been taken over by the church (see, e.g., Acts 26:18).

You who abhor idols, do you rob temples? (2:22). This is one of three specific examples of Jewish disobedience of the

A ROMAN TEMPLE

The remains of the temple of Saturn in Rome.

▼

law that Paul cites to prove that Jews do not "do" the law that they possess. The other two—stealing and committing adultery—are straightforward. But what does Paul mean by accusing the Jews of "robbing temples"? (1) If the word Paul uses here (*hierosyleō*) is given its literal meaning, than the reference is probably to Jews who robbed pagan temples of their idolatrous statues in order to melt them down and profit from their precious metals. The Old Testament specifically prohibits the practice (e.g., Deut. 7:26).

(2) Paul may be using the word metaphorically, referring to Jews who did not pay the required "temple tax." This tax, levied on all Jews wherever they lived, was designed to support the Jerusalem temple and its ministries. Jewish texts suggest that failure to pay this tax was widespread.[17]

(3) We have some evidence that the word could refer in a vague way to sacrilege.[18] Paul could, then, be accusing the Jews of elevating the law to such a place that it infringed on the rights and honor of God himself.[19] While this third alternative is attractive, the first should probably be accepted, for this view best accounts for the relationship between the first part of the statement and the second. Robbing pagan temples is a natural contrast to "abhorring idols."

▶

TEMPLE TAX

Silver shekels (top) and half shekels (bottom), which were used for the temple tax.

As it is written, "God's name is blasphemed among the Gentiles because of you" (2:24). Paul concludes his indictment of the Jews for failing to obey the law they take so much pride in with a quotation from the Old Testament. Two different prophetic passages contain language like this: Isaiah 52:5 and Ezekiel 36:20. The latter verse comes from the

---

▶ Circumcision as a "Boundary Marker"

God first instituted circumcision as a "sign of the covenant" that God entered into with Abraham and his descendants (Gen. 17:10–14). All males descended from Abraham were to be circumcised on the eighth day as a mark of their identity as the people of God.

Jews, of course, practiced the rite throughout the Old Testament period, but it became especially significant when Jews, because of the Exile, lived as a minority group in the midst of a pagan environment. To preserve their identity and to prevent intermingling with the Gentiles, they put great emphasis on "boundary marker" rituals such as circumcision, food laws, and the observance of Sab-

bath. This emphasis explains why, for instance in Galatians, it is just these rites that become the focus of debate with the Judaizers. Indeed, these external rituals became so important that some Jews fell into the habit of thinking that simply being born into the people of the Jews (marked for males by circumcision) and following these kinds of rituals would guarantee their salvation.

The rabbinic claim that "no person who is circumcised will go down to Gehenna" (*Exod. Rab.* 19 [81c]), while dating from the post-New Testament period, undoubtedly reflects the opinion of many Jews in Paul's day.

famous "new heart" and "new spirit" prophecy, which Paul uses elsewhere, including a possible allusion later in Romans. But the text of Paul's quotation is closer to the Isaiah passage. Since the sense of the two Old Testament passages is the same, the issue is not of major importance; but the allusion to Isaiah is more likely. Not only is Isaiah Paul's favorite Old Testament book, but he also quotes from this very section (Isa. 52:7) in Romans 10:15 to sketch the course of evangelistic preaching.

What makes Paul's quotation of this text interesting is that Isaiah (and Ezekiel also) ascribe the blasphemy of God's name not to Israel's sin but to her condition of exile, which has led the nations to question God's existence and faithfulness. Paul shifts the application of the text slightly to suit his larger theme in this part of Romans, "leveling the playing field" between Israel and the Gentiles.

Circumcision has value if you observe the law (2:25). In 2:25–29, Paul challenges a widespread Jewish notion that if a man was circumcised, he would ultimately be saved. The apostle attacks this attitude head-on by claiming that the outward rite of circumcision helps a person in the judgment of God only if it is accompanied by heartfelt (see 2:29) obedience to the law. Again, Paul insists, it is what the Jew *does*, not what the Jew *has*, that matters for God.

The one who is not circumcised physically and yet obeys the law will condemn you (2:27). Paul's claim is a radical one. (1) Jews in Paul's day insisted that Gentiles had to be circumcised if they wanted to become members of the people of God. Indeed, a few more "Hellenized" Jews, such as Philo of Alexandria, spiri-

tualized circumcision, along with most Jewish rituals. But they still insisted that the physical rite was essential (*Special Laws* 1.1–11, 304–6; *Abraham* 92). An intriguing story about the conversion of a Gentile king in Josephus suggests that some Jews may not have insisted on circumcision for converts.[20] But the prevailing opinion was that only circumcised Gentiles could be considered true "proselytes," that is, converts to Judaism.[21] When Paul therefore suggests that a Gentile who is not circumcised may stand in judgment over Jews, he is breaking with a basic Jewish tradition. (2) For Jews, circumcision was an indispensable part of keeping the law. Yet Paul suggests that uncircumcised Gentiles may be "obeying the law." Paul begins hinting here at a redefinition of what it means to "keep the law" that he will develop further in Romans (see esp. 3:31; 8:4; 13:8–10).

Circumcision is circumcision of the heart, by the Spirit, not by the written code (2:29). "Written code" translates a Greek

R E F L E C T I O N S

WHAT PAUL SAYS IN THESE VERSES ABOUT CIRCUMCISION is in some ways limited because of the unique status of circumcision and of the Jewish faith. For only Judaism and its institutions are rooted in God's revelation in the Old Testament. But one important point about circumcision does apply broadly to any religious ritual: Any such ritual only has value if it is accompanied by heartfelt obedience. In the Christian church, we can apply the principle to such rites as baptism and the celebration of the Lord's Supper. These are rituals instituted by Christ himself and appointed for our benefit. Yet they will only have value in our lives when they are met by faith and a commitment to make Christ the Lord of our lives. The temptation to substitute the outward form for the inward reality is always present.

word that means "letter" (*gramma*). In later Christian theology, Paul's contrast between "letter" and "spirit" was applied to the interpretation of the Old Testament. Christians, it was argued, needed to penetrate behind the "letter" of the words of the Old Testament in order to be able to understand its true, "spiritual," meaning. We preserve this same metaphor when we speak of obeying the "spirit" of the law.

But Paul has no such application of this language in view. In the three places where he uses the contrast (see also Rom. 7:6; 2 Cor. 3:3–5), "spirit" refers to the Holy Spirit, poured out by God as part of the new covenant blessing, while "letter" refers to the Old Testament law. In Romans 2:29, therefore, Paul hints again at the argument that will follow in the book, where he makes clear that only God's Spirit, empowered by God's new covenant grace, can change the heart of a person and make it acceptable to God.

God's Faithfulness and the Judgment of Jews (3:1–8)

The dialogical style of Romans, reminiscent of the ancient diatribe (see comments on 2:1ff.), is revealed in Paul's frequent pauses to respond to objections of misunderstandings of what he has just taught. Paul knows that some of his readers might draw the wrong conclusion about what he has taught in Romans 2. He seems to have eliminated any special privileges for Jews, accusing them of being just as guilty as the Gentiles of breaking God's law. But, while Gentile and Jew are equally condemned for failing to live up to God's demands of them, it is not the case that Jews have no advantage at all. It is this point that Paul briefly makes in this short paragraph. But he does not stop there. He also suggests that God's judgment of the Jews is

entirely in keeping with his covenant promises and person.

First of all, they have been entrusted with the very words of God (3:2). Paul does not follow up his "first of all" with a "second" or "third." Perhaps "first of all" means something like "most important." Or perhaps Paul started a list but was sidetracked before finishing it. But we can guess what that list would have looked like from the similar context in 9:4–5. Having access to "the very words of God" is the greatest blessing the Jews enjoy. The Greek word here (*logia*) has the connotation of "spoken words," or "oracles"; it draws attention to the fact that God himself has spoken to the Jews in his Old Testament word to them. The enormous advantage this gives to the Jews is brought out in many passages. Note, for instance: "What other nation is so great as to have such righteous decrees and laws as this body of laws I am setting before you today?" (Deut 4:8); "He has revealed his word to Jacob, his laws and decrees to Israel. He has done this for no other nation; they do not know his laws. Praise the LORD" (Ps. 147:19–20).

So that you may be proved right when you speak and prevail when you judge (3:4). Paul quotes from Psalm 51:4, part of David's acknowledgment to God that he was perfectly justified in judging David for his sin with Bathsheba. What is telling in this quotation is its emphasis on God's justice *in judgment*. Paul conceives of God's "faithfulness" (3:3), truth (3:4a), and "righteousness" (3:5) quite broadly. Many first-century Jews (and modern interpreters) think that these words all contain promises of blessing only for Israel. God will be faithful and true to his covenant with Israel, rescuing them from their enemies and saving them. But, as Paul hints in this verse, God's faithfulness has ultimately a much wider reference than to his promises of blessing to Israel. God is faithful to *all* his words—the ones that threaten judgment for disobedience as well as to the ones that promise blessing. If, then, Paul implies, God judges Israel for her sins, he is still faithful, true, and just.

The theme of God's justice in punishing his people is one found in many Jewish books of Paul's time, as the Jews tried to interpret the disasters they had suffered in light of God's word and promises. This motif is especially prominent in the first-century B.C. book *Psalms of Solomon*. See, for instance, 8:7–8: "I thought about the judgments of God since the creation of heaven and earth; I proved God right in his judgments in ages past. God exposed their sins in the full light of day; the whole earth knew the righteous judgments of God" (see also 2:18; 3:5; 4:8).

God's righteousness (3:5). In 1:17, we argued that "righteousness of God" refers to God's activity of putting sinners into right relationship with himself. This is the dominant meaning of the phrase in Romans, and Paul will use the phrase with this sense later in this chapter (3:21–22). But, as we hinted in our comments on 3:4, God's "righteousness" here is not his "saving" righteousness but his "personal" righteousness. "Righteousness," or "being in the right," implies a standard of measurement. But there can be no standard above God; God is his own standard of measurement. Therefore God's "righteousness" ultimately includes his always acting in accordance with his own nature. Paul's point is that human sin can never cancel God's faithfulness to his own standard of behavior. Israel's sin has

given God the opportunity of manifesting his righteousness in his judgment. Several Old Testament passages also use the language of "righteousness" or "justice" to make a similar point (see esp. Neh. 9:32–33):

> Now therefore, O our God, the great, mighty and awesome God, who keeps his covenant of love, do not let all this hardship seem trifling in your eyes—the hardship that has come upon us, upon our kings and leaders, upon our priests and prophets, upon our fathers and all your people, from the days of the kings of Assyria until today. In all that has happened to us, you have been just; you have acted faithfully, while we did wrong.

How could God judge the world? (3:6). Paul probably alludes to Genesis 18:25, where Abraham is pleading with God to spare the lives of people in Sodom and Gomorrah: "Far be it from you to do such a thing—to kill the righteous with the wicked, treating the righteous and the wicked alike. Far be it from you! Will not the Judge of all the earth do right?"

The Guilt of All Humanity (3:9–20)

Paul brings the threads of his indictment together in a grand conclusion. All people, Jews as well as Gentiles, are under sin's power (3:9), incapable of rescuing themselves from their plight by anything that they might do (3:20). In this way, he paves the way for his exposition of the good news of redemption through Jesus (3:21ff.).

Under sin (3:9). In a way similar to non-Western cultures today, ancient people tended to view the world in terms of dominating "powers": astral forces, general and local deities, magical spells, and so on. This worldview surfaces at many points in the Bible; and we need to appreciate it if we are to understand its message. In this text, for instance, it is not by chance that Paul claims the human dilemma consists not in the fact that people commit sins, but that they are "under sin." Paul pictures sin as a ruthless taskmaster and human beings as sin's helpless slaves. Clearly, then, what is required if people are to be rescued from this plight is not a teacher or a moral example, but a liberator. Jesus Christ, Paul will announce in 3:24, is just that liberator.

As it is written (3:10–18). In 3:10–18, Paul quotes from as many as six different Old Testament passages to buttress his claim that all people are under sin's power. Such a series of quotations is similar to the later rabbinic practice of "pearl-stringing." But we have evidence from the Dead Sea Scrolls that Jews even before the time of Christ were already collecting Old Testament "proof texts" for various key doctrinal ideas. One of the scrolls, for instance (4QTestimonia), consists entirely of quotations, with interspersed comments, about a messianic prophet. Scholars have long speculated that the early Christians put together such series of texts as an apologetic device in their witness to the truth of their faith. Some think that the quotations in 3:10–18 may come from just such a document.[22] Whether that is true or not (and proof is, in the nature of the case, not forthcoming), the series of quotations fits Paul's purpose very well. He here uses the literary device of inclusio, with the phrase "there is no" occurring in

the opening and closing lines as a frame around the whole.

Therefore no one will be declared righteous in his sight by observing the law (3:20). The phrase "observing the law" is the NIV rendering of a Greek phrase literally translated "works of the law." Paul uses this phrase seven other times (3:28; Gal. 2:16 [3x]; 3:2, 5, 10), and in each case he denies that justification (or a related concept) can be attained by these "works of the law." The NIV rendering reflects the traditional interpretation of the phrase: anything a person does in obedience to the law. No "work" that a person does, even when that work is one demanded by God himself in his holy law, is capable of putting that person in a right relationship with the God of the universe. But, noting the prominence of what we have above called "boundary markers" in first-century Judaism (see comments on Rom. 2:25), some recent interpreters think the phrase may have a more nuanced reference. Paul may be referring to the Jewish tendency to obey the law as means of establishing their own superiority over the Gentiles. The focus within this interpretation shifts from the *performance* of the law (as in the traditional interpretation) to the *possession* of the law.[23]

We think the traditional interpretation has much in its favor. The Hebrew phrase equivalent to the Greek expression that Paul uses here is found several times in the Dead Sea Scrolls (4QFlor 1:7; 1QS 5:21; 6:18; 4QMMT 3:29). It also seems similar to the rabbis' common reference to "works" or "commandments" (see also *2 Apoc. Bar.* 57:2, "the works of the commandments"). Each of these Jewish expressions has the general sense of "obeying the law." Any other nuance has to be read into the phrases from a particular reading of the broader Jewish context; and that broader reading is not convincing.

Justification and the Righteousness of God (3:21–26)

In one of the greatest paragraphs of the Bible, Paul rehearses some of the reasons why the coming of Jesus Christ is, indeed, good news. In Christ, God has acted to manifest his saving righteousness, making it possible for any person who believes to be "justified"—pronounced innocent before the judgment seat of God himself (3:21–23). This verdict of justification is possible because Christ has redeemed us from our enslavement to sin (3:24), giving himself as a sacrifice that provides atonement for all people (3:25a). But what gives this paragraph its unparalleled significance is its claim that God did all this while preserving his own righteousness (3:25b–26a). In Christ—God become man and sacrificed for us—God found a way both to "justify" undeserving sinners *and* to remain "just" as he did so (3:26b).

Apart from law . . . to which the Law and the Prophets testify (3:21). "Law" in the first phrase refers to the Mosaic law, and thus should probably be made definite: *the* law. "The Law and the Prophets," on the other hand, is a way by which Jews referred to the Old Testament as a whole (see, e.g., Matt. 5:17; 7:12).[24]

Through the redemption that came by Christ Jesus (3:24). The word "redemption" (*apolytrōsis*) means "liberation through payment of a price." Some interpreters think that this word, and its cognates, "redeem" (Gal. 3:13–14; 4:5; Titus

2:14; 1 Peter 1:18; Rev. 14:3) and "ransom" (Matt. 20:28//Mark 10:45; 1 Tim. 2:6; Heb. 9:15), have, through their use in the Old Testament, lost any sense of a "price paid." The terms simply mean "deliverance" or "deliver."[25] But this is probably not the case. Several New Testament texts keep alive the idea of a "price." The terms were widely used in the ancient world to refer to the process by which prisoners of war or slaves could be bought out of their bondage.[26] Paul, then, presents Christ's death as a price that has been paid to release human beings from their slavery to sin (see comments on Rom. 3:9). Theologians and laypeople alike have asked the question: "To whom, then, was the price paid?" But Paul gives no answer; and perhaps even asking the question pushes Paul's metaphor further than he intended.

God presented him as a sacrifice of atonement (3:25). Another significant theological term with a debated background lies behind the NIV's "sacrifice of atonement" (*hilastērion*). This word was used widely in the Greek world to refer to altars, monuments, etc., that would have the power to "propitiate" the wrath of gods. Many interpreters think this is the context from which Paul takes the term, and thus prefer to translate "propitiation."[27] But the word is also used in the

REDEMPTION

A first-century papyrus document recording the purchase of two slaves.

▼

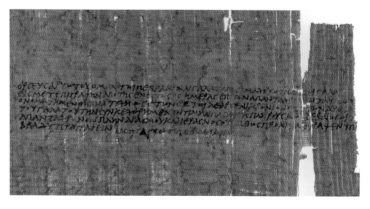

Old Testament in a more specific sense, where it refers to the "mercy seat" (KJV language), the place on the altar where blood was placed and atonement took place. In fact, so often does the term have this meaning in Leviticus 16, in the description of the Day of Atonement ritual, that it virtually takes on the meaning "place of atonement" (see Lev. 3:1, 13, 14, 15). Since the only other occurrence of the word in the New Testament has this same reference (Heb. 9:5), we should probably accept this as the reference Paul intended.

There is some reason to think Paul may here be taking over an early Christian tradition that portrayed Christ's death against the background of the Old Testament sacrificial system. The allusion would have been striking and extremely significant for believers acquainted with the Old Testament. The cross of Christ, Paul asserts, is now the place, in this new covenant age, where God deals with the

MERCY SEAT

(left) A model of the Most Holy Place with a priest sprinkling blood on the mercy seat in the Day of Atonement ritual.

(right) The mercy seat, which also serves as the lid to the ark of the covenant.

THE TABERNACLE

A model of the tabernacle showing a sacrificial scene.

sins of his people. No longer behind a veil, God's atoning work is now displayed for all to see. Since this atoning work includes (in both the Old Testament sacrificial system and in the New Testament portrayal of Christ's death) the turning away of God's wrath, we are also justified in concluding that his atoning work includes the notion of propitiation.

Because in his forbearance he had left the sins committed beforehand unpunished (3:25). "Left . . . unpunished" captures well the interesting word that Paul uses here (*paresis*), which means "postponement of punishment" or "neglect of prosecution." God did not prosecute Old Testament sinners with the full vigor of the law, but allowed them to go unpunished. Now, however, that debt must be paid; and Christ, the "sacrifice of atonement," has paid it.

"By Faith Alone" (3:27–31)

Paul now elaborates one crucial point from 3:21–26: God makes his righteousness available to people by faith alone.

Is God the God of Jews only? Is he not the God of Gentiles too? Yes, of Gentiles too, since there is only one God (3:29–30a). Perhaps the most basic of all Jewish beliefs was the confession: "Hear, O Israel: The LORD our God, the LORD is one" (Deut. 6:4). Pious Jews uttered this confession, called the *Shema* (from the opening word in Hebrew), every day. Paul here turns this confession on the Jews. For if there is only one God, then he must be God of Gentiles as well as Jews, for it would be inconceivable in the ancient mind for a people to have no god. But, Paul goes on to argue, if God is God of both Jews and Gentiles, then he must justify them in the same way (Rom. 3:30b).

"By Faith Alone": The Case of Abraham (4:1–25)

In 3:27–31 Paul establishes the point that a person can be put right with God only by faith. Now, in chapter 4, he elaborates this "faith alone" viewpoint with respect to one of the most important figures in the history of Israel: the patriarch Abraham. Despite his reputation among Jews as a strict adherent of the law, Abraham, Paul explains, has nothing to boast about. For he, too, was justified by faith alone (4:1–8). Neither his circumcision (4:9–12) nor the law (4:13–17) had anything to do with his acceptance before God. It was his faith, a faith that remained firm despite much evidence to the contrary, that enabled him to experience what God had promised (4:18–21). It is by that same faith that Christians inherit the

R E F L E C T I O N S

UNDERSTANDING AND APPLYING THE GOOD NEWS of Jesus Christ means not only understanding the first-century context but also understanding ours. We live in an age that is not comfortable with the notion of sin. The idea that God might actually be angry with people for their sin is uncongenial indeed. But we will not appreciate just why Jesus Christ is such good news for the world until we adjust our thinking to match that of the biblical authors. They knew the reality of sin; and they knew the reality of a holy God who could not tolerate sin. Only through the sacrifice of Christ, paying the debt incurred by our sin that we could never pay, could God make a way of accepting people who are by nature unacceptable to him. Those people in our day who ignore or minimize the problem of human sin in the face of a holy God do well to heed the warning of the great medieval theologian Anselm: "You have not yet considered the weight of sin."

righteousness made available in Jesus Christ (4:22–25).

Abraham, our forefather. . . . If, in fact, Abraham was justified by works (4:1–2). The Old Testament itself calls Abraham the "father" of Israel (Isa. 51:2), recognizing the role that the book of Genesis gives him as the founder of the people of promise (see Gen. 12:1–3). But Jewish tradition made Abraham even more significant and tended to attribute his unique salvation-historical status to his obedience. According to the apocryphal book Prayer of Manasseh, Abraham "did not sin" against God (v. 8); Sirach claims that "no one has been found like him in glory" (Sir. 44:19). *Jubilees* 23:10 lauds Abraham for being "perfect in all his deeds with the Lord, and well-pleasing in righteousness all the days of his life." He was even said to have perfectly obeyed the law before it had been given (*m. Qidd.* 4.14; cf. *2 Apoc. Bar.* 57:2). Paul therefore discusses Abraham not only because he is a foundational figure within the Old Testament, but also because he must combat tendencies in Judaism to attribute Abraham's righteousness and salvation-historical significance to his works.

Abraham believed God, and it was credited to him for righteousness (4:3). In order to capture Abraham for his own teaching about the righteousness of faith, Paul seizes on the crucial text of Genesis 15:6 (see also Gal. 3:6). In the Genesis story, Abraham's faith is specifically his conviction that God would send him a natural descendant (Gen. 15:4–5). But this promise of a son born to him and Sarah represents the whole promise of God to Abraham. Critical to Paul's citation of the passage is the idea of "crediting" (Gk. *logizomai + eis*). The Hebrew

construction does not indicate that Abraham's faith was itself a righteous deed (as some Jews interpreted the text), but that his faith was the means by which God graciously gave Abraham the status of righteousness. Paul seizes on this notion and plays on it throughout Romans 4. This "crediting" was on the basis of faith, not works—a matter of pure grace on God's part (4:4–8). The "crediting" was, moreover, not based on circumcision (4:9–12) or the law (4:13–17). This recurring reference to Genesis 15:6 is somewhat similar to the Jewish interpretational technique called *midrash*, in which a Scripture text becomes the basis for an extended discussion.

God who justifies the wicked (4:5). This famous assertion is particularly striking because it seems to fly in the face of explicit Old Testament teaching. God condemns human judges who "justify" the guilty (see Prov. 17:15; Isa. 5:23) and himself declares that "I will not acquit the wicked" (Ex. 23:7). But Paul is using the word "justify" (Gk. *dikaioō*) in a new way, to describe the creative act by which God, on the basis of Christ's own righteousness, gives to sinful people a status they do not have and could not earn.

David says the same thing (4:6). One feature of the midrashic technique (see comments on 4:3) is the use of texts from the Prophets or the Psalms to illuminate an original text from the law (the Pentateuch). A single word common to both texts was often enough to bring them together. Paul falls into this standard Jewish interpretational technique when he illustrates the meaning of the key word "credit" from Genesis 15:6 by citing Psalm 35:1–2 in Romans 4:7–8. The word "count" in the quotation translates the same Greek word (*logizomai*) that is translated "credit" in the Genesis text.

Under what circumstances was it credited? Was it after he was circumcised, or before? It was not after, but before! (4:10). As we made clear in our notes on 2:25, circumcision became for Jews, facing the threat of persecution and assimilation into larger Gentile populations, a key sign of Jewish identity. Paul reminds his readers that the righteous status Abraham gained with God was not based on his circumcision. The Genesis account makes this clear, for God's pronouncement of Abraham's righteousness comes in Genesis 15, while circumcision is not even introduced until chapter 17. The rabbis speculated that twenty-nine years went by between the two events.

The sign of circumcision, a seal of the righteousness that he had by faith (4:11). The Old Testament calls circumcision a "sign of the covenant" (Gen. 17:11), and Jewish texts dating from after the New Testament period also characterize circumcision as a "seal" (*b. Šabb.* 137b; *Exod. Rab.* 19 [81c]; *Tg. Ket. Cant.* 3:8). Some scholars think this language may have been current in Paul's day,[28] but others are not so sure.[29] What is clear is that Paul, against tendencies in Judaism to connect circumcision to the Mosaic covenant and to the law, insists that it was significant only as an identifying marker for the righteous status Abraham had already gained through his faith.

That he would be heir of the world (4:13). The Old Testament does not use this same language when referring to God's promise to Abraham. But Paul's language seems to be chosen to summarize the three key provisions of God's promise: that Abraham would have innumerable descendants, making a "great nation" (Gen. 12:2; cf. 13:16; 15:5; 17:4–6, 16–20; 22:17); that he would possess the "land" (13:15–17; 15:12–21; 17:8); and that he would be the means of blessing to "all the peoples of the earth" (12:3; 18:18; 22:18). Note especially the promise of 22:17, that Abraham's descendants would "take possession of the cities of their enemies." The prophet Isaiah expands the promise of the land to include the entire world (Isa. 55:3–5), and some Jewish texts use similar universal language to describe God's promise to his people. For instance, the *Book of Jubilees* presents Abraham as blessing Jacob with these words: "May he strengthen and bless you, and may you inherit all of the earth" (*Jub.* 22:14).[30]

Where there is no law there is no transgression (4:15). The key to the interpretation of this difficult assertion is the restricted meaning of the word "transgression" (*parabasis*). It refers to a "stepping over" of a specific law or custom.[31] Paul's point, then, is definitional: Only

where a specific law exists can sin take the specific form of a "transgression." In the case of Israel, the coming of the Mosaic law brought "wrath" by turning the peoples' sin into the more serious and blameworthy category of *parabasis*.

The God who gives life to the dead and calls things that are not as though they were (4:17). This description of the God in whom Abraham believed is difficult grammatically; but our concern is with some interesting parallels to the language in Jewish literature. God's power to give life is featured in the Old Testament (Deut. 32:39; 1 Sam. 2:6) and was even enshrined in one of the most common Jewish liturgies, the "Eighteen Benedictions." In light of the context, Paul probably applies the language specifically to God's creating of life in the dead womb of Sarah.

The second description of God may reflect a widespread Jewish teaching that God created the world out of nothing (*creatio ex nihilo*). The verb "call" often refers to God's creative work (see, e.g., Isa. 41:4; 48:13), and Philo often used the verb in statements about God's creative work (see, e.g., *Special Laws* 4.187: "for he called things that are not into being"). But the language of "giving life" was sometimes combined with God's call to describe conversion. Especially important is *Joseph and Aseneth* 8:9: "Lord, God of my father Israel, highest and most powerful God, who gives life to all things and calls from darkness into light, and from error into truth, and from death into life." Paul may be picking up this language to emphasize that God has the power to create new spiritual life in the midst of the deadness of human sin and alienation.[32]

Abraham in hope believed and so became the father of many nations (4:18). Paul's use of the story of the miraculous birth of Isaac in 4:18–20 to stress the strength of Abraham's faith is similar to Hebrews 11:11–12; these two texts, in turn, resemble Philo's description of Abraham and an early Christian text, *1 Clement* 10. This raises the possibility that Paul is here quoting a widespread tradition about Abraham's faith.

Without weakening in his faith, he faced the fact that his body was as good as dead (4:19). This description of Abraham's faith appears to clash with two elements in the Genesis narrative about Abraham. (1) According to Genesis 17:17, when told that Sarah would bear him a son, Abraham "fell facedown; he laughed and said to himself, 'Will a son be born to a man a hundred years old? Will Sarah bear a child at the age of ninety?'" Philo suggests that Abraham's laughter may have been an expression of joy rather than of disbelief (*Questions and Answers on Genesis* 3.55); and some of the rabbis followed suit. But the parallel reaction of Sarah in 18:12–15 and

---

R E F L E C T I O N S

ABRAHAM'S FAITH IS A MODEL FOR THE KIND OF FAITH that God is still looking for in his people. He believed "against hope," yet "in hope." His faith was "against hope" because it flew in the face of material evidence and common sense. He was too old to have children; his wife was barren. How could they possibly conceive a child? Yet Abraham did not let this evidence detract from the promise that God had given him. It was "in [the] hope" created by God's word to him that he believed God would give him and Sarah a child, even though it made no rational sense. Are we willing and able to believe God's promises when all the evidence points in the other direction?

the context make this solution unlikely. Probably Paul is making a generalization about the whole course of Abraham's life. (2) A second problem with Paul's description is the fact that Genesis 25:1–2 indicates that Abraham later produced children through another wife, Keturah. The best solution is to assume that God's gift of procreative power to Abraham remained after the birth of Isaac.

He was delivered over to death for our sins and was raised to life for our justification (4:25). This brief description of Christ's work on our behalf is carefully worded, with the parts of the statement parallel to one another. Many scholars therefore think it is likely that Paul is quoting an early Christian confession. The confession may have been modeled partly on the prophet Isaiah's description of the work of the Suffering Servant, who would be "handed over because of their sins" (Isa. 53:12 in LXX).

The Hope of Glory (5:1–11)

Paul shifts gears in this chapter. In chapters 1–4, he has outlined the heart of his gospel: that sinful people can be put right with God through their faith in Jesus Christ. Now he goes on to show (in chs. 5–8) that the person who has been justified is assured of being saved from God's wrath and delivered from the ravages of sin and death in the last day. Paul announces this theme in 5:1–11, arguing that those who are justified, though still subject to life's trials, have a secure hope for future deliverance from wrath.

We have peace with God (5:1). "Peace" is, of course, a common word in the ancient world and can have many different nuances. It generally referred, negatively,

to a cessation of hostility. But Paul's use of the word is more in keeping with the positive concept of the word found in the Old Testament: the well-being, prosperity, or salvation of the godly person. The prophets predicted a day when God would establish a new era of peace (see, e.g., Isa. 52:7, quoted in Rom. 10:15): "How beautiful on the mountains are the feet of those who bring good news, who proclaim peace, who bring good tidings, who proclaim salvation, who say to Zion, 'Your God reigns!'"

Through whom we have gained access by faith into this grace in which we now stand (5:2). The word "access" (*prosagōgē*) was used in the ancient world to refer to a person's being conducted into the presence of royalty (see LSJ, who cite Xenophon, *Cyr.* 7.5.45). Whether the word was used often enough for this situation to lead Paul's first readers to make this association is not clear. But the image is one that would have struck a note with the Christians in Rome, aware of court protocol that restricted "access" to the emperor to certain highly placed individuals. Through Jesus Christ, every believer has this kind of access to the grace of the King of heaven.

We also rejoice in our sufferings . . . knowing . . . (5:3–4). In these verses, Paul lists a series of virtues that Christians who respond to suffering in the right way can experience. Such a list, with the most important items coming at the end, resembles the ancient literary form called *sorites*. Similar claims about the beneficial effects of suffering for the Lord's sake are found elsewhere in the New Testament:

> Consider it pure joy, my brothers, whenever you face trials of many

kinds, because you know that the testing of your faith develops perseverance. Perseverance must finish its work so that you may be mature and complete, not lacking anything. (James 1:2–4)

In this you greatly rejoice, though now for a little while you may have had to suffer grief in all kinds of trials. These have come so that your faith—of greater worth than gold, which perishes even though refined by fire—may be proved genuine and may result in praise, glory and honor when Jesus Christ is revealed. (1 Peter 1:6–7)

The teaching was probably a widespread tradition in the early church that Paul here quotes to establish contact with Christians in Rome who do not know him.

And hope does not disappoint us (5:5). The word "disappoint" could be more literally translated "put to shame" (*kataischynō*). This verb is used in the Old Testament to mean "suffer judgment." Typical is Isaiah 28:16 (quoted by Paul in Rom. 9:33 and 10:11): "So this is what the Sovereign LORD says: 'See, I lay a stone in Zion, a tested stone, a precious cornerstone for a sure foundation; the one who trusts will never be dismayed [or ashamed; *kataischynthē*]" (see also Ps. 22:5: "They cried to you and were saved; in you they trusted and were not disappointed [or ashamed; *katēschynthēsan*]"). Believers have a secure hope, based in the love and activity of God in Christ, so we need have no fear of being "ashamed" in the time of judgment.

God has poured out his love into our hearts by the Holy Spirit (5:5). The language of "pouring out" reminds us of Joel's famous prophecy about God's "pouring out" his Spirit in the last days (Joel 2:28–32, quoted by Peter on the Day of Pentecost; Acts 2:17–21).

Very rarely will anyone die for a righteous man, though for a good man someone might possibly dare to die (5:7). The difference between these two assertions probably lies in a distinction between "righteous" and "good," illustrated by the gnostics, who contrasted the "righteous" god of the Old Testament with the "good" god of the New (see Irenaeus, *Haer.* 1.27.1). In order to underscore the magnitude of God's love for us, Paul reminds his readers that it is extremely rare for a human being to give his or her life for a person who is upright and moral, though one can find examples of people giving their lives for people they love. Yet God has given Christ to die for people who were hostile to him.

Since we have now been justified by his blood, how much more shall we be saved from God's wrath through him! (5:9). We can understand better why Paul so emphasizes the unbreakable connection between justification and final salvation when we appreciate the general Jewish view of justification. Jews generally believed that a person would only be justified in the last day, when God evaluated a person's life in the judgment. See, as a typical example, *Psalms of Solomon* 17:26–29:

He will gather a holy people whom he will lead in righteousness; and he will judge the tribes of the people that have been made holy by the Lord their God. He will not tolerate unrighteousness (even) to pause among them, and any person who knows wickedness shall not live with them. For he shall know them that they are children of their God. He will distribute them upon the land according to their tribes; the alien and the foreigner will no longer live near them. He will judge peoples and nations in the wisdom of his righteousness.

Jesus' own use of "justify" language is in keeping with this Jewish perspective. Note, for instance, the contrast in Matthew 12:37: "For by your words you will be acquitted [or "justified"; the verb is *dikaioō*], and by your words you will be condemned." Paul proclaims that a person can experience this end-time justifying verdict in this life, the moment he or she puts faith in the Lord Jesus. A Jewish objector might well wonder what value that verdict would have for the time of judgment. Paul affirms that justification leads infallibly to a positive verdict in the judgment. For the judgment of that last day simply ratifies the eschatological verdict God has already pronounced in favor of the believer.

The Reign of Grace and Life (5:12–21)

Paul reinforces the security of Christian hope by grounding it in the work of Jesus Christ, whose "act of righteousness" brings life to those who belong to him just as certainly as Adam brought death to all who belong to him. Throughout this text, Paul assumes that both Adam and Christ have representative significance, as he adopts popular ancient Jewish ideas of the solidarity among individuals.

Just as sin entered the world through one man (5:12). Important for our appreciation of this famous theological text is the fact that the word "man" in Hebrew (*ʾādām*) is also the name "Adam." The very name of Adam, therefore, suggests his representative significance: Adam *is* "man."

▸ Corporate Solidarity and Adam's Sin

Modern readers are often disturbed or even offended at the idea that Adam, millennia ago, might have done something to affect all people who have lived since him. The Christian philosopher Pascal called this idea—"original sin"—an "offense to reason." However, while it does not necessarily remove all the offense, it is helpful to remember that ancient people—and Jews in particular—had a strong notion of "corporate solidarity." Jews believed that people were bound to one another in various relationships and that the actions of one person could have a determinative influence on all those to whom they were related.

The classic Old Testament example is Achan, whose sin in keeping for himself some of the plunder from the battle of Jericho is also said to be "Israel's sin" (Josh. 7:1, 11) and the reason why God's anger burns against Israel as a whole (5:1). Some scholars have taken the notion too far, suggesting that Hebrew thinking merged individuals into a corporate personality. But the importance of corporate thinking for ancient Jews is generally acknowledged and should correct the tendency in the modern West to look at such texts from too "individualistic" a perspective.

Death came to all men, because all sinned (5:12). The exact relationship between the sin of Adam and the death and condemnation of all people is a matter of long-standing debate among theologians. Paul is not explicit about the relationship, and so it is appropriate to ask what he might have assumed from his Jewish background.

Unfortunately, Jewish literature does not manifest a consistent view. A few Jewish texts attribute sin and death to the devil (see, e.g., Wisd. Sol. 2:24: "through the devil's envy death entered the world, and those who belong to his company experience it"). A very few even put the blame on Eve: "From a woman sin had its beginning, and because of her we all die" (Sir. 25:24). But more typical of the Jewish perspective is the tension exhibited on this matter in the Syriac *Apocalypse of Baruch*. The writer of this second-century A.D. book can assert, on the one hand, that Adam brought death to all his descendants: "When Adam sinned a death was decreed against those who were to be born" (*Apoc. Bar.* 23:4); "What did you [Adam] do to all who were born after you?" (48:42; see also *4 Ezra* 7:118). On the other hand, he also makes every person responsible for his or her own death: "Adam is, therefore, not the cause, except only for himself, but each of us has become our own Adam" (*Apoc. Bar.* 54:19); "Although Adam sinned first and has brought death upon all who were not in his own time, yet each of them who has been born from him has prepared for himself the coming torments" (54:15; see also *Bib. Ant.* 13:8–9).

The interpreter of Romans cannot, therefore, attribute to Paul any specific view on the relationship of Adam to humankind based on Jewish literature. A few interpreters have suggested that Paul may have taken over a deterministic tra-

---

▶ **Paul and Jewish Apocalyptic**

Jewish apocalyptic tended to divide the world into two "ages," separated by the coming of the Messiah. The "old age" of Israel's sin and degradation would give way to a new age in which God would bless and vindicate his people. A good representative text is *4 Ezra* 7:112–15:

He [an angel sent to instruct Ezra] answered me and said, "This present world is not the end; the full glory does not remain in it; therefore those who were strong prayed for the weak. But the day of judgment will be the end of this age and the beginning of the immortal age to come, in which corruption has passed away, sinful indulgence has come to an end, unbelief has been cut off, and righteousness has increased and truth has appeared. Therefore no one will then be able to have mercy on someone who has been condemned in the judgment, or to harm him who is victorious."

Paul adapted this basic scheme, modifying it to suit the Christian understanding that Messiah would come not once, but twice. Accordingly, the early Christians believed that the "new age" had been inaugurated with Christ's first coming but would only be consummated at his second. So the present time was a period of "overlap" between the two ages: by faith in Christ believers belonged to the new age of salvation but still lived and were influenced by the old age of sin and death. In Romans 5–8, Paul uses this two-age scheme to explain why Christians can have joy and confidence in their salvation even as they continue to struggle against sin (ch. 6), death (chs. 5, 8), and the law (ch. 7). Paul therefore contrasts the evil powers that "reign" in the present age (sin and death) with the powers of the age that has already dawned in Christ (grace, life, and righteousness).

dition about Adam's sin popular in gnostic-oriented circles.[33] But the gnostic myths to which scholars appeal cannot be traced definitely to Paul's time.

Sin is not taken into account when there is no law (5:13). Paul reflects here the same perspective on the law that we observed in our notes on 4:15: The coming of the Mosaic law enabled God for the first time to record sin as a violation of specific commands and prohibitions. The verb "take into account" (*ellogeō*) perfectly captures this nuance, since it was used to describe the careful, precise recording of accounts necessary in bookkeeping. A second-century papyrus document has two women writing to their steward: "Put down to our account everything you expend on the cultivation of the holding."[34]

A pattern of the one to come (5:14). "Pattern" translates *typos*, from which we get the word "typology." A *typos* was the impression left by the blow of a hammer or similar implement, and therefore came to have the meaning of form, pattern, or example. Old Testament people, events, and institutions, under God's sovereign direction, can become patterns for their New Testament counterparts. So, Paul affirms, Adam, in his representative significance, is a *typos* of Christ. "The one to come" is similar to other New Testament descriptions of the Messiah as the "coming one" (cf. Matt. 11:3; 21:9; 23:39; John 4:25; 6:14; 11:27; Heb. 10:37). We have little evidence from intertestamental literature that this title was being widely used to denote the Messiah.

The many (5:15, 19). Many scholars think that Paul's use of the word "many"

in this passage reflects certain occurrences of the same word in Hebrew, where the word was a stylistic equivalent of "all." Reference is especially made to Isaiah 53:11–12: ". . . by his knowledge my righteous servant will justify many. . . . For he bore the sin of many, and made intercession for the transgressors."[35] "Many" may be equivalent to "all" in this passage. But the claim that it regularly *means* "all" is exaggerated.

How much more will those who receive God's abundant provision of grace and of the gift of righteousness reign in life through the one man, Jesus Christ (5:17). Verses 18–19 could give the impression that the scope of salvation is as wide as the scope of sin and death. But what Paul says in 5:17 corrects this possible misapprehension. For by insisting that only those who "receive" God's gift will reign in life, he makes clear that one can enjoy life in Christ only by responding to the offer of grace.

Just as sin reigned in death, so also grace might reign through righteousness (5:21). The contrast between two "reigns" in this verse reflects a fundamental structure that Paul uses throughout his letters, but especially in chapters 5–8, to interpret and explain the significance of Christ. The structure has its roots in Jewish apocalyptic, a popular and diverse approach to understanding history and the future in Paul's day. Attempts to define the essence of Jewish apocalyptic vary considerably, and any attempt to survey the movement would require considerable space.

"Dead to Sin" and "Alive to God" (6:1–14)

What Paul has said in 5:20 about grace increasing all the more where sin increased might lead readers to the wrong conclusion. They might think that God's promise to meet sin with his grace means that sin does not matter—that Christians, because they are ruled by grace, need no longer concern themselves with sin. Like the seasoned preacher that he is, Paul anticipates this incorrect inference and heads it off immediately in chapter 6.

What shall we say, then? (6:1). As we noted in our comments on chapter 2, the question and answer style of writing that Paul frequently uses in Romans is similar to the ancient style of diatribe. In this case, however, he uses the style to teach Christians, not to debate with opponents of the faith. Scholars have shown that the diatribe style was often used in the ancient world in just this educational kind of setting.[36]

All of us who were baptized into Christ Jesus were baptized into his death (6:3). Paul's teaching that baptized believers become participants in Jesus' death and resurrection (cf. 6:5) has led to a long and contentious search for the background that might have led him to this idea. In the late 1800s and early 1900s, many scholars, persuaded that Paul's interpretation of Christ was deeply indebted to Greco-Roman influences, thought his conception of baptism into Christ's death came from the so-called mystery religions. These religions, which adherents joined by undergoing a secret rite of ini-

▶

"BAPTISMAL" POOL

A traditional Jewish purification bath (*miqveh*) discovered near Herod's palace in Jericho.

tiation, or *mystērion*, sometimes offered people the opportunity to be mystically joined to a dying and rising god. Paul, it was thought, adopted this idea and applied it to the Christian's union with Jesus in his death and resurrection through baptism. However, most scholars today don't think that the mystery religions had much influence on the early Christians' conception of Christ and his benefits. As A. J. M. Wedderburn has argued, it is improbable that Paul's presentation of the Christian's identification with Christ in his death and resurrection through baptism in Romans 6 has much to do with the mystery religions.[37]

What does inform Paul's notion of the believer's identification with Christ is his "second Adam Christology." As we have seen, Romans 5 presents Adam as representative head of the human race. Because all people are represented in Adam, his sin can at the same time be the sin of all people. Now Paul, of course, presents Christ as a representative figure similar to Adam. He can, then, portray Christians dying *with* Christ and being buried *with* him because he thinks of believers participating in Christ's acts of redemption. Baptism, as we will see, is Pauline shorthand in this text for the conversion experience.

Also debated is what Paul means by claiming that baptism is "*into* Christ Jesus." Paul may simply be abbreviating the common formula "in the name of Christ/Jesus," used several times in the New Testament in relationship to baptism (see Matt. 28:19; Acts 8:16; 19:5; cf. 1 Cor. 1:13, 15). But the "name" in the culture of that day represented the person himself or herself. Thus, this concept inevitably shades into the other idea, that Paul views believers as incorporated into Christ through baptism. At least one rab-

binic text (*b. Yebam.* 45b) suggests that "wash in the name of" signifies being bound to the person in whose name one is washed.

We were therefore buried with him through baptism (6:4). An important concept in 6:4–8 is the notion that Christians were "with" Christ in his death/crucifixion (6:5, 6, 8), burial (6:4), and resurrection (6:5, 8). How are we to understand this "withness"? Many scholars appeal to the general religious notion of "mysticism" to explain the idea. The identification with a god who died and rose to new life each year (imitating the cycle of nature) in the mystery religions (see above) would be one example of such a mystical concept. But the notion of some kind of merging of personality between a person and a god was found in many ancient Near-Eastern religions as well.

The basic concept that informs Paul's language here, however, should not be labeled "mysticism." As we noted in our comments on 5:12–21, Paul's teaching grows out of the Old Testament/Jewish notion of corporate solidarity. This notion is not properly "mystical," since it does not posit any merging of personalities. The solidarity is judicial or forensic. This is particularly clear with respect to Adam, who is, of course, not a god but an individual human being, whose significance for others is as their representative. This notion carries over into Romans 6 and explains how Paul can claim that believers were "with" Christ in his death, burial, and resurrection. As Adam in his sin represents all people, so Christ in his redemptive work represents people. Death, burial, and resurrection are singled out here because these three events were part of the core early Christian tradition about Christ's redemptive work. Note, for example, 1 Corinthians 15:3–4: "For what I received I passed on to you as of first importance: that Christ died for our sins according to the Scriptures, that he was buried, that he was raised on the third day according to the Scriptures."

In order that . . . we too may live a new life (6:4). A literal translation would be: "in order that . . . we too may walk in newness of life." Paul's use of the word "walk" to describe a person's lifestyle reflects a widespread Jewish metaphor (using the Hebrew word *hlk*). See, for example, Deuteronomy 26:17: "You have declared this day that the LORD is your God and that you will walk in his ways, that you will keep his decrees, commands and laws, and that you will obey him."

If we have been united with him like this in his death, we will certainly also be united with him in his resurrection (6:5). "United with" comes from a verb that means "grow together" (*symphyō*) and is often used in horticulture. Many interpreters, therefore, conclude that Paul may be alluding to Jesus' famous illustration of the vine and the branches (John 15). However, the word is used in many contexts, most of them not horticultural. We have no reason to think that this particular connotation of the word would have been in Paul's mind at this point.

Our old self was crucified with him (6:6). Paul uses the language of the "old self" or "old man" also in Ephesians 4:22–24 and Colossians 3:9–11. In both of these, the "old self," which Christians "put off," is contrasted with the "new self," which they have put on (Col. 3) or are to put on (Eph. 4). Modern interpreters often give the imagery an individualistic interpretation, as if the "old self" were the believer's sinful "nature" and the "new self" the renewed nature given at conversion. But Paul's idea is probably more corporate than this. We must again remember what he said about Adam's representative significance in chapter 5. With this notion present in the context, we are probably right to think of the "old self" as essentially Adam himself. Christ is then the "new self" (see Eph. 2:15; 4:13). What is crucified with Christ, then, is not some part, or nature, of us, but, as J. R. W. Stott puts it, "the whole of me as I was before I was converted."[38] When a person comes to Christ, that person is no longer under the domination of (though still influenced by) the nexus of sin and death brought into the world by Adam.

REFLECTIONS

SOME POPULAR EXPLANATIONS OF THE CHRISTIAN life use Paul's language of "old self" and "new self" to conceptualize the biblical teaching. One view, for instance, holds that when a person is converted, they lose the "old self" and become entirely a "new self." Another maintains that the "new self" is simply added to the "old self" when a person comes to Christ. Neither explanation does justice to all the biblical data or to our own experience. The former view cannot explain why Paul calls on Christians to "put off your old self" (Eph. 4:22–24) and has a hard time explaining the reality of continuing sinfulness in the believer. The latter, by contrast, does not do justice to the decisive change in our status that verses like Romans 6:6 teach. A better approach, then, is to think of the "old self" as Adam (cf. Rom. 5) and the "new self" as Christ. When we come to Christ, our servitude to the "old self" (or, better, "old man"), Adam, is broken, and we are tied inextricably to the "new self," Jesus Christ. So a decisive change occurs, but a change that does not make us immune from the continuing influence of our old Adamic self.

Anyone who has died has been freed from sin (6:7). "Freed [from]" actually translates the verb that is regularly translated "justify" (*dikaioō*). Many commentators think this translation should be preserved here. If so, then this verse is claiming that the believer's freedom from sin's power (6:6) is based on (note the "because" at the beginning of 6:7) the believer's justification (from sin's penalty). This idea may be theologically quite acceptable. But the NIV rendering has a lot to be said for it. Only here in his writings does Paul use the preposition "from" (*apo*) after the verb "justify" (though cf. Acts 13:38). More important, Paul may well be reflecting here a Jewish tradition, preserved in *b. Šabb.* 151b: "When a man is dead he is freed from fulfilling the law."[39]

The death he died, he died to sin once for all (6:10). The believer's death "to sin" is the ruling idea of this paragraph (see 6:2). It is a metaphor Paul uses to indicate the believer's complete break with the domination or mastery of sin. Being "dead to sin" means that Christians are no longer "slaves to sin" (6:6); sin is no longer our master (6:14). But why would Christ have had to "die to sin," as 6:10 claims? Some commentators think Paul may be using the metaphor in a different way here, to depict the redemptive benefits of Christ's death on our behalf. But we can maintain the same basic significance of the metaphor when we remember that Paul is writing in the context of his ruling "two-age" salvation-historical scheme (see comments on 5:21). In his incarnation, Christ took on our humanity and entered into the present evil age. Sin rules this age, and so Christ was subject to its power throughout his earthly life. To be sure, he never succumbed to that power and actually sinned. But he did need to be released from its power; and his death was that release. The main line of Paul's argument in these verses thus becomes clear:

- Christ died to sin (6:10).
- We died with Christ (6:5, 6, 8).
- Therefore, we have died to sin (6:2).

In Christ Jesus (6:11). Paul's salvation-historical conception, rooted in Jewish apocalyptic, can again explain his claim that believers are "in" Christ. This idea, widespread in his letters, is again often thought to reflect ancient religious mystical notions. A. Deissmann, who popularized the notion in the early 1900s, argued that Paul viewed Christ as the "medium" or "ether" in which the Christian lives. But such a conception tends to depersonalize Christ and therefore runs counter to New Testament views of Jesus. A better explanation is to refer again to Paul's belief that Christ is the representative head of the new age of salvation. He incorporates within himself all who belong to him by faith. To be "in Christ," then, means to be identified with Christ as our representative and to have all the benefits he has won in his redemptive work applied to us.[40]

You are not under law, but under grace (6:14). Failure to appreciate the background of Paul's teaching can lead casual readers of Romans to misunderstand this assertion badly. Some might think that Paul proclaims believers to be free from any code of ethics at all. Those who have some knowledge of the history of theology might conclude that Paul proclaims the freedom of the believer from any divine commands—"law" in the sense the word is used in Lutheran theology, as the contrast to the gospel.

But, as we have seen earlier (see comments on 2:12), "law" (*nomos*) in Paul, a first-century Jew, almost always refers to the Mosaic law, the Torah. Paul is not claiming that believers are free from any divine commands (such as those we find in the teaching of Jesus or the New Testament letters). What he means is that believers are no longer bound to the Mosaic law. A new era in God's plan of salvation has dawned, an era in which God's eschatological grace is being poured out. With the coming of this new era, the old era has ceased to be the one to which we belong. The law of Moses was part of that old era. (Paul develops this argument in great detail in Gal. 3:15–4:7.) Paul's statement here is similar, then, to John's claim: "The law was given through Moses; grace and truth came through Jesus Christ" (John 1:17).

Freed from Sin's Power to Serve Righteousness (6:15–23)

Paul's focus in 6:1–14 has been on the negative: Believers are no longer slaves of sin (6:6). In 6:15–23, he broadens the perspective by including the positive side as well: Set free from sin, believers are now slaves of righteousness and of God.

Don't you know that when you offer yourselves to someone to obey him as slaves, you are slaves to the one you obey (6:16). Slavery was one of the best-known institutions in the ancient world. Almost 35–40 percent of the inhabitants of Rome and the peninsula of Italy in the first century were slaves; and the situation in the provinces may have been comparable.[41] So Paul's analogy would have been one that all his readers could immediately have identified with. Making the analogy even more exact is the fact that people in the ancient world could sell themselves into slavery (e.g., to avoid a ruinous debt).[42] Similarly, Paul suggests, believers who constantly obey sin rather than God might find themselves to be slaves of sin again, doomed to eternal death.

You have been set free from sin and have become slaves to righteousness (6:18). Modern people, especially in the West, prize their autonomy. As heirs of the humanism of the Enlightenment, they assume that the noblest human being is the one who is subject to nothing but his or her own rational considerations. Ancient people, however, had a much stronger belief in the degree to which all human beings were under the control of outside powers—whether they be gods, the stars, or fate in general. The biblical writers certainly share this conviction. Nowhere in this paragraph does Paul suggest a person might not be a slave of something. Either he or she is dominated by sin or by righteousness and God—there is no middle ground. Jesus reflects the same perspective when he claims that "no one can serve two masters. Either he will hate the one and love the

RECEIPT FOR DELIVERY OF A SLAVE

This receipt is written on a pottery shard (*ostracon*) discovered in Egypt.

other, or he will be devoted to the one and despise the other. You cannot serve both God and Money" (Matt. 6:24).

Offer them in slavery to righteousness leading to holiness (6:19). "Holiness" (which suggests the state of being holy) can also be translated "sanctification" (which suggests the process of becoming holy). In either case, Paul picks up the imagery from the Old Testament, where the root *qds* is widely used to denote the idea of being "set apart" from the world for the service of the Lord. As Christians give themselves in slavery to righteousness, they will progress further and further on the path of becoming different from the world and closer to the Lord's own holiness.

The wages of sin is death (6:23). "Wages" translates *opsōnia*, a word that means "provisions," but which is often used of money paid for services rendered. It was particularly applied to the pay given to soldiers (all three uses in the LXX have this sense [1 Esd. 4:56; 1 Macc. 3:28; 14:32]). The specific imagery in this verse, therefore, might be sin, as a commanding officer, paying a wage to his soldiers.

Released from the Law, Joined to Christ (7:1–6)

As Paul has suggested in 6:14 (see comments), the law of Moses belongs to the old age. In order to belong to the new age, therefore, believers must be released from the domination of the Mosaic law. In this paragraph Paul asserts that release and explains its consequences.

I am speaking to men who know the law (7:1). The "law" here, as throughout

chapter 7, is probably the Mosaic law. We might therefore conclude that "[those] who know the law" must be Jews. But this is not necessarily the case. A substantial number of Gentiles in the ancient world were attracted to the Jewish religion. They regularly attended synagogue meetings, knew the Old Testament, and endeavored to follow the law as much as possible. But they were not considered Jews because they stopped short of becoming circumcised. These Gentile sympathizers, called "God-fearers" (see, e.g., Acts 13:26), were probably numerous in the early Christian churches, and many of the Gentiles Paul addresses in Rome were probably drawn from their number.

The law has authority over a man only as long as he lives (7:1). Paul refers to what may have been a well-known maxim in his day. See, for instance, *b. Šabb.* 30a: "If a person is dead, he is free from the Torah and the fulfilling of the commandments."[43]

If she marries another man (7:3). The Greek phrase means, literally, "become to a man" (*ginomai andri*). It is a colloquialism for "marry," as the LXX reveals, so the NIV rendering is accurate.[44] But Paul may use this particular wording so that he can create a better parallel with the believer's being "joined to" Christ (7:4, the Greek there is the same).

When we were controlled by the sinful nature (7:5). "Sinful nature" is the NIV rendering of the Greek word *sarx*, whose literal meaning is "flesh." The word has this literal meaning in the New Testament (e.g., 1 Cor. 15:39), but Paul particularly often uses *sarx* as a metaphor to denote the sinful tendency that governs people apart from Christ. As in this verse, the NIV generally chooses to translate this word with the phrase "sinful nature" when it has this metaphorical connotation.

Paul's use of this particular word in this way is striking and has created considerable controversy. A few scholars have thought that Paul might be influenced by certain Greek traditions that tended to view the physical body as evil. But a more likely background is the Old Testament use of the Hebrew word *bāsār* ("flesh") to denote the human being, and particularly the human being in his or her weakness, frailty, and proneness to sin (see Gen. 6:3, 12; Ps. 78:39). This background makes it clear that "flesh" is not a *part* of the human being (as the NIV translation may suggest), but the whole person looked upon as tied to this world, with its sin and corruption. Paul extends this basic sense a bit further, conceiving of *sarx* as virtually a power that exercises control over people outside of Christ. This, in turn, fits nicely into his two-age salvation-historical scheme. *Sarx* becomes another one of those ruling powers of the old age, from which believers are released through conversion to Christ. This is why Paul can in this verse describe our pre-Christian past as, literally, the time when we were "in the flesh."

The Coming of the Law (7:7–12)

The beginning of Romans 7 is the climax in Paul's negative assessment of the Mosaic law in Romans (see also 3:20, 28; 4:15; 5:20; 6:14, 15). Like sin, the law is something that people must "die to" if they are to enjoy the benefits of incorporation into Christ. As a seasoned preacher and teacher, Paul well knows the conclusion that people might draw

from this negative assessment. So he himself brings this faulty inference out into the open at the beginning of this paragraph: "What shall we say, then? Is the law sin?" He then shows why the inference is a faulty one, arguing that sin, not the law, is at fault in bringing about the human plight of death.

I would not have known what sin was except through the law (7:7). The Hebrew verb for "know" (*yd*ˁ) often has the sense "experience, be in relationship with." The NIV obscures this sense of "know" by choosing other English renderings where the verb has this sense. But a more literal translation quickly reveals this usage. See, for instance, Jeremiah 9:6: "'You live in the midst of deception; in their deceit they refuse to *know* [NIV acknowledge] me,' declares the LORD." What the Lord is rebuking the people for is their failure to maintain their relationship with him. This same meaning occurs frequently in the New Testament with the comparable Greek verbs for "know." Second Corinthians 5:21, which claims that Christ did not "know" sin, is a good example.

Some interpreters apply this meaning to the verbs in this verse. Paul is then claiming that Israel did not "experience" sin until the law came. But this experien-

tial sense of the verbs is by no means common in the New Testament. Nevertheless, Paul seems to be claiming more than that the law simply "defined" what sin was. What he probably means is that the law gave to Israel a sense for what sin really is, in all its heinousness (see Rom. 7:13).

"Do not covet" (7:7). A few scholars, thinking that Paul refers to the experience of Adam and Eve throughout this paragraph, argue that Paul here refers to the prohibition that the Lord gave to the first human pair in the Garden of Eden. They note that the Aramaic targum *Neofiti I* uses a word that could be translated "desire" in Genesis 3:6 and that a rabbinic text claims that "desire" was injected into Eve by the serpent.[45] But these connections are tenuous at best. The words are

---

▶ The Use of "I" in Light of Paul's Corporate Solidarity with Israel

Throughout 7:7–25, Paul writes in the first person singular: "I," "me," "my," etc. The modern reader would naturally conclude that Paul does so because he is describing his own experience in these verses. Perhaps the modern reader is right. But the ancient world also furnishes some rhetorical models that suggest a different conclusion. Some scholars have drawn attention to texts in which the "I" is "fictive"; that is, an author writes in the first-person singular to describe a situation or experience without including himself or herself at all. A familiar example comes from Paul himself: "If I speak in the tongues of men and of angels, but have not love, I am only a resounding gong or a clanging cymbal. If I have the gift of prophecy and can fathom all mysteries and all knowledge, and if I have a faith that can move mountains, but have not love, I am nothing. If I give all I possess to the poor and surrender my body to the flames, but have not love, I gain nothing" (1 Cor. 13:1–3).[A-4] However, these texts are not close in nature to Romans 7. They are almost always cast in a hypothetical mold (as is the Corinthians text cited above) or include the author.

Closer in nature to Romans 7 and more relevant to Paul's own background and the context of Romans are Old Testament and Jewish texts that use "I" to depict the people of Israel. Note, for example, Micah 7:8–10, in which "I" is the nation of Israel, lamenting its judgment and expressing its hope:

> Do not gloat over me, my enemy!
> Though I have fallen, I will rise.

> Though I sit in darkness,
>   the LORD will be my light.
> Because I have sinned against him,
>   I will bear the LORD's wrath,
> until he pleads my case
>   and establishes my right.
> He will bring me out into the light;
>   I will see his righteousness.
> Then my enemy will see it
>   and will be covered with shame,
> she who said to me,
>   "Where is the LORD your God?"
> My eyes will see her downfall;
>   even now she will be trampled underfoot
>   like mire in the streets.[A-5]

Since Paul is writing in these verses about the coming of the Mosaic law (not "law" in general), a reference to the people of Israel makes good sense here. But this is not to exclude Paul himself. In the kind of solidarity viewpoint typical of these chapters, he identifies himself with the history of his own people Israel. Their experience is, in a real sense, his also. What happened when God gave the law to Israel at Sinai has also affected Paul. Such a close identification with the history of Israel is also typical of first-century Jews. In the yearly Passover ritual, every Jew confessed that he or she was a slave in Egypt and experienced the Lord's deliverance from bondage (see, e.g., *m. Pesaḥ* 10).

almost certainly an abbreviated citation of the tenth commandment of the Decalogue (Ex. 20:17; Deut. 5:21). There is Jewish precedent for such an abbreviation.[46] Paul probably quotes this commandment because some Jews viewed "coveting," or illicit desire, as the root evil.[47] The prohibition could then become a representative summation of the Mosaic law as a whole.[48] Paul uses the commandment in just this sense. He is writing about Israel's experience with the Mosaic law as a whole—not one person's experience (the "I") with one commandment.

Produced in me every kind of covetous desire (7:8). This language has been taken to refer to Paul's own sexual awakening at the time of his puberty.[49] But the word "desire" (*epithymeō*) generally has a broader meaning in Paul; moreover, as we have seen, a reference to Paul's individual experience in this paragraph is unlikely. Several other interpreters have suggested that Paul may be thinking of his *bar mitzvah*. But the ceremony was unknown in Paul's day; it was a medieval creation.[50]

The very commandment that was intended to bring life actually brought death (7:10). Interpreters who think Paul is describing the experience of Adam (as a representative person) in this paragraph argue that this language can only properly be applied to Adam and Eve. For only they actually experienced death when "the commandment came" and they sinned against the Lord. All other human beings since them were born in sin, condemned to death already.

But the commandment, in light of the context, must refer to a representative commandment from the Mosaic law (see 7:7). To be sure, Jewish tradition sometimes claimed that Adam and Eve were subject to the law itself. One of the Aramaic paraphrases of the Old Testament, *Neofiti I*, translates Genesis 2:15–16: "And the Lord God took man and caused him to dwell in the Garden of Eden, in order to keep the Law and to follow his commandments." But it is vital to Paul's understanding of salvation history to claim that the law came only with Moses, introduced 430 years after Abraham (Gal. 3:17). He would hardly give up such a vital point here.

What we must understand is that Paul is writing to counteract a certain Jewish tradition about the Mosaic law. That tradition, rooted in the Old Testament itself (Lev. 18:5; Ps. 19:7–10; Ezek. 20:11), ascribed virtual salvific power to the law (see, e.g., *t. Šabb.* 15.17: "The commands were given only that men should live through them, not that men should die through them"[51]). Paul turns this tradition on its head: The law brought not life, but death. Paul does not mean that the people of Israel experienced spiritual death for the first time when the law came. But what he does mean is that they were driven more deeply into spiritual helplessness because of the way the law so clearly spelled out the divine demands. When failure to meet these demands inevitably ensued, Israel's penalty for its sin was simply made all the greater (see also Rom. 4:15; 5:13–14).

Sin . . . deceived me (7:11). Advocates of the "Adamic" interpretation of these verses view this assertion as an allusion to Genesis 3:13, in which Eve claims that "the serpent deceived me, and I ate" (note that Paul uses this same verb to describe Eve's deception in 2 Cor. 11:13; 1 Tim. 2:14). Paul puts sin in the role of the serpent. But Paul uses the verb elsewhere with no allusion to the Fall.[52] That some allusion to the experience of Adam might be present in these verses need not be denied. In fact, Jewish tradition sometimes paralleled Adam and Israel. But Paul's main focus is on the Mosaic law and therefore on Israel, not Adam.

Life Under the Law (7:13–25)

Scholars and laypeople have debated for centuries over the interpretation of this passage. This commentary is not the place to discuss the matter. Suffice it to say that we think Paul is referring to the experience of the Jewish people (before Christ) under the law.[53] In 7:7–12, he describes what happened when the law "came" to the people of Israel. Now he turns to the nature of their experience living under that law.

Sold as a slave to sin (7:14). The NIV "as a slave" is an inference from one common application of the verb that Paul uses here. The verb itself means simply "sell," but it refers specifically to the selling of slaves in eleven of its twenty-four LXX occurrences and in one of its nine New Testament uses (Matt. 18:25). The slave imagery is further suggested by Paul's use of a preposition (*hypo*) that means "under" (see 3:9).

What I want to do I do not do, but what I hate I do (7:15). This confession of frustration at not being able to put into practice what one knows to be the right thing to do is similar to many found in the ancient world. Certainly the most famous comes from the Latin writer Ovid: "I see and approve the better course, but I follow the worse."[54]

That is, in my sinful nature (7:18). Or "flesh" (*sarx*); see comments on 7:5.

I see another law at work in the members of my body (7:23). Paul's introduction of a second "law," alongside "God's law" (7:22), is problematic. What is this "another law"? Since Paul has consistently used the word "law" to refer to the Mosaic law throughout this passage, this other law may simply be the Mosaic law in another guise. As a revelation of God's righteous will for his people, this law is "holy, righteous and good" (7:12). But when perverted by sin, that same law brings frustration and death (7:7–11). However, the word "another" makes it difficult to think that this second law has any relationship to the Mosaic law. Paul seems to be talking about a different law altogether. Ancient writers could sometimes use the word "law" (*nomos*) to refer to a general authority, norm, or power (see comments on 2:12). A contrast between God's law and an evil "law" is found elsewhere in Jewish literature, as in *T. Naph.* 2.6: "As a person's strength, so also is his work . . . as is his soul, so also

REFLECTIONS

IF ROMANS 7 IS ABOUT THE EXPERIENCE OF ISRAEL with the Mosaic law, what value does the chapter have for the Gentile Christian? For Gentiles have never been "under" the law of Moses. But Paul regards Israel's experience with the Mosaic law as typical of the experience of all people with "law" of any kind. Even God's own good and righteous commandments could not rescue Israel from her sin; how much less will other laws, be they moral codes or private resolutions, deliver us from our human plight. For law, in its very nature, tells us what to do but does not give us the power to do it. As long as we are held captive by sin, law will only reveal more clearly our problem and frustrate our efforts to live up to its standards. Deliverance from this dilemma, as Paul makes clear in 7:25, comes only through "Jesus Christ our Lord."

is this thought, whether on the Law of the Lord or on the law of Beliar."

What a wretched man I am! (7:24). "Wretched" (*talaipōros*) is a strong word. This word and its cognates are used several times in the Old Testament to refer to the "misery" or "distress" that come on the wicked in God's judgment (e.g., Isa. 47:11; Jer. 6:7).[55]

The Spirit of Life (8:1–13)

In chapters 6 and 7, Paul has answered possible objections to his teaching in chapter 5 that Christians who have been justified by faith have full assurance of being saved in the last day. Neither sin (ch. 6) nor the law (ch. 7) can stand in the way of our ultimate vindication. In chapter 8, Paul takes up the theme of assurance once again. "No condemnation" is the great claim that stands over all of the chapter. Especially important is the introduction of a new "power" on the scene: the Holy Spirit. Mentioned in passing in 7:6, the Spirit's work is the focal point of the chapter. It is because of the Spirit's powerful influence that the believer can experience the blessings of salvation both now and into the future.

In Christ Jesus (8:1). The language of incorporation into Christ reminds us of the teaching of 5:12–21. As all human beings are "in Adam" and so suffer the death that his sin introduced into the world, so believers are "in Christ" and enjoy the benefits of the righteousness and life that his work on the cross secured.

The law of the Spirit of life (8:2). As Paul has done twice earlier in the letter (3:27; 7:23), he contrasts one "law" with another "law." The "law of the Spirit" could be a reference to the Mosaic law as it is used and actuated by the Holy Spirit. Appeal can be made here to a prophecy that was influential on the early Christian understanding of the new age: Jeremiah 31:31–34 and its close parallel, Ezekiel 36:24–32. These texts predict that God will one day write his law on the hearts of his people and put his Spirit in their hearts in such a way that they will be able to obey that law. "The law of the Spirit" may be Paul's way of referring to that internalized, Spirit-influenced law.

However, while the prophets looked for a day when God's people would be able to follow his law, they do not present that law as the liberating power (as Paul here presents "the law of the Spirit"). Nor does Paul ever suggest that the law would have such a role. It is better, then, to think that the word "law" in the phrase "law of the Spirit" has the meaning of "authority" or "power" (see comments on 2:12 and 7:23). The second "law" in this verse, "the law of sin and death," may be the Mosaic law, since Paul in chapter 7 has shown how that law was used by sin to bring death. But "law of sin" in 7:23 is not the Mosaic law, but a rhetorical counterpart to God's law. So here also "the law of sin and death" is probably the power of sin, leading to death, that holds people in its sway.

Sinful nature . . . sinful man (8:3). In both cases (as the NIV note indicates), these phrases translate a single Greek word, *sarx* ("flesh"). As we have seen (see comments on 7:5), Paul picks up the Old Testament use of this word to refer to human weakness and bondage to sin. What he is affirming, then, is that God has won the victory over the "flesh" in the "flesh" itself. By sending his Son to become fully human, God entered the arena of "flesh" and overcame its power to prevent people from obeying God and his law.

Sin offering (8:3). The Greek words here (*peri hamartias*) could be translated simply "concerning sin." But in the LXX, the phrase usually refers to a sacrificial offering; and three of the eight New Testament occurrences also have this meaning (Heb. 10:6, 8; 13:11). Christ is himself the sin offering that effects forgiveness and the turning away of God's wrath. God condemned sin in Christ, our substitute, so that we could escape condemnation.

The righteous requirements of the law (8:4). The NIV plural "requirements" is interpretive; the Greek word (*dikaiōma*) is singular. The plural of this word is common in the Old Testament to refer to the "statutes" of the law, a usage continued in the New Testament.[56] In the light of this usage, Paul's use of the word in the singular here must be deliberate. He is thinking not of the way Spirit-led Christians obey the detailed requirements of the law, but of the way believers, because they are in Christ, fulfill the overall demand of the law.

Who do not live according to the sinful nature but according to the Spirit (8:4). Dominating 8:4–11 is the contrast between the Spirit and the "flesh" (*sarx*, rendered "sinful nature" or "sinful mind" or simply "sinful" in the NIV). The Greek way of conceptualizing the human being has exerted a strong influence on those of us who live in the West. We naturally bring that conception into our Christian faith. The Greeks tended to take a dualistic view of human beings. That is, they divided, often quite sharply, the "material part" of the human being—the body or the flesh—from the "immaterial part"—the soul or the spirit. Under this influence, we can easily read 8:4–11 as if Paul were calling on believers to live according to their immaterial spirit and not according to their material body.

But such a reading badly misrepresents Paul's argument. (1) While some dualism is apparent in the New Testament view of the human being (for the soul can be separated from the body at death), the early Christians generally adopted the Old Testament/mainstream Jewish view of the human being as a fundamental unity. Indeed, it is this essentially unitary way of looking at people that requires resurrection: The body and soul cannot be separated forever.

(2) *Sarx*, when used to describe human proneness to sin in Paul, is not a part of the human being, but a perspective from which the whole human being is viewed. It is not that one part of us is sinful; we are, apart from Christ, sinful throughout—in mind, body, and soul.

SIN OFFERING

A model of a Jewish sacrificial scene at the tabernacle.

▼

(3) The "spirit" in this passage is the Holy Spirit, not the human spirit. Note that the NIV capitalizes every occurrence of "spirit" (*pneuma*) in these verses except one (8:10). Even this one probably should be capitalized, for the text is best translated "the Spirit is life." Reading these verses against their appropriate Old Testament/mainstream Jewish/early Christian background, then, makes clear that Paul is working throughout with a contrast between God's Spirit, the power of the new age that he sends into the lives of his people, and the human propensity to sin and evil. God's Spirit inevitably wins this battle. In this life he plants within us a new way of thinking (8:5–7) that must infallibly lead to a new way of living (8:4). Ultimately, that same Spirit will raise and transform our bodies themselves (8:11).

Have their minds set . . . the mind (8:5–6). The Greek words behind these translations (*phroneō* and *phronēma*) refer not just to the mental process of thinking, but to the general direction of the will.

The mind controlled by the Spirit is life and peace (8:6). The peace Paul refers to here is not the subjective "peace of mind," but the objective state of peace between God and his people and the general well-being that this relationship brings. Informing this concept is the Old Testament use of *shalom* to denote the eschatological blessing that God promises to his people (see comments on 5:1).

You, however, are controlled not by the sinful nature but by the Spirit (8:9). The NIV rendering is accurate enough. But a literal translation reveals the "two-age" salvation-historical conception that again informs Paul's teaching: "You are not in the flesh but in the Spirit." To be "in" the flesh is to belong to the sphere or realm of sinful, depraved humanity. All people, because of Adam's sin, begin life trapped in this realm, destined to spiritual death. But in his grace, God removes us from that realm and puts us in another realm, ruled by Christ, righteousness, life, and the Spirit. All Christians, by definition, are therefore "in" the Spirit—living in the realm dominated by God's Holy Spirit.

If the Spirit . . . lives in you (8:9). Paul's shift from the idea of believers being "in the Spirit" to the Spirit being "in" believers reveals that both are figures of speech, metaphors used to convey the truth that believers are ruled over and empowered by the Spirit.

He who raised Christ from the dead will also give life to your mortal bodies (8:11). Paul here reflects a key underlying tension in his celebration of the believer's blessings in Christ. Through the sacrifice of his son and the work of his Spirit, God has given his people "life" in the present: freedom from condemnation (8:1–9). But that "life" is not complete. The blessing of the new age has begun, but it is not yet here in its fullness. Believers must still face the reality of physical death, in that our bodies are still "mortal." Therefore, God's life-giving work is not finished until the body has been raised.

We have an obligation (8:12). Here Paul reflects the important "correction" that he makes to the simple Jewish idea of the "two ages." No longer is the transition from the one to the other a sharp, one-time event. The new age has dawned with the coming of Christ, and believers enjoy the benefits of that age, or realm, even now. But the old age has not disappeared. It has been judged and defeated, but will not be finally vanquished until the return of Christ in glory. With all the blessings we have received, therefore, believers still have a battle to fight. Sin and the flesh can still exert a powerful influence on us, an influence that must be resisted.

The Spirit of Adoption (8:14–17)

The Spirit gives life (8:1–13); he also confers on believers the status of God's own children. That new status is a source of joy in the present; but also a source of confidence for the future.

Sons of God (8:14). In the Old Testament and Judaism, "son of God" was used to depict Israel as the people whom God has called to be his own. See, for instance, Hosea 11:1 (quoted in Matt. 2:15): "When Israel was a child, I loved him, and out of Egypt I called my son."[57] The plural "sons of God" is less often used of the people of Israel, but it occurs often enough to justify our thinking that this background has influenced Paul's use of the phrase here (see Deut. 14:1; Isa. 43:6).[58] Paul therefore implies that Christians now take on the status and privileges of the people of Israel. This attribution to Christians of blessings once held by the people of Israel becomes an important theme in Romans 8 and sets up the problem Paul begins to deal with in chapter 9: Has God simply disenfranchised Israel?

The Spirit of sonship (8:15). The Greek word behind "sonship" can also be translated "adoption" (*huiothesia*). "Sonship" denotes the state of being God's own

children; "adoption" refers to the process that leads to that state. Since almost all of the uses of the word outside the New Testament mean "adoption," that is probably the best rendering here.[59]

The process of adoption was unknown among Jews, but was common in the Greek, and especially the Roman, world. It was a legal institution by which a person could adopt a child and confer on that child all the legal rights and privileges that would accrue to a natural child.[60] One of the most famous "adoptions" in the Roman world was Julius Caesar's adoption of Octavian, who became Emperor Augustus. Paul's readers in Rome would naturally have thought immediately of this institution when they read these verses. The language would have conveyed to them the amazing grace of God in taking sinful human beings, making them his own children, and conferring on them all the rights and privileges of heaven itself (see also 8:23; Gal. 4:5; Eph. 1:5). But, while the language Paul uses here undoubtedly points to this Roman

◀

ADOPTION

Octavian (Caesar Augustus), who is pictured here, was adopted by Julius Caesar.

institution, the word also indirectly conjures up the Old Testament and Jewish background we sketched above. Israel herself, Paul affirms in Romans 9:4, experienced this same "adoption." Here again is a blessing given to Israel that is now "transferred" to Christians.

And by him we cry, "Abba, Father" (8:15). "Cry" or "cry out" (*krazō*) is used in the Gospels of people who "cry out" under the influence of demons (e.g., Mark 3:11; 5:5, 7). We find the same usage in some ancient magical texts, in which a demon, or someone possessed, is said to "cry out." Since Paul has been describing the believer as a person, in a sense, "possessed" by the Spirit, we may view this "crying out" here as "ecstatic" in nature. If so, however, we must carefully qualify the idea to make clear that this exclamation is the product not of mindless possession but of conscious understanding. Note the emphasis in Romans 8:16 on the "testifying" work of the Spirit. Another background is suggested in the Psalms, where worshipers are frequently portrayed as crying out to God in praise or in supplication (see, e.g., Ps. 55:16: "But I call to God, and the LORD saves me"). Nevertheless, properly nuanced, the former option makes better sense in this context.

The Spirit himself testifies with our spirit that we are God's children (8:16). This is the only place in chapter 8 where the word "spirit" refers to the human spirit rather than to the Holy Spirit of God ("spirit" in 8:15 is not the human spirit, but a rhetorical counterpart to the Holy Spirit). The translation "testifies with" is not certain. The verb Paul uses (*symmartyreō*) can also mean simply "testify to." But the "with" idea is preserved in a second-century A.D. papyrus, where each person who adds his signature to attest the truth of the document claims to be "joining in witness."[61] This idea makes good sense here. God's own Spirit adds his voice to our own inner conviction that we are God's own dear children. Paul may even want to follow the biblical legal requirement of at least two witnesses (see Deut. 19:15: "One witness is not enough to convict a man accused of any crime or offense he may have committed. A matter must be established by the testimony of two or three witnesses").

Now if we are children, then we are heirs (8:17). The move from being "children" to being "heirs" is a most appropriate way to introduce the idea of Christian hope. As Paul argues elsewhere (see esp. Gal. 4:1–3), a child is by definition not yet at

---

▶ "Abba" as "Daddy"?

Many Christians know that the word *Abba* is an Aramaic word that means "father, daddy." Jesus himself must have used this word in addressing God, for the New Testament authors, writing in Greek, nevertheless preserved this word in their text (see Mark 14:36). The word generally connotes an intimate relationship and suggests the close familial union of believers with their God. However, the claim that Jews never used this word for God or that it always has the informal sense conveyed by a word like our "Daddy" is exaggerated. Jews could use *Abba* in prayers to God, and it is not always used by little children.[A-6]

the legal age to come into all the rights and privileges of family membership. So also, he suggests, the Christian, while adopted into God's family, does not yet experience all the blessings of that relationship. Only when Christ returns in glory will the final transformation into the image of Christ, God's Son, be complete.

Paul's readers would be familiar with the rules of inheritance from the Roman law of their time.[62] But, in addition to this "everyday" background to the inheritance idea, another background may also figure into Paul's imagery here. The Old Testament regularly depicts God's promise to his people as an "inheritance." In the early stages of the Old Testament, this inheritance was identified particularly with the land of Israel. See, for example, Numbers 34:2: "Command the Israelites and say to them: 'When you enter Canaan, the land that will be allotted to you as an inheritance will have these boundaries.'"[63] In later Judaism, however, "inheritance" could also describe the life that God will give his people in these last days: "But the devout of the Lord will inherit life in happiness" (*Pss. Sol.* 14:10).[64]

The Spirit of Glory (8:18–30)

The "glory" that the believer will experience as his or her inheritance on the last day is the theme of this section. The text begins on this note—"the glory that will be revealed in us"—and ends on it—"those he justified, he also glorified." In between, Paul shows how the glory of God's children is the goal of all creation (8:18–25) and how God is working during this life to give the believer confidence for that last day (8:26–30).

The glory that will be revealed in us (8:18). The sequence of present suffering leading to future glory is common in Jewish literature. See, for example, *2 Apoc. Bar.* 15:8: "For this world is to them [the righteous] a struggle and an effort and much trouble. And that accordingly which will come, a crown with great glory." However, because Paul looked back at the realization of God's promises in Christ, he put more stress than Jewish writers did on the participation of the believer in that eventual glory. We will not only be ushered into a state of glory; we will share in Christ's own glory.

The creation waits in eager expectation (8:19). Paul's reference to "creation" in this context is debated. Since he claims that creation "waits" (8:19), "was subjected to frustration" (8:20), and has been "groaning" (8:22), many interpreters think that he must have in mind human beings. But Paul seems to contrast creation with believers (see 8:23); and he never portrays unbelievers as having hope for the future. Probably, then, "creation" in these verses denotes the subhuman world. Sufficient precedent for Paul's vivid personification of creation here is found in the Old Testament, which depicts the hills, meadows, and valleys as shouting for joy and singing (Ps. 65:12–13), and the earth itself as mourning (Isa. 24:4; Jer. 4:28; 12:4).

The creation was subjected to frustration, not by its own choice, but by the will of the one who subjected it (8:20). When Adam and Eve fell into sin, Genesis 3 tells us, the earth itself was "cursed" (Gen. 3:17–18). It is this curse to which Paul refers when he claims that creation has been "subjected to frustration": that is, it has not attained the ends for which God first made it. Since God is the One who uttered the curse, it is his will that so subjected it. But human sin was the immediate occasion for the curse, and Jewish literature frequently alludes to the connection between sin and the earth's fallen condition. See, for example, *4 Ezra* 7:11–12:

> For I made the world for their sake, and when Adam transgressed my statutes, what had been made was judged. And so the entrances of this world were made narrow and sorrowful and toilsome; they are few and evil, full of dangers and involved in great hardships.

The creation itself will be liberated from its bondage to decay (8:21). Along with the fall of the earth through human sin, Jewish writers also celebrated the earth's eventual renewal. This theme is especially prominent in Jewish apocalyptic, and Paul seems to derive some of his ideas in this section from that influential strand of Jewish thinking. As a typical example, sharing also the personification of creation that we find in Romans 8, see *1 Enoch* 51:4–5:

> In those days, mountains shall dance like rams; and the hills shall leap like kids satiated with milk. And the faces of all the angels in heaven shall glow with joy, because on that day the Elect One has arisen. And the earth shall rejoice; and the righteous ones shall dwell upon her and the elect ones shall walk upon her.[65]

While human beings are the focus of God's attention in his plan of salvation, the earth itself will also be rescued from the effects of the Fall. If one adopts a pre-millennial eschatology, then the Millennium may be regarded as that period when the earth is restored to its original "good" condition.

The whole creation has been groaning as in the pains of childbirth (8:22). The pain of labor is a natural metaphor for Christian hope. In each case the suffering is momentary, leading to joy at the end. See especially John 16:20b–22:

> You will grieve, but your grief will turn to joy. A woman giving birth to a child has pain because her time has come; but when her baby is born she forgets the anguish because of her joy that a child is born into the world. So with you: Now is your time of grief, but I will see you again and you will rejoice, and no one will take away your joy. (Note also Matt. 24:8; Mark 13:8).

We ourselves, who have the firstfruits of the Spirit, groan inwardly (8:23). "Firstfruits" is used repeatedly in the Old Testament to describe the initial part of the harvest offered to the Lord and to his priests.[66] It is hard to know whether this background plays a significant role in the New Testament use of the term, where it refers to the first stage of a series—the

REFLECTIONS

AN ISSUE THAT LOOMS EVER LARGER AS DEBATES about the extent of "global warming" heat up is the Christian attitude toward the environment. Horrified by the excesses of radical environmentalists, who often deny the special nature of human beings as created in the image of God, many Christians have taken a strong anti-environmental position. It is true that the New Testament says little about the world of nature. It focuses mainly on the redemption and growth in grace of people. But passages such as Romans 8 remind us that God has a concern for the world of nature in itself. He created it, and he plans to redeem it one day. The environment, therefore, has value in itself, and Christians need to practice good stewardship of that environment. We are called under God to resist the materialism that makes our own comfort the standard by which we make decisions and to give God's creation the protection it deserves.

first converts in an area (Rom. 16:5; 1 Cor. 16:15), the first steps in God's redemptive plan, and Christ himself, the first to be raised from the dead.[67] In each case, however, the idea of "firstfruits" implies the certainty of more to come.

"Groan" is a keyword in these verses. Creation groans (8:22), Christians groan (8:23), and the Holy Spirit groans (8:26). Paul may use the word in this context where hope is so prominent because righteous sufferers in the Old Testament frequently describe themselves as "groaning" in their present sufferings as they call out to God for deliverance (see Ex. 2:24; 6:5).[68] The word, therefore, nicely captures the combination of frustrated longing for final deliverance that characterizes this passage.

The Spirit helps us in our weakness (8:26). As long as we are in this life, we are "weak," incapable of finally overcoming sin and destined to die. But God sends help for us during this time of waiting for our hope to reach its fruition. The Spirit's ministry is one of the most important sources of help and support. The word "help" in the NIV translates a verb that can be rendered "bear a burden along with" (*synantilambanomai*).[69] A few interpreters have suggested that Paul may have derived his idea of the intercession of the Spirit from Hellenistic religions or even Gnosticism. But a more likely source is the Old Testament and especially apocalyptic Judaism, which emphasized the importance of angelic and other mediators.[70]

He who searches our hearts knows the mind of the Spirit (8:27). Paul's language picks up Old Testament descriptions of God as the One who "knows" or "judges" the hearts of his people (e.g., 1 Sam. 16:7; 1 Kings 8:39).[71]

God works for the good (8:28). Many Christians misinterpret this verse, thinking that God here promises to give us all kinds of "good" things: jobs, money, health, and so on. But, as the context makes clear, "good" is primarily the glory God will one day enable us to share with Christ, our Lord. In the Old Testament, "good" sometimes has a similar focus, denoting the blessings of the age to come.[72]

Those God foreknew he predestined (8:29). Theologians have debated for many years just what Paul means by "foreknow." In Greek generally, the verb means "know something ahead of time." Some scholars thus think that Paul is teaching that God knew ahead of time about the faith people would have and predestined those who would believe. But a characteristic biblical use of the verb "know" raises another possibility. This verb often connotes not mental "knowledge" but an intimate relationship. See, for instance, Genesis 18:19, where the NIV translates "for I have chosen him [Abraham]," although the verb is the usual Hebrew word for "know" (*ydʿ*; see also, e.g., Jer. 1:5; Amos 3:2). Most of the other New Testament occurrences of "foreknow" have this sense.[73] Since Paul here does not say that God knew anything about us but rather that he knew *us,* the idea "choose ahead of time" makes the best sense.

The firstborn among many brothers (8:29). "Firstborn" is similar to the idea of "firstfruits" (see comments on 8:23). As the first to be raised from the dead and enter into the state of glory, Christ paves the way for his brothers and sisters to follow. Also possibly contributing to the imagery of this verse is the use of "firstborn" in the Old Testament to refer to the Messiah (Ps. 89:27).

Celebration of the Believer's Security (8:31–39)

Paul now reflects on the wonder of the confidence believers have, as he has outlined this assurance in chapters 5–8. The series of questions in 8:31–35 invite the reader to join in with the celebration.

He who did not spare his own Son, but gave him up for us all (8:32). The wording of this sentence is similar to that

found in the famous story about Abraham's offering of Isaac. God commends Abraham for not "sparing" his own son (Gen. 22:12, 16; the NIV translates "withhold" in these verses, but the Greek verb in the LXX is the same verb Paul uses). In later rabbinic tradition, Abraham's offering of Isaac grew into an elaborate tradition, called the *Aqedah* ("binding"; the name derives from the fact that Abraham "bound" Isaac with ropes [Gen. 22:9]). But the tradition does not seem to have existed in Paul's day; the earliest evidence for it comes from the Amoraic (post A.D. 200) period.

As it is written, "For your sake we face death all day long; we are considered as sheep to be slaughtered" (8:36). Paul quotes Psalm 44:22 to show that God's people have always had to face opposition from the ungodly. Paul writes before the great persecution of Christians in Rome under Nero, but the terrible trial these Roman Christians were destined to experience illustrates the degree of opposition that God's people may sometimes face in this fallen world. The appropriateness of this citation is suggested by the

▶

THE ROMAN COLOSSEUM

Outside and inside view. The bottom photo shows the hallways and rooms under the Colosseum floor (no longer visible).

▶

fact that the later rabbis applied this text to the death of the martyrs.[74]

Neither height nor depth (8:39). These words, and other words like them, were used in the ancient world to denote the celestial space above and below the horizon.[75] Since spiritual beings were thought to reside in the heavens, these terms could also be applied to spiritual beings. But there is little lexical evidence that these terms have such a denotation. Probably, as in Ephesians 3:18, the imagery is simply spatial: Nothing in the heavens above or on the earth below can separate believers from God's love for them in Christ.

God's Promises and Israel's Plight (9:1–5)

In chapter 9, Paul's argument enters a new phase. He has shown that the gospel of Jesus Christ provides justification for anyone who believes (chs. 1–4) and that this divine verdict will hold good at the judgment of God (chs. 5–8). Throughout this argument, a key subtheme has been that Gentiles have equal access with Jews to this new work of God. The blessings God promised to his people in the Old Testament are now available for any Christian. Believers, whether Jew or Gentile, are children of Abraham (ch. 4), children and heirs of God (8:14–17), destined for glory (8:18–30).

But all this raises an insistent question: What about God's promises to Israel? Paul seems to be affirming that what God first promised Israel he has given to the church. Israel, as a whole, remains in her sin (9:1–3); what, then, of all her privileges (9:4–5)? The gospel Paul preaches, therefore, creates an apparent problem for the faithfulness of God to his word. This issue, enunciated

in 9:6, is the driving issue of chapters 9–11. Paul must show that his interpretation of the gospel is consistent with the Old Testament promises to Israel. Not surprisingly, he turns to the Old Testament itself to make his case. Almost one-third of Paul's quotations from the Old Testament occur in these three chapters of Romans.

Conscience (9:1). This word is one of the few that Paul takes from the Hellenistic world.[76] The Greek word used here (*syneidēsis*) appears only once in the canonical books of the Old Testament (Eccl. 10:20 LXX). "Conscience" played an important role in Stoic philosophy, but Paul shows no dependence on the technical use of the word. He seems instead to use it in its more "everyday" meaning, to denote the faculty within us that monitors our agreement with moral norms.

I have great sorrow and unceasing anguish in my heart (9:2). Paul's grief over the spiritual state of his fellow Israelites reminds us of the Old Testament prophets, who lamented the sin and resulting judgment of God on the people of Israel in their own day. See, for example, Jeremiah 4:19–22:

> Oh, my anguish, my anguish!
>   I writhe in pain.
> Oh, the agony of my heart!
>   My heart pounds within me,
>   I cannot keep silent.
> For I have heard the sound of the
>   trumpet;
>   I have heard the battle cry.
> Disaster follows disaster;
>   the whole land lies in ruins.
> In an instant my tents are destroyed,
>   my shelter in a moment.
> How long must I see the battle standard
>   and hear the sound of the trumpet?

My people are fools;
they do not know me.
They are senseless children;
they have no understanding.
They are skilled in doing evil;
they know not how to do good.

Cursed (9:3). The Greek word is *anathema*, which has been taken into English as a way of denoting something or someone rejected and denied status. The Greek word itself translates the Hebrew *ḥerem*, "something set apart for God." What is set apart for God may have a positive purpose, as when sacrifices are called "anathema."[77] But the word usually has a negative sense, referring to something or someone set aside by God for destruction. For instance, the city of Jericho and the Canaanite cities conquered by Israel are said to be "anathema."[78] The rabbis later used the same word to refer to those who were excommunicated from the faith.[79]

I could wish that I myself were . . . cut off from Christ for the sake of my brothers (9:3). Paul takes on a role here similar to that of Moses with respect to the people of Israel after their sin in worshiping the golden calf. Moses asks that God would blot his name out of "the book" if he would not forgive the people (Ex. 32:30–32). So also Paul is ready to sacrifice his own salvation for the sake of his "brothers," the people of Israel who have not responded to the gospel.

The people of Israel (9:4). Paul's use here of the word "Israelites" (NASB; Gk. *Israēlitai*) marks a significant shift from his use of "Jew" or "Jews" in chapters 1–8 (1:16; 2:9, 10, 17, 28, 29; 3:1, 9, 29). "Jew" (*Ioudaios*), deriving from the territory of Judea, is a politically and nationally oriented term. It is the word that most people in the Roman Empire used to denote people who lived in the land of Israel. But "Israelite" often has a more theological connotation. This word, of course, goes back to the name that God bestowed on Jacob (Gen. 32:28; 35:10) and passed down to his offspring (32:32; 46:8). It therefore hints at the favored status of the people of Israel in the eyes of God.

Several intertestamental books preserve this distinction between the words. In 1 Maccabees, for instance, "Jew" is used in letters to foreign nations or when the focus is on politics. But "Israel" is used when the focus is on the people's religious status in relationship to other nations. Simply by shifting from "Jew" to "Israelites," then, Paul signals his intent to consider seriously the special position and promises enjoyed by that people.

Adoption as sons (9:4). In 8:15 and 23, Paul used the word "adoption" or "sonship" (*huiothesia*) to describe Christians' special blessing as God's own children. In applying that same word here to unbelieving Israel, Paul shifts the meaning a bit. God "adopted" Israel as a nation in the sense that he selected that nation to be the recipient of his old covenant blessing and to act as the conduit of his blessing to the rest of the world (see Ex. 4:22–23; Deut. 14:1–2).[80]

The divine glory (9:4). In chapter 8, Paul has also attributed "glory" to Christians (e.g., 8:18, 30). We must again assume that the "glory" ascribed here to Israel is different from the eschatological glory Christians are destined for. The Old Testament repeatedly speaks of the appearance of "the glory of the LORD" on special occasions and in the temple (e.g.,

Ex. 16:7, 10).[81] Thus, what Paul probably refers to here is the divine presence of the Lord with his people.

The covenants (9:4). The plural form of the word is unusual. We generally think of one "old" covenant and one "new." Paul could be referring to both of these here, but he seems to be describing the privileges of Israel apart from their fulfillment in Christ. In other words, Paul is probably thinking of the several covenants that God made with various Old Testament people (e.g., Noah, Abraham, Israel at Sinai, and David [cf. 2 Sam. 23:5]).

The temple worship (9:4). The regular offering of sacrifices in the temple in Jerusalem was a central focus of Jewish religious life. As a famous text from the Mishnah proclaims, "By three things is the world sustained: by the Law, by the [Temple-]service, and by deeds of loving-kindness."[82] Jews who lived close enough were expected to travel to Jerusalem for the great pilgrimage festivals every year, and Jews in the Diaspora were to contribute yearly to a fund to maintain the temple service.

The patriarchs (9:5). The promises that God gave Abraham, Isaac, and Jacob became the focal point of Israel's identity as a nation and her blessings before the Lord. Reference to the "patriarchs" (lit., "fathers") brackets Paul's argument in these chapters (see also 11:28), focusing attention on Israel's special status.

Defining the Promise (1): God's Sovereign Election (9:6–29)

As the first step in Paul's defense of God's faithfulness to his promises to Israel, he uses the Old Testament itself to show just what God has promised Israel. His key point is that God never promised salvation to every individual Jew. All along, Paul demonstrates, God's own sovereign act of "calling" was what brought the Jew to salvation. Throughout this section, Paul is responding to the popular Jewish view of election, which held that God's covenant with Abraham, renewed through Moses, guaranteed salvation to every Jew who did not separate himself or herself (e.g., by renouncing the law) from Israel. Paul's response, to quote the phrase of N. T. Wright, is that "what counts is grace, not race."[83]

Paul's extensive use of the Old Testament throughout this section is similar in some ways to the Jewish practice of

REFLECTIONS

WE HAVE NOT COMMENTED ON THE VERY END OF Romans 9:5 because the text does not have significant "background" issues. But we should not pass by the verse without noting the significance of the text for Christology. The NIV renders the end of the verse "and from them is traced the human ancestry of Christ, who is God over all, forever praised." With the comma after "Christ," this translation attributed the title "God" to Jesus—an explicit statement of his deity.

But note the RSV rendering of the same text: "and of their race, according to the flesh, is the Christ. God who is over all be blessed forever. Amen!" Here we find a period after "Christ," making the last blessing one that applies to God the Father. The problem here is that our earliest Greek manuscripts (for the most part) had no punctuation at all. The Greek letters run continuously without breaks between words. So modern editors, commentators, and translators have to decide where to put punctuation marks and what marks to use. A good case can be made here for either the comma or the period after "Christ." But the evidence leans toward the comma, suggested by the fact that the NRSV has gone that direction. On the most probable interpretation, therefore, Romans 9:5 is an important New Testament testimony to the deity of Christ.

scriptural commentary called *midrash*. To be sure, Paul uses certain techniques found among Jewish *midrashim*, such as bringing together texts on the basis of common words ("descendants"/"offspring" in Gen. 21:12 [9:7] and Isa. 1:9 [9:29]). But, the overall integration of Scripture into Paul's own argument is quite different than the more strictly "commentary" format of the Jewish midrashic writers.

Not all who are descended from Israel are Israel (9:6). The first occurrence of "Israel" refers to "physical" Israel: All the people descended from Jacob, whose name, we might recall, was changed to "Israel" (Gen. 32:28). The second "Israel" in the verse must, however, have a spiritual significance, referring to people who truly have a relationship with the Lord. But how broadly does Paul intend the word to apply? While it is debated, Galatians 6:16 seems to suggest that Paul could use the word "Israel" to refer to everyone who belonged to the Lord, Gentile or Jew. But this "transfer" of the term from physical Israel to the church is rare; we have no other example until the second century. Because of this, and because of the nature of the argument in these chapters, then, it is better to think of this spiritual Israel here as an Israel *within* Israel: those Jews truly saved within the larger nation.

Abraham's children (9:7). Paul's defense of the proposition that only some Jews are truly Jews in the spiritual sense begins, naturally enough, with Abraham. For, as we noted in our comments on chapter 4, the Old Testament makes God's call and promise to Abraham the starting point of the people of Israel (Gen. 12:1–3; 15:1–5, 18–21).[84] The

true, spiritual "descendants" (or "offspring," *sperma*) of Abraham are those who are "reckoned" to be so through Isaac. For the Old Testament teaches that Abraham had other natural children, through the slave woman, Hagar. Yet they do not participate in the promise of God. Genesis 21:12, the verse that Paul quotes here, was God's assurance to Abraham that he would have children through Isaac and that these children would inherit the promise.

In other words (9:8). The NIV rendering paraphrases the Greek, which, literally translated, is "that is." This phrase is similar to the one used by the sectarians at Qumran to introduce a contemporary application of the Old Testament. The Hebrew phrase is *pesharo*, from which is derived the name given to the method of Old Testament interpretation in the Dead Sea Scrolls, *pesher*. Paul therefore signals that 9:8 is his "interpretation" of the passage he has quoted in 9:7.

At the appointed time I will return, and Sarah will have a son (9:9). This quotation is a mixture of Genesis 18:10 and 14, in which God insists that he will take the initiative in bringing a son to Abraham through Sarah.

Rebekah's children had one and the same father (9:10). An objector to Paul's argument might point out that the distinction between Isaac and Ishmael did have a physical component to it, in that they had different mothers. Thus, to make his point crystal clear, Paul moves down a generation, reminding his readers that both Jacob and Esau were born to the same mother, Rebekah, and father, Isaac. Indeed, Paul goes even further. While not clear from the NIV, the Greek

Paul uses here (*koitē*, from which we get the word "coitus") probably means "semen."[85] In other words, Paul reminds us that Jacob and Esau were conceived in one act of sexual intercourse. How much less basis, physically, could there be for a distinction between them?

Paul's argument picks up certain emphases within Judaism itself, as *4 Ezra* 3:13–16 makes clear:

> And when they were committing iniquity in your sight, you chose for yourself one of them, whose name was Abraham; you loved him, and to him alone you revealed the end of the times, secretly by night. You made an everlasting covenant with him, and promised him that you would never forsake his descendants; and you gave him Isaac, and to Isaac you gave Jacob and Esau. You set apart Jacob for yourself, but Esau you rejected; and Jacob became a great multitude.

God's purpose in election (9:11). "Purpose" translates a word (*prothesis*) that emphasizes God's plan as predetermined (see 8:28). The Dead Sea Scrolls use a parallel Hebrew word (*mahahsabâ*) in a similar way. See, for example, 1QS 3:15–16a:

> From the God of knowledge stems all there is and all there shall be. Before they existed he made all their plans and when they came into being they will execute all their works in compliance with his instructions, according to his glorious design without altering anything.

Not by works but by him who calls (9:12). Modern scholars are not agreed about just what the Jewish view of election may have been. But there is a grow-ing consensus that there was not a single doctrine, but a variety of views. At least one strand of Judaism linked God's election to human works. A particularly interesting text from Philo comments on the distinction between Jacob and Esau and attributes it, at least in part, to their works, which God had foreseen:

> Once again, of Jacob and Esau, when still in the womb, God declares that the one is a ruler and leader and master, but that Esau is a subject and slave. For God the Maker of living beings knows well the different pieces of his own handwork, even before he has thoroughly chiseled and consummated them, and the faculties which they are to display at a later time, in a word their deeds and experiences. And so when Rebecca, the soul that waits on God, goes to inquire of God, he tells her in reply, "Two nations are in your womb, and two peoples shall be separated from your belly, and one people shall be above the other people, and the elder shall serve the younger."[86]

Jacob I loved, but Esau I hated (9:13). This famous—and difficult!—quotation is from Malachi 1:2–3. A quick glance at Malachi reveals that the prophet is not talking about the individuals Jacob and Esau. He is using these names to refer to the nations founded by these individuals: Israel and Edom, respectively. The words that come immediately before the text that Paul quotes in Romans 9:12 (Gen. 25:23) move in the same direction: "Two nations are in your womb, and two peoples from within you will be separated; one people will be stronger than the other, and the older will serve the younger."

With this Old Testament background in view, many scholars think Paul is speaking throughout this chapter about

God's calling of nations and their place in his plan of salvation. He is not—as so many interpreters have thought—teaching anything about the salvation of individuals. The Old Testament context of Paul's quotations forces us to reckon seriously with the possibility that Paul's focus is corporate and not individual. But many features from within Romans 9 are difficult to reconcile with the corporate interpretation: the focus on the identity of God's children (9:7–9, 29); the contrast between wrath and glory in 9:22–23; and the whole point of the discussion, which is to demonstrate which people from within the single nation of Israel are really chosen by God. Probably, then, Paul is choosing Old Testament texts about God's sovereign and gracious election to illustrate the point about the salvation of individuals that is the heart of Romans 9.[87]

The verbs "love" and "hate" in Malachi are covenantal terms. They do not express God's emotions about Israel and Edom but his actions with respect to them. We might paraphrase, "Jacob I have chosen, but Esau I have rejected."

Is God unjust? (9:14). The modern reader immediately assumes the issue

here is about God's "fairness": his justice in acting as he has toward Jacob and Esau. But the Greek word used here (*adikia*) comes from a root that is used throughout the Old and New Testaments to designate God's "righteousness," a term that often refers to God's faithfulness to his covenant with Israel or, more basically, to his commitment to his own person and name. Rather than raising the notion of God's "fairness" here, then, Paul may be asking whether God's actions in regard to Jacob and Esau contradict his own nature. And, of course, it is ultimately only by the standard of God's own nature that his "fairness" can be properly measured.

It does not, therefore, depend on man's desire or effort (9:16). "Effort" translates the verb *trechō*, "to run." Paul's metaphor may come from Greco-Roman athletics, since he elsewhere uses language drawn from that sphere.[88] But the Jews also spoke of "walking" or "running" in the way of the law (cf. Ps. 119:32).

The Scripture says to Pharaoh: "I raised you up for this very purpose" (9:17). "I raised you up" has the connotation "appoint to a significant role in salvation history" (cf. Jer. 50:41 [LXX 27:41]; Hab. 1:6; Zech. 11:16).

He hardens whom he wants to harden (9:18). In secular Greek, the verb "harden" (*sklērynō*) usually occurs in medical contexts, with reference to the hardness of bones. But the specific background for Paul's use of the word is Exodus 4–14, where the verb occurs fourteen times to denote the spiritual insensitivity that God brought on Pharaoh (e.g. Ex. 4:21; 7:22).[89] Paul expects us to understand the general method of God's hardening in light of the Exodus story.

But what does the Exodus story teach us about God's hardening? Some scholars insist that God's hardening of Pharaoh is a response to Pharaoh's previous decision to harden himself. They note that reference to God's hardening of Pharaoh's heart (9:12) occurs only after references to Pharaoh's hardening of his own heart (8:15, 32). Thus, it can be concluded, God only hardens people who have already made themselves insensitive to his will. However, the Exodus narrative is not so clear on this matter. Before Pharaoh hardens his own heart, five times we read that Pharaoh's heart "was hardened" (Ex. 7:13, 14, 22; 8:15, 32). The subject of these passive verbs may be God, since the narrative opens with predictions that God would himself harden Pharaoh (4:21 and 7:3). The upshot is that the Exodus story does not tip the scales decisively one way or the other about how we should integrate God's hardening with peoples' own sinful obstinacy.

One of you will say to me (9:19). The diatribe style of question and answer becomes more pronounced at this point, as Paul deals with objections to his strong emphasis on God's sovereignty in 9:14–18. As we have seen (see comments in introduction and on 2:1), this style need not have a specific objector in view. But Paul may well be reflecting in these verses his own "take" on a current debate within Judaism about God's sovereignty and human free will.

Shall what is formed say to him who formed it, "Why did you make me like this?" Does not the potter have the right . . . ? (9:20–21). Few household items were as common as the pottery jar. So

◄
POTTER

59

Romans

▶ The Debate on Sovereignty and Free Will in First-Century Judaism

Though Josephus may be trying to "dress up" Jewish views in philosophical terms more appealing to his Greek audience, what he says about the differences among the Jewish groups of his day is still likely to reflect a genuine debate:

Now at this time there were three schools of thought among the Jews, which held different opinions concerning human affairs; the first being that of the Pharisees, the second that of the Sadducees, and the third that of the Essenes. As for the Pharisees, they say that certain events are the work of Fate, but not all; as to other events, it depends upon ourselves whether they shall take place or not. The sect of the Essenes, however, declares that Fate is mistress of all things, and that nothing befalls men unless it be in accordance with her decree. But the Sadducees do away with Fate, holding that there is no such thing and that human actions are not achieved in accordance with her decree, but that all things lie within our own power, so that we ourselves are responsible for our well-being, while we suffer misfortune through our own thoughtlessness.[A-7]

the imagery of potter and clay would have been immediately accessible to all Paul's readers. The Old Testament frequently applies this imagery to God's control over his creation.[90] Jewish writers followed suit. See, for example, Sirach 33:13: "Like clay in the hand of the potter, to be molded as he pleases, so all are in the hand of their Maker, to be given whatever he decides." In Romans 9:20, Paul quotes from Isaiah 29:16, with probable allusion also to Isaiah 45:9. But the imagery was familiar enough that no single text can be identified as the one Paul definitively had in mind here.

What if God . . . bore with great patience his objects of wrath . . . to make the riches of his glory known to the objects of his mercy (9:22–23). Verses 22–23 are difficult to understand. The syntax is complicated and the theology debated. But one strand of Jewish thinking may illuminate Paul's purpose. According to some Jewish authors, God's decision to wait until the end to judge the nations of the world was for the purpose that they might fill up the full measure of their sins and so receive the full force of his wrath. See, for instance, 2 Maccabees 6:12–14, where the author seeks to comfort the people of Israel as they go through severe persecution:

> Now I urge those who read this book not to be depressed by such calamities, but to recognize that these punishments were designed not to destroy but to discipline our people. In fact, it is a sign of great kindness not to let the impious alone for long, but to punish them immediately. For in the case of the other nations the Lord waits patiently to punish them until they have reached the full measure of their sins; but he does not deal in this way with us.[91]

As he says in Hosea (9:25–26). Paul quotes two verses from Hosea (2:23 in 9:25; 1:10 [LXX 2:1] in 9:26) to buttress his claim that Gentiles are now among those being "called" (9:24) as "objects of his mercy" (9:23). Note, however, that Hosea is not predicting the conversion of Gentiles but the return of the "lost" ten northern tribes to the people of Israel. Paul reflects here a hermeneutical axiom that he assumes throughout his interpretation of the Old Testament: Predictions about a renewed Israel can be fulfilled in God's new "Israel," the church.

▶

SODOM AND GOMORRAH

Bab edh-Dhra and the Lisan peninsula—the possible site of Sodom.

Isaiah cries out concerning Israel: "Though the number of the Israelites be like the sand by the sea, only the remnant will be saved" (9:27). The "remnant" concept develops in the Prophets, who pronounce doom on Israel as a whole because of her sin but promise blessing for a smaller number on whom God would have mercy in the end. The concept fits perfectly Paul's overall purpose of proving that the relatively small number of Jews being saved in his day does not contradict God's promise to Israel. Paul's attention may have been drawn to this text especially because it uses a phrase—"the number of the Israelites"—that occurs in the verse that Paul has just cited in 9:26 (Hos. 1:10).

We would have become like Sodom, we would have been like Gomorrah (9:29). The prophet Isaiah, from whom Paul is quoting (Isa. 1:9), uses the fate of the cities of Sodom and Gomorrah (see Gen. 19) as a striking example of God's judgment on sin. The imagery is natural and common in Scripture (e.g. Isa. 3:9; 13:19).[92]

Christ, the Climax of Salvation History (9:30–10:21)

In this section Paul deviates a bit from his main argument. He will continue to outline his understanding of God's election of Israel and its consequences for the present in chapter 11. But before he does so, he pauses to analyze in more detail the somewhat unexpected turn that salvation history has taken. Most Jews, the ones to whom the promises were made, have rejected their Messiah and the salvation he offers; many Gentiles, by contrast, are streaming into God's new covenant people. Why has this hap-pened? Because, Paul claims, Israel stubbornly refused to recognize God's offer of righteousness in Christ, the climax of salvation history.

Israel, who pursued a law of righteousness, has not attained it (9:31). Behind the pair of verbs "pursue" and "attain" may lie the imagery of the runner who seeks the prize at the end of the race. In the Old Testament, this pair of verbs usually refers to people who pursue others in order to overtake them, especially in battle (e.g., Gen. 31:23; Ex. 15:9).[93] Israel, Paul suggests, earnestly and sincerely pursued the law as a means of attaining righteousness. But she has not been able to achieve this status, for the power of sin prevents people from finding salvation through the law or the works it demands (cf. 9:32).

They stumbled over the "stumbling stone." As it is written . . . (9:32–33). Paul takes language from two different verses in Isaiah (28:16 and 8:14) to characterize Christ as a "roadblock" in Israel's pursuit of the law of righteousness. He begins with language from Isaiah 28:16—"See, I lay a stone in Zion"—but quickly turns to the negative portrayal of the "stumbling stone" in Isaiah 8:14 to complete the idea. He then returns to Isaiah 28:16 at the end, promising that the person who trusts in Christ, the stone, will "never be put to shame." What is especially interesting about this combination is that Peter also juxtaposes these same two verses, along with another "stone" verse, Psalm 118:22 (cf. Matt. 21:42). This combination of texts probably existed in the early church as a way of viewing Christ in light of the Old Testament. Some scholars, indeed, postulate that the church might have put together "testimony books" containing Old Testament texts especially relevant to the church's interpretation of Jesus and his significance.[94]

They are zealous for God (10:2). "Zeal" emerged as an especially commendable virtue among Jews in the intertestamental period, when the existence of the Jewish faith was threatened by both external enemies and (more seriously) by internal compromise. Mattathias, the first leader of the most famous Jewish resistance movement, the Maccabees, called followers in these words: "Let every one who is zealous for the law and supports the covenant come out with me!" (1 Macc. 2:27). Phinehas, who killed a Jewish woman and her pagan lover for their flaunting of the law (Num. 25), was the prototypical "zealot." The New Testament therefore uniformly praises "zeal," and this verse is no exception. Paul is thankful for Israel's zeal; the problem is that it is misdirected.[95]

Since they did not know the righteousness that comes from God and sought to establish their own (10:3). "Their own" righteousness can have two different meanings. It may refer to what some contemporary scholars call "national righteousness"—the tendency of Jews to keep their covenant relationship with God very much to themselves, to focus exclusively on their own privileges, and to ignore their mission to the world at large. That this was a problem among Jews in Paul's day is clear. But Paul's use of this same kind of language in Philippians 3:6–9 points in a different direction. When Paul contrasts "a righteousness of my own that comes from the law" with "that which is through faith in Christ—the righteousness that comes

from God and is by faith," he seems to imply that "his own" righteousness was a standing before God that he thought he could maintain by his obedience to the law. So Israel, Paul here suggests, was seeking to make the law into a "law of righteousness" (Rom. 9:31), a means of marking out those whom God would save in the last day. They were therefore ignoring the Lord's warning to the people of Israel when they entered the Promised Land:

> After the LORD your God has driven them out before you, do not say to yourself, "The LORD has brought me here to take possession of this land because of my righteousness." No, it is on account of the wickedness of these nations that the LORD is going to drive them out before you. It is not because of your righteousness or your integrity that you are going in to take possession of their land; but on account of the wickedness of these nations, the LORD your God will drive them out before you, to accomplish what he swore to your fathers, to Abraham, Isaac and Jacob. Understand, then, that it is not because of your righteousness that the LORD your God is giving you this good land to possess, for you are a stiff-necked people (Deut. 9:4–6).

They did not submit to God's righteousness (10:3). Paul's use of "submit" in this sense here is similar to the use we find in *2 Apoc. Bar.* 54:5: "[You] reveal the secrets to those who are spotless, to those who subjected themselves to you and your Law in faith."

Christ is the end of the law (10:4). The English word "end" is ambiguous; but it can be taken to mean "termination," as in "The end of class finally came!" The Greek word here, *telos*, however, has the added nuance of "goal." Paul presents Christ as both end and goal of the law, much like the finish line of a race course. When the runner reaches that finish line, the race is ended; but crossing the finish line is also the goal. So God intended all along that the law would find its end and goal—its climax or culmination—in Christ. He ends the era of the law's rule even as he ushers in the times of fulfillment to which the law itself always pointed.

The man who does these things will live by them (10:5). Paul quotes Leviticus 18:5 to describe "the righteousness that is by the law." This Old Testament verse comes in a series of commands from the Lord through Moses to the people of Israel. In its original context, the "life" that the Lord promises in response to obedience is not eternal life, but the enjoyment of blessing in the Promised Land (for this use of "life" see also Deut. 30:15, 19). Paul is probably not, then, suggesting that Moses offered people salvation by means of obedience to the law. His point simply is that what the law promises can be had only through obedience to that law. Thus, any righteousness that the law promises (see Rom. 9:31) can come only through works. But our always imperfect and inconsistent works can never bring us into relationship with a perfect and holy God.

The connection between obedience and life established in Leviticus 18:5 becomes almost proverbial in the Old Testament and Judaism. See, for instance, Ezekiel 20:13:

> Yet the people of Israel rebelled against me in the desert. They did not follow my decrees but rejected my laws—although the man who obeys them will live by them—and they utterly desecrated my Sabbaths. So I said I would pour out my wrath on them and destroy them in the desert.[96]

But the righteousness that is by faith says (10:6–8). In contrast to the righteousness that is by the law (10:5) is "the righteousness that is by faith." In a striking personification, Paul puts language from two passages in Deuteronomy on the lips of this personified righteousness. The opening words, "Do not say in your heart," come from Deuteronomy 9:4, the text we cited above to illustrate the idea of "their own righteousness" (see 10:3). Paul then goes on to use phrases from Deuteronomy 30:11–14. His application of this language to the righteousness of faith is puzzling, because in the Deuteronomy passage, Moses is encouraging the Israelites to obey the law:

> Now what I am commanding you today is not too difficult for you or beyond your reach. It is not up in heaven, so that you have to ask, "Who will ascend into heaven to get it and proclaim it to us so we may obey it?" Nor is it beyond the sea, so that you have to ask, "Who will cross the sea to get it and proclaim it to us so we may obey it?" No, the word is very near you; it is in your mouth and in your heart so you may obey it.

How could Paul take this language and apply it to the righteousness by faith in contrast to the law? Some commentators think that Paul may merely be using the language of the text with no intent to "quote" it—as we will sometimes lift words from a Shakespeare play without regard to their original context.[97] But the repeated "that is" formula points to an intention to quote this text. Others think

Paul might have been influenced by the early Christian identification of Christ with the Old Testament figure of "wisdom."[98] Baruch 3:29–30 uses language from Deuteronomy 30 to describe wisdom: "Who has gone up into heaven, and taken her, and brought her down from the clouds? Who has gone over the sea, and found her, and will buy her for pure gold?" But little in the context prepares us for a Christ-wisdom connection. Probably, then, Paul wants to claim that the new covenant offer of righteousness is now that "word" that is near to the people: accessible and available for all who respond in faith.

Two further notes on the details of the quotation. (1) The language of "ascending into heaven" (10:6) is proverbial for a humanly impossible task.[99] (2) Paul's quotation of this Deuteronomy text differs from the original at one point. Where Deuteronomy 30:13 asks "who will cross the sea to get it?" Paul asks "Who will descend into the deep?" Paul may be influenced by the wording of

Psalm 107:26: "They mounted up to the heavens and went down to the depths; in their peril their courage melted away." "Sea" and the "depths" (or "abyss") were often interchanged in the Old Testament and Judaism. An early Aramaic paraphrase of Deuteronomy 30:13 combined both images: "Neither is the Law beyond the Great Sea that one may say: Would that we had one like the prophet Jonah who would descend into the depths of the Great Sea and bring it up for us."[100] The reference to Jonah reminds us also of Christ's appeal to Jonah's experience in the belly of the great fish to illuminate his own death and resurrection (Matt. 12:40). Jonah 2:3–10 parallels "sea" and "abyss" in describing Jonah's experience.

Anyone who trusts in [me] will never be put to shame (10:11). Paul quotes again from Isaiah 28:16 (see 9:33). "Put to shame" refers to a negative verdict at the judgment. Note the contrasting parallelism in Isaiah 50:7b–8a: "I know I will not be put to shame. He who vindicates me is near."

Everyone who calls on the name of the Lord will be saved (10:13). To call on someone in secular Greek referred to an appeal (especially to a god) for assistance and favor. But the language was also common in the LXX and Jewish literature.[101] The early Christians "called on" both God and Christ for mercy and favor.[102]

Paul is again here quoting the Old Testament: Joel 2:32 (3:5 in the LXX). The "Lord" in Joel is, of course, Yahweh. But Paul applies the text to believers who call on the name of Jesus (see "Jesus is Lord" in 10:9 and the context of 10:10–12). The way the early Christians applied language from the Old Testament about Jehovah God to Jesus conveys an impor-

REFLECTIONS

IN THE OLD COVENANT, GOD GRACIOUSLY BRINGS his word "near" to his people. He informs them about who he is, enters into relationship with them, and requires them to keep his law in order to maintain their status as his people. But the Old Testament is one long description of the people's failure to keep God's law. It becomes clear that human beings are not capable of obeying God apart from a special work of his grace. It is that special work that the new covenant promises. God comes "near" to us in a new way, sending his Spirit to enable obedience to him. Jesus himself has done what seemed to be impossible: risen from the dead to provide the basis for a new life. It is the good news we preach that mediates this new experience of grace. Throughout this passage, therefore, Paul highlights the importance of preaching as an indispensable stage in God's gracious plan of redemption.

Isaiah 52:7 to support the need for preachers of the good news and implicitly suggests that God has himself sent these preachers. Crucial to Paul's application is the use in the Isaiah text of the critical "good news" language (*euangelizomai*).

Their voice has gone out into all the earth, their words to the ends of the world (10:18). Paul cites Psalm 19:4 to prove that the Israelites have indeed heard the good news about Christ. But the application is by no means an obvious one. For Psalm 19 is about the revelation of God in nature and history. Does Paul really think that this psalm refers to the preaching of the good news? Probably not. He may be using the words from the psalm verse to create an analogy: As the message about God went out everywhere in nature, so now the message about God's work in Christ has been broadcast worldwide—or at least empire-wide. The Greek word behind "world" (*oikoumenē*) may refer to the Roman empire rather than to the entire inhabited world.

I will make you envious by those who are not a nation; I will make you angry by a nation that has no understanding (10:19). Israel should have understood what God was doing in Christ, for he had predicted it in the Old Testament. This quotation comes from the Song of Moses in Deuteronomy 32, a passage Paul uses a lot in this part of Romans. What probably draws his attention to this particular verse was the language of "not a nation," or "no people" (*laos*), which is identical to the language of Hosea 1:10 and 2:23 (which Paul quotes in Rom. 9:25–26). "Not a nation" refers, then, to the Gentiles, for God had not called them and

tant clue about the divine status they implicitly accorded to Jesus. To be sure, pre-Christian manuscripts of the Greek Old Testament almost universally avoided the Greek work *kyrios* ("Lord") in translating the tetragrammaton (the four Hebrew consonants that constitute the biblical name for God); they simply transliterated the Hebrew. So we do not have much written evidence that the Greek word *kyrios* was being applied to Yahweh. But we do have evidence that Greek-speaking Jews supplied the word *kyrios* when passages with the transliterated tetragrammaton were read aloud.[103] On the whole, then, the application of *kyrios* language from the Old Testament to Jesus does suggest his deity.

How beautiful are the feet of those who bring good news (10:15). In 10:14–21, Paul is showing that Israel's ignorance about God's righteousness in Christ (10:2) is inexcusable. God has sent preachers to Israel, and they have had ample opportunity to come to know the essence of God's plan. Here he quotes

formed them into a people as he had Israel.

A Summary: Israel, the "Elect," and the "Hardened" (11:1–10)

Having explored in more detail in 9:30–10:21 the reasons why so many Jews have not responded to Christ and so many Gentiles have, Paul now returns to the theme of 9:6–29, summarizing the situation in salvation history of his day. He begins with the theme that will sound throughout chapter 11: Despite Israel's disobedience (10:21), God has not rejected his people (11:2). Israel as a whole has not experienced the messianic salvation; most of them have been "hardened." But the "elect," chosen by grace, are enjoying the fulfillment of God's promise to be faithful to his people Israel.

From the tribe of Benjamin (11:1). Paul cites himself as an example of a believing Jew, illustrating the truth that God has not rejected his people. It is obvious why he would call himself an "Israelite" and "a descendant of Abraham." But why would he claim to be from the tribe of Benjamin? Rabbinic tradition claims that the tribe of Benjamin was the first to cross the "Sea of Reeds" at the time of the Exodus and that its restoration would be the sign of the renewal of all Israel.[104] But it is not clear that either of these traditions dates to the time of Paul. Perhaps he mentions his tribal derivation simply to reinforce his Jewish identity (see Phil. 3:5).

God did not reject his people, whom he foreknew (11:2). The wording of this key assertion reflects the language of Psalm 94:14 ("For the LORD will not reject his people; he will never forsake his inheritance") and 1 Samuel 12:22 ("For the

sake of his great name the LORD will not reject his people, because the LORD was pleased to make you his own"). Particularly significant for the direction of Paul's argument is his emphasis on God's concern for his own name in the latter text. Israel, despite her sin, remains the object of God's concern and blessing because of his great grace. As in Romans 8:29, "foreknew" means "chose ahead of time" (see comments on that verse).

The passage about Elijah (11:2). The Greek has simply "in Elijah." Identifying a text of Scripture by reference to a key figure within the narrative is a standard Jewish practice. The rabbis, for instance, introduce a reference to 1 Chronicles 29:14 with the words "It is written in David" (*b. ʾAbot* 3:7; in the New Testament see also Mark 12:26 [Luke 20:37], which lit. translates "in the bush," i.e., "in the passage about the burning bush").

The passage to which Paul refers is 1 Kings 19:1–8, which relates King Ahab's attack on the prophets of the Lord. The king's wife, the infamous Jezebel, threatens Elijah with the same death suffered by the other prophets. Elijah flees into the desert, where the Lord comforts him by assuring him that, against all the evidence, God is working out his plan for Israel and the surrounding nations (Rom. 11:15–18). Paul quotes Elijah's lament about being left alone (11:3), with the prophets of Baal apparently in control of matters, and the Lord's concluding reassurance to Elijah about the "seven thousand" whom he had "reserved for [himself]" (11:4; see 1 Kings 19:18). This Old Testament passage introduces the concept of the "remnant," a body of true believers whom the Lord preserves in the midst of an apostate nation. Paul goes on to affirm that God

As it is written (11:8). Paul here uses quotations from the Old Testament to show that God himself is responsible for the hardening of so many Jews. He has given them "a spirit of stupor" (11:8), and it is he who has responded to the imprecatory prayers of the psalmist (11:9–10). Paul follows the rabbinic *haraz* method in choosing citations from every major part of the Old Testament: the "Law" (Deut. 29:4 in Rom. 11:8a); the "Prophets" (Isa. 29:10 in Rom. 11:8b); and the "Writings" (Ps. 69:22–23 in Rom. 11:9–10).

Defining the Promise (2): The Future of Israel (11:11–36)

Paul began his defense of God's faithfulness to his word of promise in chapters 9–11 by explaining how a correct understanding of God's promise made sense of the present situation of Israel. Since God had from the beginning chosen only some from within Israel to be his true, spiritual people, the small number of Jewish believers in Paul's day did not contradict God's Word (9:6–29). Now Paul returns to that word of promise, showing what it means for the future of Israel. He argues that the great incursion of Gentiles into the people of God will ultimately have a positive effect on Israel itself.

Salvation has come to the Gentiles to make Israel envious (11:11). Paul's idea is drawn from Deuteronomy 32:21, which he quotes in Romans 10:19: "I will make you envious by those who are not a nation; I will make you angry by a nation that has no understanding." "Make you envious" translates a word (*parazē-loō*) that denotes God's jealousy for his people or a human being's jealousy of

has graciously preserved such a remnant of true believers within Israel right up to his own day (Rom. 11:5–6).

What Israel sought so earnestly it did not obtain, but the elect did. The others were hardened (11:7). Paul neatly summarizes the situation of the Jewish people in his own time. The nation as a whole, though seeking righteousness (see 9:31), has not attained it. Yet, as Paul has just argued, God has preserved a remnant, chosen by grace, who have reached this goal. But most of Israel is "hardened." The verb Paul uses here (*pōroō*) is rare in biblical Greek (see Job 17:7; Prov. 10:20).[105] In secular Greek the word occurs especially often in medical contexts, where it refers to the forming of a "hard sphere" in the body (e.g., a stone in the bladder) or to the "hardening" of a bone after it is broken. So also do people become "hard" with respect to things of the Lord, stubbornly rejecting his grace in Christ. Paul uses a different Greek word to denote this spiritual "hardening" in Romans 9:18, but the idea is the same.[106]

another human being.[107] Paul finds in these words of Moses in Deuteronomy hope for Israel. For, as Romans 11:14 makes clear, Paul hopes that the envy of Israel will lead ultimately to her salvation. While he is not explicit about the matter, Paul evidently thinks that the Gentiles' enjoyment of the blessings of salvation will lead Jews to desire those same blessings and so accept Jesus as their Messiah and Savior.

How much greater riches will their fullness bring! (11:12). The word "fullness" (Gk. *plērōma*) is sometimes given a quantitative meaning, as in TEV: "the complete number of Jews." But the word almost never has such a meaning. It usually (and always in biblical Greek) has a qualitative sense: "completeness" (cf. NASB). Paul is apparently referring to the full restoration to Israel of her kingdom blessings. Israel's "loss"—that is, her refusal to acknowledge Jesus as Messiah—has meant "riches for the Gentiles." Her "fullness" should bring an even greater blessing to the world.

What will their acceptance be but life from the dead? (11:15). What is this "life from the dead" that Israel's acceptance into God's kingdom will effect? Paul, of course, often pictures Christian experience in terms of new life; and he even uses language similar to this earlier in Romans to depict conversion: "Offer yourselves to God, as those who have been brought from death to life" (6:13). However, Paul more often uses this kind of language to denote the bodily resurrection of the dead. A consideration of the background of Paul's thinking in this passage also points to this meaning. One of the most influential streams in Jewish theology during this era was apocalyptic.

Apocalyptic is not easy to define; but for our purposes, we can characterize it as an attempt to make sense of history by appealing to "revelation" (the meaning of the Gk. *apokalypsis*) of heavenly mysteries. Many of the books that take an apocalyptic approach to Israel's situation focus on the events of the end. They often look for a restoration of Israel at the end of history, when the resurrection of the dead takes place.[108]

If the part of the dough offered as firstfruits is holy, then the whole batch is holy (11:16). Paul alludes to Numbers 15:17–21, where the Lord commands the people to offer to the Lord "a cake from the first of your ground meal." The word "firstfruits" (*aparchē*) is common in both secular Greek and the Old Testament to denote the initial or representative portion of a commodity to be offered in sacrifice (e.g., Lev. 2:12; 23:10; Deut. 18:4). Paul applies the imagery to the situation of Israel. Some part within Israel (the "firstfruits") is still holy; and the holiness of that initial portion makes holy the rest of Israel as well. This holy part within Israel might be the remnant of Jewish believers in Paul's day (see Rom. 11:5–7). But the following image makes it more likely that Paul is referring to the patriarchs.

If the root is holy, so are the branches (11:16). Jewish writers sometimes referred to the patriarchs as the "root." See, for example, Philo, *Who Is the Heir?* 279: "Surely he [Abraham] is indeed the founder of the nation and the race, since from him as root sprang the young plant called Israel."[109] Paul explicitly rests his hope for Israel's future on God's promise to the patriarchs (Rom. 11:28; cf. 9:5). Since he suggests that the holiness of the patriarchs makes the rest of Israel holy, one might conclude that the text teaches that all Jews will be saved. But Paul is using the word "holy" here in the way it is used in Old Testament sacrificial texts. It does not mean "set apart for salvation" (as usually in the New Testament), but "set apart" for God's special attention (see also 1 Cor. 7:14).

Branches . . . wild olive shoot . . . olive root (11:17). In 11:17–24, Paul uses different parts of an olive tree to represent key figures in the salvation history that he sketches in this chapter. The "root," as we have seen (11:16), stands for the patriarchs. The (natural) branches are the Jewish people, descended physically from the patriarchs. The wild olive shoots are Gentile Christians, grafted into the

olive tree "contrary to nature" (11:24) by God's grace. Paul perhaps chooses to use the olive tree for his comparison because it was the most widely cultivated fruit tree in the Mediterranean basin. But the olive tree also symbolizes Israel in the Old Testament and in Jewish literature (Jer. 11:16; Hos. 14:5–6).[110]

The imagery of wild olive shoots being grafted into a cultivated olive tree is not, however, realistic. Farmers, in fact, do just the reverse; they graft branches from cultivated trees into wild ones in order to improve their production. Some scholars claim that Paul, an urban man from Tarsus, simply did not understand the usual technique. Others cite evidence that farmers might occasionally graft a wild olive shoot into a cultivated tree.[111] Still others think that Paul is deliberately reversing the usual procedure in order to highlight the role of God's grace in the process. But none of these suggestions is necessary. Writers will choose illustrations that represent the reality they are trying to depict—but rarely will the analogy match the reality in every respect. So

◀
OLIVE TREE

elements that stretch or do not exactly correspond to the reality of the analogy are often introduced.

Consider therefore the kindness and sternness of God (11:22). Paul may be influenced in his use of the word "sternness" (*apotomos*) here by Wisdom of Solomon, which uses this word and its cognates to describe the nature of God's judgment. See, for example, Wisdom of Solomon 6:5: "He will come upon you terribly and swiftly, because severe judgment falls on those in high places" (see also 5:20, 22; 11:10; 12:9; 18:15).

I do not want you to be ignorant of this mystery (11:25). Paul uses the word "mystery" (*mystērion*) with a technical theological meaning derived from Jewish apocalyptic. Books that reflect this perspective use "mystery" to refer to events of the end times that have already been determined by God—and so, in that

sense already exist in heaven—and which are finally revealed by God to his people for their encouragement and understanding.

This general usage of *mystērion* appears first in Daniel, with reference to the dreams of King Nebuchadnezzar. It is "God in heaven" who reveals the mysteries of these dreams through Daniel to the king (cf. 2:28). A good example from Jewish apocalyptic is *T. Levi* 2:10: "And when you [Levi, being addressed by an angel] have mounted up there [to another heaven], you shall stand near the Lord. You shall be his priest and you shall tell forth his mysteries to men. You shall announce the one who is about to redeem Israel."[112] This concept was especially prominent in the Dead Sea Scrolls.[113] The sequence by which God planned to bring salvation to both Jews and Gentiles had not been revealed to God's people before this time. Paul is now the instrument through whom the Lord discloses the details of his plan.

Until the full number of the Gentiles has come in (11:25). "Full number" translates the same Greek word (*plērōma*) translated "fullness" in 11:12 (see comments). As we noted in commenting on that verse, the word almost always has a qualitative meaning. Is the quantitative rendering of the NIV here therefore wrong? Probably not. For the "fullness" or "completeness" that Paul ascribes to the Gentiles has in this context probably a strong numerical component. "Come in" is likely shorthand for "come into the kingdom of God" (see Matt. 7:13; 23:13; Luke 13:24). Paul is perhaps reflecting certain Jewish traditions about a fixed number of people who would enter the kingdom before the end. *Fourth Ezra* 4:35–37 is a representative text:

Did not the souls of the righteous in their chambers ask about these matters, saying, "How long are we to remain here? And when will the harvest of our reward come?" And the archangel Jeremiel answered them and said, "When the number of those like yourselves is completed; for he has weighed the age in the balance, and measured the times by measure, and numbered the times by number; and he will not move or arouse them until that measure is fulfilled."

And so all Israel will be saved (11:26). In the context, which so carefully distinguishes Gentiles and Jews, "Israel" probably refers here to national Israel. The apocalyptic background against which he writes suggests that the salvation of "all Israel" will occur in the end time (see esp. 11:15 and comments there). But how many Jews are included in the "all Israel" to be saved? Here it is important to note that this phrase in the Old Testament frequently has a collective sense, referring not to every single Israelite but to a significant or even simply representative number.

Two examples might be cited: Joshua 7:25: "Joshua said, 'Why have you brought this trouble on us? The LORD will bring trouble on you today.' Then all Israel stoned [Achan], and after they had stoned the rest, they burned them"; 2 Samuel 16:22: "So they pitched a tent for Absalom on the roof, and he lay with his father's concubines in the sight of all Israel." It is unlikely that every single Israelite alive in Joshua's day cast a stone at Achan; or that all the Jews in David's day saw the sexual dalliances of Absalom. "All Israel" in each text is representative, in that enough Jews were involved so as to give the events national significance. Thus Romans 11:26 does not promise salvation for every Jew alive at the time of Christ's return. What it promises is that a significant number, representative of the nation as a whole, will find salvation in Jesus their Messiah.[114]

The deliverer will come from Zion (11:26). To buttress his claim that "all Israel will be saved," Paul offers a quotation made up of phrases from two or three Old Testament texts. The initial

◄

MOUNT ZION

A view of Old Jerusalem in the direction of Mount Zion from the Mount of Olives.

words come from Isaiah 59:20, which was given a messianic interpretation in the targum, though the late date of that Aramaic paraphrase renders it uncertain whether the tradition was alive in Paul's day. A comparison between Isaiah 59:20 and Paul's version of the text reveals an interesting change. Whereas Isaiah predicts that the deliverer will come "to" Zion, Paul quotes him as saying that the deliverer will come "from" Zion. Paul may be depending on a form of the LXX that had the equivalent to the word "from" in it. But it is more likely that Paul, as he does elsewhere, changes the text slightly to make a theological point. What is that point? We cannot be certain, but Hebrews 12:22 associates "Zion" with the heavenly Jerusalem, the site of Jesus' high-priestly ministry. Perhaps, then, Paul changes the text to bring out a bit more clearly a reference to the Parousia.

How unsearchable his judgments, and his paths beyond tracing out! (11:33). In response to his sketch of the plan of sal-vation for both Jews and Gentiles, Paul celebrates the wisdom and power of God. "Judgments" refer not to God's role as judge but to his role as the executor of salvation history; they are the decrees he has issued in order to bring about his plan for the world.[115] Paul's attempt to explain the plight of Israel in his own day is rooted in his desire to demonstrate the agreement between God's Old Testament promise and the gospel.

Other Jewish writers in Paul's day struggled in similar ways with the plan of God in relation to the plight of Israel. The author of the book we call *2 Baruch* was one of those, and he expresses his awe at God's plan in terms similar to Paul's: "O Lord, my Lord, who can understand your judgment? Or who can explore the depth of your way? Or who can discern the majesty of your path? Or who can discern the beginning and the end of your wisdom?"[116]

From him and through him and to him are all things (11:36). The idea of God as

ST. PETER'S
SQUARE IN
MODERN ROME

the source, sustainer, and goal of all things was especially common among Greco-Roman Stoic philosophers. See, for example, the words of the second-century Roman emperor Marcus Aurelius: "From you are all things, in you are all things, for you are all things."[117] Hellenistic Jews picked up this language and applied it to their God.[118] Paul, therefore, probably knew the language from the synagogue. By the time it reaches him, of course, it has left behind the metaphysical baggage of its Stoic origin. When placed into a Christian worldview, the language appropriately emphasizes the ultimacy of God.

The Transforming Power of the Gospel (12:1–2)

The gospel has the power of rescuing any human being—Jew or Gentile—from sin's power and establishing that person in a new "right" relationship with God. But the gospel is also intended to transform the way people live. In 12:3–15:13, Paul sketches a few of the characteristics of the transformed believer. But, first, in 12:1–2, he issues a general call for believers to respond to that transforming power of God.

I urge you (12:1). The Greek behind the NIV "urge" is *parakaleō*. The word is stronger than "ask" and weaker than "command." It is the perfect word to express the moral imperative of the gospel. This word was widely used in ancient Greek moral treatises, where it often signaled a shift from one topic to another.[119]

Living sacrifices (12:1). The sacrifice of animals was central to most ancient religions, including, of course, Judaism. In call-

ing for Christians to present themselves to God as "living sacrifices," therefore, Paul is employing a metaphor that is universally understood in his day. Nor is Paul the first to use the language of sacrifice in a metaphorical way. Such metaphors are common in both the Old Testament and Judaism.[120] But Paul takes the metaphor a step further. Old Testament or Jewish use of the sacrificial metaphor implies, of course, that literal sacrifices will continue to be offered. But for Paul and the other early Christians, Jesus' once-for-all death on the cross puts an end to any further sacrifice (cf. Heb. 10:1–14).

This is your spiritual act of worship (12:1). The NIV "spiritual" translates a Greek word (*logikēn*) that is difficult to render in English (note the NIV footnote, "reasonable"). The word itself is rare in the New Testament, occurring elsewhere only in 1 Peter 2:2 (where its meaning is also debated). But the word does have a rich background in Greek and Hellenistic Jewish philosophy and religion. Arguing that God and human beings share *logos*, some Greek philosophers argued that only *logikos* worship could be pleasing to God. They contrasted this "rational" worship with what they considered to be the silly superstitions of many Greek and Near Eastern religions. Two texts can serve to demonstrate this idea:

> If I were a nightingale, I should be singing as a nightingale; if a swan, as a swan. But as it is I am a rational [*logikos*] being, therefore I must be singing hymns of praise to God.[121]

> That which is precious in the sight of God is not the number of victims immolated but the true purity of a rational [*logikon*] spirit in him who makes the sacrifice.[122]

The word "spiritual" can bring out this sense, but perhaps better is the rendering "rational." The worship God seeks from us in our everyday lives is a worship offered with a full understanding of the gospel and its implications. It flows from a renewed heart *and* mind.

Humility and Mutual Service (12:3–8)

One way in which believers reveal their transformed way of thinking is in an attitude of realistic humility toward themselves and of dedicated service to the community.

Think of yourself with sober judgment (12:3). "Think" translates a verb (*phroneō*)

that indicates the basic orientation of a person (in Romans, see also 8:5; 11:20; the cognate noun occurs in 8:6, 7, 27, and a cognate adjective in 11:25). It indicates not just one's mental state, but one's "mind-set" or attitude. Paul wants believers to form an accurate picture of themselves in their own minds. They should not consider themselves more important than they are; but neither should they think too little of themselves. Sincere and unreserved service of God and the church begins with a realistic appraisal of one's own strengths and weaknesses.

In Christ we who are many form one body (12:5). Paul's comparison of the church to the human body is well known. But the source of this comparison is not clear. The significance of Christ's own body, given in sacrifice on the cross and memorialized frequently in the celebration of the Lord's Supper, must have been a key factor. But the use of the human body to illustrate the unity and diversity of a group of people was known from other sources in the ancient world. The Roman historian Livy cites a parable of Menenius Agrippa that compares the body politic of his day with a human body.[123]

In proportion to his faith (12:6). Paul cites the different gifts God has given the church to illustrate the diversity of the Christian church. He urges those who have been given such gifts to use them effectively to serve the community. The prophet is to use his gift "in proportion to his faith." "Proportion" translates *analogia*, a word drawn from the world of mathematics and logic, where it denoted the correct proportion or right relationship. Josephus, for instance, claims that the porticos of the temple in Jerusalem were in

R E F L E C T I O N S

THE "WORSHIP" PAUL IS TALKING ABOUT IN ROMANS 12:2 applies to the whole of life. His point is that we are to consider every part of our existence as an opportunity to serve God by living out the principles of the new age to which we belong. The division with which we sometimes operate between the sphere of the "secular" and the "religious" is one Paul would simply not have recognized. Nevertheless, what Paul says here about the life of worship certainly applies to the corporate gathering for weekly praise that we call the worship "service."

The modern church is convulsed over what this service should be like, some churches insisting on organs, choirs, and hymnals and others on guitars, worship teams, and overhead transparencies. But the Bible itself says nothing about the kind of music we use or the instruments that accompany it. What texts like Romans 12:2 insist on, however, is that true worship of God must always flow from minds that have grasped and been impressed by the truth of God. Whether we sing to the accompaniment of guitars or organs, then, the *words* we sing should be carefully chosen to present an aspect of God's character to us so that we can respond with thoughtful, sincere worship.

"right proportion" to the temple as a whole.[124] The language of this text has furnished theology with its slogan "the analogy of faith," the principle that Scripture must always be interpreted in light of other Scripture. But Paul simply means that the prophet should exercise his or her gift in "right proportion" to the faith about the prophecy that God has given the prophet. Prophets should say no more and no less than what God has given them.

Let him give generously (12:8). The person with the gift of giving should exercise that gift by giving "with *haplotēs*." This word is usually translated "generously" (see NIV); but its root meaning is simply "singleness."[125] Some intertestamental Jewish texts hold up this quality of "singleness" as a key moral virtue (the entire *T. Iss.* is about this virtue). Those who give, suggests Paul, should do so with a single, undivided intent. No ulterior motives or secondary concerns should be involved.

Love and Its Manifestations (12:9–21)

This section of Paul's exhortations to the Roman Christians appears to unfold rather haphazardly. No clear theme dominates the section. Paul seems to move back and forth between admonitions about believers' relationships to other believers (12:9–13, 15–16) and to unbelievers (12:14, 17–21). The lack of clear organization may reflect Paul's use of a popular ancient style, called *paraenesis*. Found in both Greek and Jewish sources, paraenesis "strings together admonitions of a general ethical content."[126] The writer moves quickly through a variety of themes and issues, not always relating them to one another.

Paraenesis is characterized by another feature that is prominent in 12:9–21: eclecticism, or borrowing from a variety of sources. Paul quotes the Old Testament in this passage (12:19, 20), and much of what he says has parallels in Jewish and Greek ethical and wisdom sayings. But particularly striking are the parallels between 12:9–21 and the teaching of Jesus (see esp. 12:14, 17, 18, and 21). Paul absorbs some of the key ethical emphases into his own instruction and passes them on to the Romans.

Love must be sincere (12:9). The NIV, along with most English versions, supplies a verb where, in fact, none appears in the Greek text. The addition may be justified; but it is also possible that Paul views the simple "Sincere Love" as the heading for the exhortations that follow. "Love" translates the well-known Greek word *agapē*. One sometimes hears that this word is a distinctive term for the Christian conception of love. But that claim must be carefully nuanced. The word was certainly not invented by the early Christians; it occurs twenty times in the LXX, while the cognate verb is found over 250 times. But it may be true that the early Christians used this word in preference to other Greek words for "love" because it lacked some of the "baggage" (sexual and other) that other terms carried.

"Sincere" translates *anypokritos*, which is more literally translated "without hypocrisy" or "without playing a role" (such as an actor does on stage).

Be devoted to one another in brotherly love (12:10). "Brotherly love" reflects another basic Greek word for love: *philia*, here in a compound form, *philadephia*. No difference between the concept of love denoted by *philia* and that denoted by *agapē* is evident here. But the word does remind readers that the church is to be characterized by the tender love evident in the best of human families. The word "devoted" (*philostorgoi*) conveys the same nuance. See *4 Maccabees* 15:13: "O sacred nature and affection of parental love, *yearning of parents* toward offspring, nurture and indomitable suffering by mothers!"

Practice hospitality (12:13). Hospitality was especially important in the first-century world, where motels and hotels were virtually unknown. Christians traveling on ordinary business and in the service of the church depended on fellow Christians for lodging and food. Paul not only commands believers to exercise hospitality; he urges them to "pursue" it.

Bless those who persecute you; bless and do not curse (12:14). Paul's admonition echoes the teaching of Jesus, combining versions found in Matthew and Luke:

> "But I tell you: Love your enemies and pray for *those who persecute you*" (Matt. 5:44).

> "But I tell you who hear me: Love your enemies, do good to those who hate you, *bless* those who curse you, pray for those who mistreat you" (Luke 6:27–28).

Jesus' command that his followers respond to persecution and hatred with love and blessing was unprecedented in the ancient world, so Paul's dependence on Jesus is almost certain. Paul has no need to introduce the words as a quotation since they would have been well known in the early church.

Rejoice with those who rejoice; mourn with those who mourn (12:15). After

instructing Christians to respond to outsiders with love and forgiveness, Paul now turns back to the Christian community, enjoining a sincere identification with others whatever their state might be. Note how Paul's commands here echo what he says about relations within the body of Christ in 1 Corinthians 12:26: "If one part suffers, every part suffers with it; if one part is honored, every part rejoices with it." But the need for such mutual identification is found in Jewish sources as well. See, for instance, Sirach 7:34: "Do not avoid those who weep, but mourn with those who mourn."[127]

Be willing to associate with people of low position (12:16). "People of low position" can also be translated "humble activities" (the Gk. word can be either masculine or neuter). If Paul's reference is to people who rank low on the world's socioeconomic scale, he is urging Christians to imitate their Father in heaven, who frequently stresses his own concern for the "down and out" (e.g., Judg. 6:15; Ps. 10:18).[128]

Do not repay anyone evil for evil (12:17). Prohibitions of retaliation are found widely in Judaism; see, for instance, *Joseph and Aseneth* 23:9: "And we are men who worship God, and it does not befit us to repay evil with evil." But other references to Jesus' teaching in this same context argue that Paul depends directly here on Jesus' prohibition of retaliation from the Sermon on the Mount (Matt. 5:38–42).

You will heap burning coals on his head (12:20). These words come from Proverbs 25:21–22a, which Paul quotes as the response that believers are to make to their enemies. The words "coals" and "fire" in the Old Testament are usually used metaphorically to refer to God's awesome presence and especially to his judgment.[129] A few scholars, therefore, think that the Proverbs text refers to God's judgment and that Paul views the believers' kindness to enemies as ultimately increasing the degree of judgment that they will receive.[130] But the context seems to require that "heap[ing] burning coals" has a positive rather than a negative impact on the unbeliever. Thus, some scholars have theorized that the imagery in Proverbs may go back to an Egyptian ritual, in which a penitent carried coals of fire on the head as a sign of repentance.[131]

The Christian and Secular Rulers (13:1–7)

Paul interrupts his outline of the various workings of "sincere love," continued in 13:8–10, with this paragraph requiring submission to the governmental rulers.

Everyone must submit himself to the governing authorities (13:1). When Paul uses the word "authority" (*exousia*) in the plural, he elsewhere refers to spiritual "authorities"—angelic beings, whether good or evil.[132] In this text, it is clear that the word refers to human beings who have been placed—ultimately by God—in positions of authority in the government (cf. "rulers" in 13:3). But a few scholars have thought that some allusion to spiritual authorities may nevertheless be intended; that is, that Paul is referring at the same time both to human rulers and to the spiritual powers that stand behind them. Paul would thus be assuming the widespread worldview of his day, according to which spiritual beings influenced

77

Romans

▶ The Social-Political Setting of Paul's Appeal to Obey the Government

What motivates Paul to address the topic of the Christian's attitude toward the government? One reason may be theological: Paul is worried that Christians will take his demand not to "conform . . . to the pattern of this world" (12:2) too far, lumping government into the category of "this world" and therefore refusing to respect its legitimate, divinely ordained position and function. But three other specific historical movements may have contributed to "anti-government" thinking among the Roman Christians.

(1) The Jewish Christians in Rome had experienced a severe disruption in their lives when Emperor Claudius expelled all the Jews (including Jewish Christians) from the city in A.D. 49 (see the introduction). This event may well have led to resentment against the government in Rome.

(2) The decade of the 50s saw a spectacular increase in Jewish Zealot activity and popularity. The Zealots were the political terrorists of their day.

They preached insurrection against the Roman government, insisting that Israel's subjection under foreign domination was contrary to her calling to be a theocracy. The Zealots eventually won enough people to their side to incite a violent four-year insurrection against Rome (A.D. 66–70; in fact, the last holdouts, at Masada, were not defeated until A.D. 73). We do not have much evidence of Zealot sympathy among Roman Jews in these years,[A-8] but it is possible that the movement indirectly influenced attitudes of the Roman Christians.

(3) The Roman historian Tacitus mentions resistance against the payment of indirect taxes in the middle 50s in Rome.[A-9] The resistance culminated in a tax revolt against the government in A.D. 58, a year or two after Paul wrote Romans. Some of the Roman Christians may well have shared these sentiments; note how Paul climaxes his call to submit to the authorities with commands to pay taxes (13:7).

the course of human affairs, especially the affairs of nations.[133]

But this suggestion is unlikely. The word *exousia* was a normal way of referring to human rulers in Paul's day; it translated the Latin *potestates*, which was used to refer to a broad range of Roman government officials. Moreover, in all the places except one where Paul uses the plural *exousiai* to refer to spiritual authorities it is coupled with *archai*, "rulers." There is nothing in this passage to suggest a dual reference.

"Submit" translates the Gk. *hypotassō*, a verb Paul uses to denote the appropriate response of people who recognize their place in a hierarchical order. Thus, Christians are urged to "submit" to governing authorities, to their spiritual leaders, and to one another.[134] Similarly, slaves are to submit to their masters, Christian prophets to other prophets, and wives to husbands.[135] Assumed in each hierarchy is that the highest authority is always God, whose claims must always take precedence.

There is no authority except that which God has established (13:1). Paul's teaching about the divine ordination of government in general and of individual rulers in particular echoes a consistent biblical theme. Daniel, for instance, tells the arrogant King Nebuchadnezzar that God was teaching him that "the Most High is sovereign over the kingdoms of men and gives them to anyone he wishes and sets over them the lowliest of men" (Dan. 4:17).[136] Despite the disasters Israel suffered at the hands of foreign powers, this teaching remained basic throughout the intertestamental period. Note Wisdom of Solomon 6:1–3: "Listen, therefore, O kings, and understand; learn, O judges of the ends of the earth. Give ear, you that rule over

multitudes, and boast of many nations. For your dominion was given you from the Lord, and your sovereignty from the Most High; he will search out your works and inquire into your plans."

Do what is right and he will commend you (13:3). Paul may be thinking here specifically of the practice of Roman authorities to publish in inscriptions the names of "benefactors" of society. "Do what is right" may then refer in turn to the activities of Christians as "good citizens" in their own society.[137]

He is God's servant to do you good (13:4). "Servant" translates *diakonos*, a word that Paul usually uses to refer to Christians as "servants" of God and of the gospel. But the word in secular Greek was used to denote a secular official of various kinds.[138] The idea that secular rulers dispense divine justice is, of course, deeply rooted in Scripture; but it is also found in secular sources of the time. See, for instance, Plutarch: "Rulers are ministers of God for the care and safety of mankind, that they may distribute or hold in safe keeping the blessings and benefits which God gives to man."[139]

He does not bear the sword for nothing (13:4). Scholars have advanced several specific suggestions for Paul's reference here. Several point to the Roman *ius gladii*, the authority possessed of all higher magistrates of inflicting the sentence of death.[140] But the authority seems to have been confined to Roman provincial governors and restricted to their power to condemn to death Roman citizens serving in the military.[141] Others note Philo's use of the term "swordbearers" to refer to Egyptian police officials; and still others to Roman mili-

▶ Paul and Government

One of the striking elements of this passage is Paul's rosy view of government. According to him, civil authorities "hold no terror for those who do right, but for those who do wrong" (13:3). Paul may be reflecting to some extent his own experience with Roman authorities, which, on the whole, was quite positive. He used his Roman citizenship to his advantage; and when brought before the Roman governor of Achaia, his right to preach the gospel was vindicated (Acts 18:12–17).

But Paul could hardly be naive about the potential for governments to be unjust. He would have known that his people's history was littered with persecution from foreign governments. He was proclaiming as Lord of the universe One who was unjustly executed by the Roman authorities. Paul well knew that some governmental officials rewarded evildoers and punished those who did good. Probably, then, what Paul is doing in Romans 13:3–4 is describing how governments *are supposed to function* under their divine mandate. Perhaps he also implies that the submission of Christians to rulers need not take the form of obedience when governments do not implement divine justice.

tary power (to put down insurrection).[142] But Paul's rather vague wording does not enable us to pinpoint any of these situations as that to which he is referring. The most that can be said is that he refers generally to the right of governments to punish those who violate its laws.

Because of conscience (13:5). "Conscience" (*syneidēsis*) is a word that Paul takes from the world of Greco-Roman philosophy and religion (see comments on 9:1). In its original sense, *syneidēsis* referred to the painful knowledge that came after breaking a law or custom. Some scholars argue that Paul always uses it with this meaning. If that were the case here, he would be urging believers to submit to government so that they can avoid that sense of wrongdoing. But New Testament writers frequently "extend" the meanings of words that they borrow from another sphere. In the case of *syneidēsis*, there is good evidence that this has happened—that the word can also denote "consciousness" of God and his

demands (cf. 2:15). This meaning fits well in the present context. It is because the believer is conscious of God's ordaining of governmental authorities that he or she will willingly submit to them.

The authorities are God's servants (13:6). In 13:4, Paul called the ruler a *diakonos* ("servant"; see comments on 13:4). But the word for "servant" here is a different one—*leitourgos*. It and its cognates occur frequently in the LXX to denote people who served in the temple, and in the New Testament the word group always refers to religious service or servants of some kind.[143] A strong case can therefore be made here that Paul views secular authorities as having religious significance. However, *leitourgos* was used in secular Greek to denote public officials of various kinds (cf. our "public servant"), and the word occurs with this meaning in the LXX as well.[144]

If you owe taxes, pay taxes; if revenue, then revenue (13:7). "Taxes" (Gk. *phoros*;

Lat. *tributa*) denotes direct taxes (cf. also Luke 20:22; 23:2), while "revenue" (Gk. *telos*; Lat. *portoria*) refers to "indirect" governmental taxes, such as fees for various services and customs duties (cf. Matt. 17:25, where the NIV translates "duty").

Love and the Law (13:8–10)

After his "excursus" about the Christian's responsibility to the government, Paul returns to the subject that has dominated 12:9–21: love. He now highlights love as the virtue that brings all the commandments of the Mosaic law to their ultimate fulfillment.

The commandments, "Do not commit adultery," "Do not murder," "Do not steal," "Do not covet" (13:9). In both Exodus 20:1–17 and Deuteronomy 5:6–21, the prohibition of murder comes before the prohibition of adultery. However, at least one important LXX manuscript of Deuteronomy (Vaticanus) has them in the same order as Paul, and this order is attested also in the Nash Papyrus (a first or second-century B.C. scrap of text with the Ten Commandments) and in several Jewish and early Christian texts.[145] This may, therefore, have been the order of commandments popular in certain circles of Diaspora Judaism.

Are summed up in the one rule, "Love your neighbor as yourself" (13:9). The Greek word for "rule" is simply *logos*, "word." There is precedent in Judaism to use this word to refer to commandments, and especially the Ten Commandments, which were often called the "Ten Words."[146]

The love command of Leviticus 19:18 had been singled out by some Jews as central to the demands of the law; Paul

is, of course, borrowing here again from the teaching of Jesus, who claimed that "all the Law and the Prophets" hung on this command and the command to love the Lord God.[147] Some Jews interpreted "neighbor" (*ra'*) in the command to refer to fellow Israelites only[148]; others gave a broader interpretation.[149] Jesus and Paul assume the broader interpretation.

Living in Light of "the Day" (13:11–14)

Paul wraps up this general section of his ethical exhortations by returning to the theme of salvation history with which he began. Believers are to avoid conformity to "this age" (cf. 12:2), because it is an age of darkness that is passing away, to be replaced by a new age of light and salvation (13:11–14).

The hour has come for you to wake up from your slumber (13:11). Sleep is

often a metaphor for spiritual insensitivity in the ancient world.[150]

The night is nearly over; the day is almost here. So let us put aside the deeds of darkness and put on the armor of light (13:12). Darkness veils the activities of criminals and is also the time for drinking bouts, carousing, and sexual dalliance. It is therefore almost universally associated with evil. To that extent, Paul's imagery communicates rather clearly to any audience. But the Old Testament and Judaism supply a further, theological

▶ The "Weak" and the "Strong" in Rome

Applying Paul's plea for tolerance in these chapters requires that we understand something about just what the underlying issue in all these divisions may have been. What particular set of values or beliefs led to the dissensions over food, wine, and holy days that Paul mentions in these verses? Scholars suggest several scenarios, but two deserve consideration.

1. The "weak" may have been Gentile Christians who brought into their practice of Christianity certain ascetic practices from their pagan background. A popular philosophical/religious group of the time, for instance, were the neo-Pythagoreans, who avoided eating anything that had a "soul" (including, in their view, animals).[A-10] Some of the later gnostics also avoided eating "flesh," and certain ideas that later became part of the system of "Gnosticism" were already circulating in the first century. Pagans also had superstitions about "lucky" and "unlucky" days, and several Greco-Roman religious cults also observed special days. However, specific language within 14:1–15:13 as well as the tenor of Romans as a whole make it much more likely that the specific problems Paul treats in these chapters had their roots in debates about the continuing relevance of the Torah.

2. This leads us to the second alternative: that the "weak in faith" abstained from meat, observed special days, and avoided wine out of a concern to maintain Jewish "purity." The Torah itself did not require Jews to refrain from eating all meat or from wine. But Jews who lived in dominantly pagan cultures often refrained from such food out of concern that it was not "kosher." The notable biblical example, of course, is Daniel, who "resolved not to defile himself with the royal food and wine, and he asked the chief official for permission not to defile himself this way" (Dan. 1:8).[A-11] Pious Jews often abstained from wine out of fear that it had been contaminated by the pagan practice of offering wine as a libation to the gods.[A-12] We know from many Jewish sources that matters such as the food laws and the observance of Sabbath and other festivals took on a heightened importance in the intertestamental period, as Jews sought to hold on to their distinct identity in the midst of persecution and an often hostile Gentile environment.

Ascetic tendencies found in other ancient religions may have encouraged such decisions on the part of Jews. Note, for instance, Philo's description of the Therapeutae, a Jewish sect of the pre-Christian era:

> For as nature has set hunger and thirst as mistresses over mortal kind they propitiate them without using anything to curry favour but only such things as are actually needed and without which life cannot be maintained. Therefore they eat enough to keep from hunger and drink enough to keep from thirst but abhor surfeiting as a malignant enemy both to soul and body.[A-13]

Reflections of the influence of this ascetic tendency surface elsewhere in the New Testament.[A-14] Early church historians report that some Jewish Christians at a later day abstained from eating flesh.[A-15] On this hypothesis, the "days" that the weak were observing probably included the Sabbath and the annual Jewish festivals.

dimension to the night/day imagery used here. The Old Testament prophets frequently used the expression "the day of the LORD" to denote the time when God would intervene decisively to save his people and judge their enemies.[151] This phrase is taken over and adapted by the New Testament writers, who spoke of the "day of Christ," and so on. Since, therefore, the era of salvation and blessing can be called "the day," "the night" may represent this present evil age. Note, for instance, *1 Enoch* 58:

> The righteous ones shall be in the light of the sun and the elect ones in the light of eternal life which has no end [v. 2]. . . . The sun has shined upon the earth and the darkness is over. There shall be a light that has no end. . . . For already darkness has been destroyed, light shall be permanent before the Lord of the Spirits, and the light of uprightness shall stand firm

forever and ever before the Lord of the Spirits [v. 6].

The Qumran covenanters called themselves "the children of light" and their enemies, the unspiritual, the "children of darkness." In light of this background, Paul must be seen to be urging believers to live in accordance with the new age of salvation that has already been inaugurated by Christ but remains to be consummated in the future.

A Plea for Tolerance (14:1–12)

In 14:1–15:13, Paul rebukes the Roman Christians for standing in judgment over one another. They have divided into two "camps" over certain issues. Those whom Paul labels "weak in faith" (cf. 14:1) hold that believers should not eat meat (14:2), that they should regard certain days as more "holy" than others (cf. 14:5), and, perhaps, that they should not drink wine (cf. 14:21). The "strong" (cf. 15:1), by contrast, feel free to eat meat, to drink wine, and to treat every day alike. Paul comes down on the side of the strong (14:14, 20; 15:1), but his main concern is the disunity that these issues are creating within the Christian community. He wants both weak and strong to respect the views of the others and to cease the mutual recriminations that are tearing apart the community.

Accept him whose faith is weak (14:1). At both the beginning and end of chapter 14 (see 14:22–23), Paul characterizes the "weak" with respect to their "faith." Paul's use of the word throughout Romans requires that it refers to that "trust in Christ" that is fundamental to the gospel. Yet, as 14:2 makes clear, this faith is being looked at here from a spe-

R E F L E C T I O N S

IF OUR IDENTIFICATION OF THE ROOT PROBLEM IN Rome is correct, then the source of division between the "weak" and "strong" had to do with certain Jewish customs that the "weak" thought important to retain in living out their new life in Christ. What is especially significant for contemporary application is the recognition that such practices are neither required nor condemned in the New Testament. Jewish Christians who wanted to continue to observe the foods laws and Sabbath were entirely free to do so; but they could not insist that other Jewish Christians or Gentile Christians follow suit. The issue that Paul deals with in Romans 14–15, therefore, falls into the category we call *adiaphora*: things neither required nor prohibited. Paul's plea for tolerance, therefore, cannot be extended to other kinds of issues. The apostle could be very intolerant when the truth of the gospel was at stake (see, e.g., Galatians).

cific angle: what one thinks one's faith in Christ allows one to do. The person "weak in faith," therefore, is not necessarily one who is immature in his or her faith. It is, rather, a person who has not yet come to the conviction—because of the "pull" of a life spent in Judaism—that the Christian faith allows him or her to eat meat, drink wine, and ignore Jewish holy days.

One man considers one day more sacred than another (14:5). As we argued above, the "sacred" days are probably Jewish holy days, which the weak insisted carried over into the Christian era. Just what these holy days may have included is not clear. Jews, of course, celebrated annually several great festivals inaugurated in both the Old Testament (e.g., the Day of Atonement, Passover) and in the intertestamental period (e.g., Purim, Hanukkah). Many Jews observed regular days of fasting; the Pharisees fasted twice a week. And, of course, the weekly Sabbath was central to Jewish life.

That the Sabbath was one of the days in dispute is probable from two circumstances. (1) Sabbath observance became a key identification marker for Jews in Paul's day and was therefore likely a point of contention between Jewish and Gentile Christians. (2) Colossians 2:16, where Paul deals with a somewhat similar issue, specifically mentions the Sabbath as one of the holy days at issue.

He who eats meat, eats to the Lord, for he gives thanks to God; and he who abstains, does so to the Lord and gives thanks to God (14:6). This is the earliest mention in Christian literature of the practice of giving thanks at mealtime.[152] It is, of course, a continuation of the Jewish practice.[153] The "Lord" in this verse

may be God the Father. But the fact that the "Lord" in Romans 14:9 is Christ suggests that Paul is thinking of Christ as the Lord throughout these verses.

Christ died and returned to life (14:9). Paul cites bedrock Christian tradition: "For what I received I passed on to you as of first importance: that Christ died for our sins according to the Scriptures, that he was buried, that he was raised on the third day according to the Scriptures."[154] Only here, however, do we have in this tradition the language of "come to life" rather than "raised." Paul tailors the wording to suit his context, in which he will note that Christ is the Lord of both "the dead and the living."

We will all stand before God's judgment seat (14:10). Paul is the only New Testament author to put a theological twist on the well-known *bēma*, the scene of secular judgment.[155] In 2 Corinthians 5:10, he refers to the "judgment seat of Christ," but the variant in divine name should not suggest that he thinks of a different setting, or time, of judgment.

"As surely as I live," says the Lord, "every knee shall bow before me; every tongue will confess to God" (14:11). The bulk of this quotation is from Isaiah 45:23, a text apropos to the issue Paul is discussing here, since the verse is surrounded with claims of the Lord's unique sovereignty: "I am God, and there is no other" (45:22); "In the LORD alone are righteousness and strength" (45:24). The opening words of the quotation, "As surely as I live," do not come from Isaiah 45. This phrase, however, does occur twenty-two times in the Old Testament, including Isaiah 49:18, which may be Paul's specific reference. Why does he add these words? Perhaps to suggest that the "Lord" of the quotation from Isaiah 45:23 is none other than the Lord Christ, who died and was raised.

Limiting Liberty by Love (14:13–23)

Most of 14:13–23 is directed to the "strong," as Paul is urging them not to insist on the exercise of their own rights at the expense of the spiritual health of the "weak."

Let us stop passing judgment on one another (14:13). Paul may be alluding to Jesus' teaching: "Do not judge, or you too will be judged" (Matt. 7:1). Absolute prohibitions of judging are rare in Judaism, and Paul consistently alludes to Jesus' teaching in this part of Romans.

Stumbling block (14:13). The Greek word *proskomma* refers to any obstacle that might cause a person to trip or stumble. It is therefore a perfect metaphor for a practice or word that might cause a believer to "stumble" in his or her walk with the Lord. This is its significance throughout the New Testament.[156]

Obstacle (14:13). The Greek word here is *skandalon*, which originally denoted a "trap." But the word also became a metaphor for the idea of "occasion of misfortune" or "cause of ruin." All fourteen New Testament occurrences of this word have this significance. Leviticus 19:14 ("Do not curse the deaf or put a stumbling block in front of the blind, but fear your God. I am the LORD") may have been the seminal text for this metaphorical significance in the Scripture.

No food is unclean in itself (14:14). "Unclean" translates *koinos*, which means "common"; it is the word used to describe the Greek of the New Testament period: *koinē*, or "common" (i.e., widespread) Greek. The Jews began to use this word to denote food that was "common," that is, secular and therefore to be avoided by the zealous Jew.[157]

Approved by men (14:18). "Approved" (*dokimos*) can also be translated here "esteemed." The word normally denotes the quality of having been approved through a test.[158] But there is some evidence that the word could also mean "esteemed" or "respected."[159]

R E F L E C T I O N S

NEW TESTAMENT CLAIMS SUCH AS PAUL'S IN 14:20, that "all food is clean," are sometimes taken by Christians to mean that they do not need to observe any limitations of any kind on their food or activities. If an activity is not expressly forbidden in Scripture, they claim, they have a complete right to do it.

But such Christians miss two important counterpoints in Scripture. (1) The essence of New Testament ethics is to encourage God's people to embody certain key moral principles that will direct their activity. Thus, many practices not forbidden in Scripture might be forbidden because of an extension of these principles. Most believers, for instance, are convinced that the recreational use of drugs is wrong, not because it is prohibited in Scripture, but because it violates the principle that we are to honor God with our bodies.

(2) Each of us comes to our Christianity with different backgrounds and make-ups, and therefore with different weaknesses. We are called on by God to exercise wisdom in identifying activities that may be without harm in themselves but which could become a temptation to ourselves. The principle that Paul enunciates in 1 Corinthians 6:12 is an important one to set alongside of Romans 14:20: " 'Everything is permissible for me'—but not everything is beneficial. 'Everything is permissible for me'—but I will not be mastered by anything."

All food is clean (14:20). The Old Testament uses the word "clean" to denote food that was uncontaminated and therefore acceptable for Jews to eat (see, e.g., Gen. 7:2–3, 8; 8:20).[160]

Or drink wine (14:21). Since Paul introduces the drinking of wine as an example of his own behavior, it is not clear whether it was one of the points dividing the weak and the strong. We do know that many Jews abstained from wine in pagan contexts out of fear that it had been involved in ritual libations to the gods.

Unity Through Mutual Respect (15:1–13)

Paul now calls on the strong to imitate Christ in pleasing other people rather than themselves (15:1–6). He then climaxes his appeal for tolerance and mutual respect in the Roman Christian community by calling on each group to "accept" the other and so fulfill the plan of God, set forth in the Old Testament, to bring Jews and Gentiles together in one people of God (15:7–13).

We who are strong ought to bear with the failings of the weak (15:1). The word "strong" here comes from a Greek word that means "powerful" or "capable" (*dynatos*), while "weak" translates *adynaton*, "incapable." The *dynatoi* are those Christians, like Paul himself, who are "capable" of understanding that their faith in Christ frees them from requirements of observing ritual aspects of the law of Moses. But others, with strong emotional ties perhaps to their Jewish upbringing, are not "capable" of living out this freedom. While Paul therefore shifts vocabulary here, he is continuing to address the same issue as he did in chapter 14.

Each of us should please his neighbor for his good (15:2). The unexpected use of the word "neighbor" reveals that Paul has the "love command" of Leviticus 19:18 in mind: "Love your neighbor as yourself." Following the lead of Jesus (e.g., Matt. 22:34–40), Paul finds in this command the essence of new covenant ethics (see Rom. 13:8–10). An allusion to the command is especially appropriate in a context dealing with tolerance toward fellow Christians, for the love command is preceded in Leviticus 19:18 by a prohibition of negative attitudes toward other Israelites: "Do not seek revenge or bear a grudge against one of your people."

For even Christ did not please himself but, as it is written, "The insults of those who insult you have fallen on me" (Rom. 15:3). Paul puts words from Psalm 69:9b on the lips of Jesus. The "you" in the quotation is therefore God, while the "me" is Christ himself. Language from Psalm 69 is often applied in the New Testament to the suffering of Christ on the cross.[161] Paul thus makes two points via this quotation. (1) If Jesus could endure the insults of others, his followers should certainly be willing to put up with the minor irritations occasioned by Christians with different viewpoints. (2) Jesus'

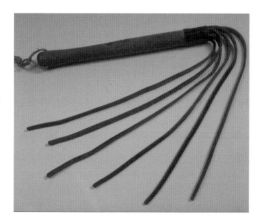

◀
ROMAN WHIP

own suffering on the cross serves as the preeminent example of pleasing others rather than oneself.

So that through endurance and the encouragement of the Scriptures we might have hope (15:4). A perhaps preferable rendering is "through endurance and the comfort that comes from the Scriptures." This alternative takes the Greek word *paraklēsis* to mean "comfort" rather than "encouragement" and attaches the genitive *tōn graphōn* (as a genitive of source) to that word only rather than to both nouns. One argument for this rendering is the possible influence of Jewish texts on Paul's wording here. Note 1 Maccabees 12:9: "since we have as encouragement [*paraklēsin*] the holy books that are in our hands." Paul seems to stray from his main point a bit here, writing more generally about the sufferings that believers, following their Lord, are destined to experience. In their midst, Paul reminds us, the Scriptures comfort us as we read about God's sovereign control of the world and his promises to his people.

Christ has become a servant of the Jews on behalf of God's truth, to confirm the promises made to the patriarchs so that the Gentiles may glorify God for his mercy (15:8b–9a). While the structure of this sentence is debated, the NIV has probably accurately captured its basic sense. The ministry of Messiah ("Christ") Jesus to Israel fulfills God's promises to his people and at the same time opens the way for Gentiles to be admitted into the people of God. Paul succinctly summarizes a key motif of the letter to the Romans.

Throughout the letter, the apostle has labored to show that the Abrahamic promise includes Gentiles (cf. ch. 4) without canceling Israel's own privileges and blessings (cf. chs. 9–11). The "truth" (*alētheia*) of God in 15:8 can perhaps more accurately be translated the "faithfulness" of God. The translators of the LXX frequently used this Greek word to render Hebrew words meaning "faithfulness." A good example is Psalm 36:5: "Your love, O LORD, reaches to the heavens, your faithfulness [LXX *alētheia*] to the skies" (cf. also Rom. 3:7). In light of the argument of Romans 4, "the promise made to the patriarchs" might include faithful Gentiles. But Paul has brought the language of "promise" and "fathers" together in Romans 9–11 (cf. 9:5 and 11:28) to refer to the things promised by God to the Jewish people specifically. This is probably his intention here also.

As it is written (15:9). The four quotations from the Old Testament in 15:9b–12 all contain the key word "Gentiles." Paul's purpose is to confirm from Scripture that Gentiles were all along included in God's gracious promise to create and bless a people for his own name. Paul follows Jewish custom in quoting from every part of the Old Testament canon: the Law, the Prophets, and the Writings.[162]

I will praise you among the Gentiles (15:9b). These words come from Psalm 18:49 (or possibly 2 Sam. 22:50, which has these identical words). In this psalm, the speaker is David, who praises God for the victory that the Lord has given him over the Gentile nations. As he did in quoting Psalm 69 in Romans 15:3, Paul again puts these words of David on the lips of Jesus. It is Messiah Jesus who has finally subdued the nations and brought them under the benefits of his kingdom reign.

Rejoice, O Gentiles, with his people (15:10). The careful student of Scripture, who compares Paul's quotations with their Old Testament originals, will be perplexed here. For the Hebrew text of Deuteronomy 32:43, which Paul is quoting, is translated, "Make his people rejoice, O nations." Paul's wording is found in the LXX version. This is not in itself surprising; Paul usually quotes the Old Testament according to the LXX. But in this case, by following the Greek translation, Paul may be misquoting the text and thereby making an incorrect application of the text.

This problem is a difficult one in some New Testament texts. But it might not be so difficult here. Note how most English versions (including the NIV) follow the LXX reading in translating Deuteronomy 32:43. They do so partly because a Hebrew manuscript containing this verse has been found at Qumran (4QDeut^a) that agrees with the LXX rendering. In this case, therefore, there is good reason to think that the LXX has preserved the original Hebrew text.

Praise the Lord, all you Gentiles, and sing praises to him, all you peoples (15:11). Paying careful attention to the Old Testament context of the words that Paul quotes often sheds light on his purpose. In this case, Paul is probably drawn to these opening words from Psalm 117 because verse 2 (the only other verse in this psalm) goes on to cite God's "mercy" (*eleos*) and "truth" (*alētheia*) as reasons for the psalmist's praise. God's "truth," or "faithfulness," demonstrated to Israel and his "mercy" revealed to the Gentiles are the lead ideas that govern these quotations (15:8–9).

The Root of Jesse will spring up (15:12). "Root" is a common messianic designation, usually found in conjunction with the name David (see, e.g., Jer. 23:5; 33:15).[163]

Paul's Ministry and Travel Plans (15:14–33)

Paul typically closes his letters with some personal notes, referring to his own plans

87

Romans

MEDITERRANEAN WORLD

Jerusalem, Illyricum, and Spain were part of Paul's ministry goals.
▼

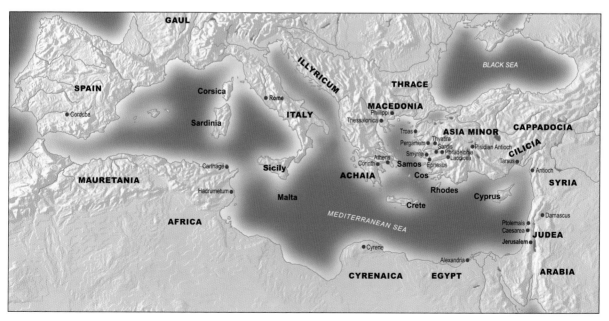

and asking prayer for them. Typical of Romans is the long elaboration of these points that we find in these verses. Paul rehearses his past travels in 15:14–21, focusing on his ministry among the Gentiles. In 15:22–29, he announces his future travel plans: to go to Spain via Jerusalem and Rome. He then requests prayer for the collection he is bringing to the Jewish Christians in Jerusalem in 15:30–33.

You yourselves are full of goodness, complete in knowledge and competent to instruct one another (15:14). Without suggesting that Paul indulges in insincere flattery, he may here be using a popular ancient literary device, the *captatio benevolentiae*, an expression of confidence in his readers. Ancient writers frequently used such flattery of their readers to gain adherence for their ideas.[164]

A minister of Christ Jesus . . . with the priestly duty of proclaiming the gospel of God, so that the Gentiles might become an offering acceptable to God, sanctified by the Holy Spirit (15:16). Paul's description of his ministry in this verse is remarkable for its extended use of priestly metaphors. It is important to note that they are metaphors. Paul does not consider himself a "priest" but compares his gospel ministry of proclamation in word and deed to the ministry of a priest. The word "minister" itself, at the beginning of the verse, probably has priestly connotations. The Greek word is *leitourgos*. While it can mean simply "servant" (see comments on 13:6), the other cultic terms in the verse suggest that it has the meaning of "priest," as it often does in the Old Testament and Jewish writings.[165]

"The priestly duty of proclaiming the gospel of God" renders a difficult Greek phrase, with "gospel" as the object of the verb "offer sacrifice." But a parallel is found in *4 Maccabees* 7:8, which speaks of "administrators of the law" (lit., "those who serve the law as priests"). The sacrifice Paul offers in his priestly ministry is the Gentiles themselves. Paul is probably reflecting here Isaiah's prediction of an influx of Gentiles into God's kingdom on the Day of the Lord in Isaiah 66:19–20:

"I will set a sign among them, and I will send some of those who survive to the nations—to Tarshish, to the Libyans and Lydians (famous as archers), to Tubal and Greece, and to the distant islands that have not heard of my fame or seen my glory. They will proclaim my glory among the nations. And they will bring all your brothers, from all the nations, to my holy mountain in Jerusalem as an offering to the LORD—on horses, in chariots and wagons, and on mules and camels," says the LORD. "They will bring them, as the Israelites bring their grain offerings, to the temple of the LORD in ceremonially clean vessels."

Paul reflects here the typical New Testament eschatological transformation

---

REFLECTIONS

PAUL IDENTIFIES THE GENTILES themselves as the offering he hopes to make to God (15:16). He reminds us that people are what ministry is all about. We can easily become preoccupied with the programs we administer, the subject matter that we are teaching, the books we are writing. We can forget that the purpose of programs, classes, and books is the formation of strong Christians, sanctified, and therefore an acceptable offering to God.

of the sacrificial system of the Old Testament: Animal sacrifices are replaced by obedient Christians (cf. 12:1 and comments) and the praise they offer God (cf. Heb. 13:15), and the priest is replaced by Christian ministers.

By the power of signs and miracles (15:19). "Signs and miracles" (or the more usual rendering "signs and wonders"; *sēmeia kai terata*) is standard biblical terminology for miracles. The phrase occurs particularly often in the account of the Exodus (15 of the 29 occurrences of the phrase refer to the Exodus events); see, for example, Deuteronomy 4:34: "Has any god ever tried to take for himself one nation out of another nation, by testings, by miraculous signs and wonders, by war, by a mighty hand and an outstretched arm, or by great and awesome deeds, like all the things the LORD your God did for you in Egypt before your very eyes?" Some scholars think Paul deliberately uses this language in order implicitly to put himself on a par with Moses in his salvation-historical significance.

From Jerusalem all the way around to Illyricum (15:19). Paul probably chooses Jerusalem as the starting point for his ministry because it was the center of Judaism. Both Paul (Gal. 1:18–19, 22) and Luke (Acts 9:26–30; cf. 26:20) affirm Paul's ministry in Jerusalem. Why Paul chooses Illyricum is harder to say, since neither he nor Luke ever explicitly indicate that Paul ministered there. But Illyricum, the Roman province covering the area today known as northern Albania and much of Yugoslavia and Bosnia-Herzegovina, was located on the Egnatian Way, a road that Paul traveled as he preached the gospel in Phillipi and Thessalonica.[166] Considering, then, Paul's preference of sticking to well-traveled Roman roads, he may well have preached in Illyricum during the movements mentioned in Acts 20:1–2.

When I go to Spain (15:24). Parts of Spain (which in ancient times included all of the Iberian Peninsula) had been occupied by Roman troops since about 200 B.C. But Rome fully organized Spain as a province only in Paul's lifetime. Scholars used to think that there was a significant Jewish presence in Spain at this time, but this is now doubted.[167] Why did Paul choose Spain as the next target of his pioneer church-planting ministry? It may be simply because it was a relatively new "Romanized" area. But it may also be that Paul thought of Spain as identical to the Old Testament "Tarshish," the "ends of the earth" that Isaiah predicted would be the culmination of God's eschatological work among the Gentiles (see Isa. 66:19, quoted above).[168]

Whether Paul ever got to Spain is not clear. If, as we think, the Pastoral Letters were written after Paul's release from his first Roman imprisonment (Acts 28), it is perhaps unlikely; for these letters reveal Paul back in the eastern Mediterranean. Yet one early Christian text, *1 Clement* 5:7, seems to suggest that Paul did eventually reach Spain.

To have you assist me on my journey (15:24). The NIV pretty well captures the nuance of the verb *propempō* that Paul uses here, for it became almost a technical early Christian word for missionary support.[169] Paul makes clear that he expects the Romans to offer him material assistance for his plans to evangelize Spain.

In the service of the saints there (15:25). Here and in the following verses Paul refers to his famous "collection" for the impoverished Jerusalem Christians. During his third missionary journey, Paul gathered money from his Gentile churches to be sent as an offering to Jerusalem.[170] Paul saw this collection not only as a practical demonstration of Christian charity, but also as an opportunity to close the growing rift between Gentile and Jewish Christians.

Macedonia and Achaia were pleased to make a contribution (15:26). Paul refers to the churches he planted in Philippi, Thessalonica, and Berea (all in the Roman province of Macedonia) and in Corinth (in Achaia).

The poor among the saints (15:26). This phrase can also be translated "the poor who are the saints" (taking *tōn hagiōn* as an epexegetic genitive). In this case the word "poor" is a technical description of the righteous ones. Such a designation is possible, since "poor" becomes almost a technical way of denoting God's people in some Old Testament and Jewish texts. But it is probably not called for here. The NIV rendering makes better sense.

After I . . . have made sure that they have received this fruit (15:28). A literal rendering of the Greek is "having sealed for them this fruit." The idea of sealing suggests an official proclamation of authenticity (e.g., Est. 8:8, 10; John 3:33); a papyrus text speaks of "sealing [sacks] of grain" in order to guarantee their contents.[171] Paul, the apostle to the Gentiles, will accompany the collection to Jerusalem to ensure its integrity and interpret its significance.

Join me in my struggle (15:30). Paul probably reflects the Jewish use of the word "struggle" to depict the spiritual striving of the righteous in this world.[172]

Greetings and Epistolary Conclusion (16:1–23)

In this section Paul continues with the items typical of the closing parts of his letters: a commendation of a fellow Christian (16:1–2), greetings (16:3–15, 16b, 21–23), a promise of spiritual victory (16:20a), and a benediction (16:20b). But somewhat unexpected is his sudden condemnation of false teachers (16:17–19), as well as the number of people he greets (since Paul has never visited Rome before).

I commend to you our sister Phoebe (16:1). Letters of commendation were common in the ancient world.[173] Travelers could not count on public facilities for food or lodging, so they had to rely on networks of personal relationships. Phoebe is a fellow Christian whom Paul has gotten to know during his ministry in Corinth. She is traveling to Rome, perhaps on business, so Paul wants to introduce her and to give her his stamp of approval.

A servant of the church in Cenchrea (16:1). The city of Corinth, where Paul spent considerable time on both his second and third missionary journeys, was situated about one and a half miles inland from its closest seaport (Lechaeum). The Gulf of Corinth lies to the northwest and the Saronic Gulf to the northeast. Cenchrea is located roughly five miles due east of Corinth on the Saronic Gulf and served as the main seaport for Corinth. In Paul's day the cities were linked by a series of forts.[174] We can presume that Phoebe, frequently in Corinth on business, had become converted through the ministry of the church there and was well known to Paul.

But what does Paul intend in calling her a "servant"? The Greek word (*diakonos*) is often used in the New Testament to denote any Christian, called to serve the Lord and minister to his people. Note especially 1 Peter 4:10, where the cognate verb is used: "Each one should use whatever gift he has received to serve [*diakoneō*] others, faithfully administering God's grace in its various forms."[175] Thus, Paul may here mean no more than that Phoebe is a fellow Christian.

But the phrase "*diakonos* of the church" suggests a more official role. This word is also used to refer to a specific position of ministry in the early church: the "deacon" (in Paul, see Phil. 1:1; 1 Tim. 3:8, 12). Probably Paul identifies Phoebe as one of the deacons in the Cenchrean church. In later centuries, the office of "deaconess" was officially recognized.[176] But the masculine *diakonos* was also applied to female office-holders in the early church.[177] The New Testament reveals little about the role of deacons in the church, but many scholars suspect that they are particularly involved in visiting the sick, providing for the needy, and caring for the financial and material needs of the church in general. Such a function would suit well Phoebe's apparent secular position (see below).

She has been a great help to many people, including me (16:2). The NIV paraphrases here, since the Greek simply calls Phoebe a *prostatis* to many. This word is found only here in biblical Greek, but it comes from a verb that can mean either to care for, give aid to, or to direct, preside over. The NIV assumes the former meaning; some advocates of expanded roles for women in ministry argue for the latter, claiming that Phoebe is a "leader" of the church. But it is unlikely that Paul would acknowledge Phoebe as a leader or director of himself. A better alternative is to adopt the meaning this word sometimes has in the Greco-Roman world: "patron." The patron played an important role in society, using his or her influence and financial resources to sponsor people for various positions and promotions. We can envisage Phoebe as a prominent and wealthy woman, who used her resources and influence to assist Christians like Paul.[178]

Greet (16:3–15). Before noting some points of significance with regard to individual names, it is worth commenting on the cumulative force of the names. These names may not make interesting reading for the modern Christian or obvious material for the preacher. But for the historian of ancient Christianity, they are a gold mine. Names in the ancient world were rarely simply nice-sounding tags; they almost always carried meaning. Sometimes that meaning provides to the student of the ancient church a window into that church's socioeconomic composition. Two particular points emerge from careful study of the names in Romans 16.[179] (1) A majority of the names are Gentile, confirming the evidence from elsewhere of the mainly Gentile makeup of the Roman church. (2) Most of the names are ones usually

◄

ROMAN APARTMENT BUILDING

The remains of a multi-storied *insula* in Ostia, the port city of Rome.

given to slaves or "freemen" (persons who had been set free from slavery).

Priscilla and Aquila (16:3). The Greek actually has "Prisca [*Priska*] and Aquila"; the NIV has the practice of "normalizing" variants of the same name. "Priscilla," the form that Luke prefers, is the diminutive form of the name "Prisca." Priscilla and Aquila were from the Roman province of Pontus, in northern Asia Minor. They lived for a time in Rome but were forced to leave when Emperor Claudius banned all Jews from the city in A.D. 49 (cf. Acts 18:1–2). They ministered with Paul during his eighteen-month stay in Corinth and then left to establish a church in Ephesus (Acts 18:18), where Paul eventually rejoined them (cf. 1 Cor. 16:19). We do not know when they returned to Rome, but we do know that the ban of Jews was allowed to lapse after the death of Claudius in A.D. 54. Paul notes that they "risked their lives" for him (Rom. 16:4); perhaps at the time of the riot in Ephesus (Acts 19).

The church that meets at their house (16:5). The early Christians could not afford their own meeting places, so they met in private homes. Here Paul mentions the Christians who gathered for worship in the home of Priscilla and Aquila; and he mentions two others later (16:11, 14). The Roman "church," then, in effect, is made up of several separate "house churches"—accounting perhaps for the disunity that Paul must rebuke in chapters 14–15. The size of the ancient Roman home would also have meant that the largest congregation would have numbered no more than twenty to thirty Christians.

Andronicus and Junias . . . outstanding among the apostles (16:7). Andronicus is a male name; and so is Junias. But the latter is only one of the possible readings of the Greek name. The word is *Iounia* (found here in the accusative singular form, *Iounian*). *Iounia* can either be a female name, "Junia" (cf. KJV; NRSV; REB), or a contracted form of the male name Junianus, "Junias" (cf. NIV; RSV; NASB; TEV; NJB). A contracted form of a name would be in order, since Paul uses several others in this context. But we do not have evidence from ancient sources that Junianus was ever contracted to Junias. The feminine Latin name "Junia," by contrast, was common. Probably, then, Andronicus and Junia are another husband-and-wife ministry team (along with Priscilla and Aquila).

In calling them "apostles," Paul is almost certainly not putting them on a

REFLECTIONS

PAUL'S REFERENCES TO PHOEBE (16:1–2) AND JUNIA[S] in 16:7 have become a storm center in the recent debates about the roles of women in ministry. Both are clearly prominent women in the early church, but just what roles they actually played is debated. This debate reveals strikingly the tendency for this issue to polarize opinion and run roughshod over careful, balanced interpretation. On the one hand are many egalitarians, who insist Phoebe was "president" or "head pastor" of the church in Cenchrea and that Junia was a female "apostle," equal in rank and authority to Peter, John, and Paul. On the other are certain complementarians, who insist that Phoebe was no more than an ordinary Christian "servant" with a ministry of helps and that Junia[s] was a man (or, if a woman, was not esteemed "*among* the apostles" but esteemed "*by* the apostles").

Neither extreme does justice to the text, as we have briefly suggested in the notes above. But the extremes of opinion remind us that, especially when issues are explosive and emotions run high, we must make doubly sure that we approach the text to see what it says, not to insist on making it say what we want.

par with Peter, John, James, himself, and so on. "Apostle" (*apostolos*) also refers in the New Testament to a commissioned missionary and this usage was carried over into the early church.[180]

Those who belong to the household of Aristobulus (16:10). The ancient Greco-Roman "household" (the word does not occur in the Greek but is implied) consisted both of the immediate and perhaps extended family living in the home as well as the household servants. While we cannot be certain, the Aristobulus mentioned here may have been the brother of King Herod Agrippa I, ruler of Palestine under Roman auspices from A.D. 41–44 (his death is described in Acts 12:19b–23). Aristobulus went with Agrippa as a hostage to Rome and died in A.D. 48 or 49.[181] But servants in his household may still have been identified with their famous deceased master.

Narcissus (16:11). Narcissus was a well-known freedman who served Emperor Claudius and who committed suicide just before Paul wrote Romans.[182]

Rufus (16:13). Rufus may be the son of Simon of Cyrene, who carried the cross-bar of Christ's cross part of the way to Golgotha (cf. Mark 15:21: "A certain man from Cyrene, Simon, the father of Alexander and Rufus, was passing by on his way in from the country, and they forced him to carry the cross"). Mark was probably written from Rome, and he may therefore mention Alexander and Rufus because he has come to know them during his stay there. Yet Rufus was a common name, so we cannot be certain of the identification.

Greet one another with a holy kiss (16:16). The kiss was a common form of greeting in the ancient world generally and in Judaism in particular.[183] It is referred to often in the New Testament, and by the second century, the Christian liturgy contained a "kiss of peace" as a standard feature.[184] We don't know that this kiss was a part of worship services in Paul's day. But if so, Paul probably envisages his letter being read aloud in a worship service, concluded with such a kiss.

Watch out for those who cause divisions (16:17). The identity of the false teachers about whom Paul warns the Romans cannot be determined. He speaks of them generally, we have no evidence elsewhere in Romans of specific false teachers, and we have insufficient evidence about first-century Roman Christianity.

Such people are not serving our Lord Christ, but their own appetites (16:18). "Appetites" translates the Greek word *koilia*, "belly." The NIV, along with most commentators, take the word by metonymy to refer to the sensual urges generally. But the word may refer to the preoccupation with food laws typical of many Jews in the first century (the same issue arises in Philippians 3:19, where Paul talks of false teachers whose "god is their stomach").

The God of peace will soon crush Satan under your feet (16:20). This promise of

◀ *left*

CENCHREA AND CORINTH

eschatological victory may echo the famous "proto-evangelium" of Genesis 3:15: "And I will put enmity between you and the woman, and between your offspring and hers; he will crush your [the Serpent] head, and you will strike his heel." Some Jewish texts also seem to echo this promise.[185]

Lucius (16:21). This Lucius has sometimes been identified with Lucius of Cyrene, a prophet/teacher in the church at Syrian Antioch (Acts 13:1), or with Luke the Evangelist ("Luke" can be a variant of "Lucius"). But the name was common, and neither identification is likely.

Jason (16:21). This Jason is likely the same person who gave Paul shelter during the tumult in Thessalonica (Acts 17:5–9).

Sosipater (16:21). Sosipater is a variant of "Sopater," the name of a man from Berea who accompanied Paul when he left Greece at the end of his third missionary journey (Acts 20:4).

I, Tertius, who wrote down this letter (16:22). Tertius is otherwise unknown to us, but he here identifies himself as the "amanuensis," the trained scribe who physically copied down Paul's dictation to the Roman Christians. Amanuenses, trained to write small and neatly, were often employed in a day when paper was both scarce and expensive.

Gaius (16:23). "Gaius" is a common name, and at least three different New Testament Christians bore it: Gaius of Derbe (Acts 20:4; cf. 19:29); a Gaius from Corinth (1 Cor. 1:14); and a Gaius who was a church leader in Asia Minor (3 John 1). Since Paul writes from Corinth, the Gaius who sends greetings is probably the Corinthian Gaius.

Erastus (16:23). This Erastus may be the same Erastus whom Paul sent from Ephesus to Macedonia on an errand during the third missionary journey (Acts 19:21–22; cf. 2 Tim. 4:20). But the name of Erastus has also been discovered on an inscription from Corinth, identifying him as an *aedile* of the city. The term Paul uses to describe Erastus, *oikonomos* ("director of public works"), may be roughly equivalent.[186]

The Doxology (16:25–27)

Because this doxology appears in several different places in manuscripts of Romans, many scholars are convinced that it was added to Romans after Paul wrote the letter. But there is good reason to think that Paul himself wrote it as a fitting conclusion to his great theological treatise.

Prophetic writings (16:26). Since Paul claims the mystery is "made known" in these writings, some have identified them with the New Testament. But Paul has also shown that the Old Testament, properly interpreted, testifies to the mystery. Moreover, the phrase seems to echo the opening words of Romans: "the gospel he promised beforehand through his prophets in the Holy Scriptures."

ERASTUS
INSCRIPTION
▼

Cranfield, C. E. B. *A Critical and Exegetical Commentary on the Epistle to the Romans.* 2 vols. ICC. Edinburgh: T. & T. Clark, 1975, 1979.

Academic-level commentary especially strong on grammar, history of interpretation, and theology.

Dunn, James D. G. *Romans 1–8, Romans 9–16.* WBC. Waco, Tex.: Word, 1988.

Academic-level commentary representing the "new perspective" on Paul.

Edwards, James. *Romans.* NIBC. Peabody, Mass.: Hendrickson, 1992.

A readable exposition that does a good job of presenting current scholarly options.

Fitzmyer, Joseph. *Romans: A New Translation with Introduction and Commentary.* AB. Garden City: Doubleday, 1993.

Especially strong on introductory issues and history of interpretation.

Käsemann, Ernst. *Commentary on Romans.* Eerdmans, 1980.

A dense but important commentary emphasizing Paul's apocalyptic theology.

Moo, Douglas J. *The Epistle to the Romans.* NICNT. Grand Rapids: Eerdmans, 1996.

English-text based exposition with focus on theological meaning and application.

_____. *Romans.* NIVAC. Grand Rapids: Zondervan, 2000.

English-text based exposition with focus on application of the text to today's world.

CHAPTER NOTES

Main Text Notes

1. The *Catalogus Liberianus* (A.D. 354) claims Peter as the founder and first bishop of the Roman church, but earlier tradition associates both Peter and Paul with the founding of the church (Irenaeus, *Haer.* 3.1.2; 3.3.1).
2. See the text in *PL*, col. 46.
3. Philo (*Embassy to Gaius* 23.155) claims that the nucleus of the Roman Jewish community was made up of enslaved prisoners of war. But H. J. Leon is not disposed to accept this claim (*The Jews of Ancient Rome* [Philadelphia: Jewish Publication Society, 1960; updated edition by C. Osiek, Peabody, Mass.: Hendrickson, 1996], 4–5).
4. Leon, *Jews,* 135–70; cf. Romano Penna, "Les Juifs à Rome au temps de l'apôtre Paul," *NTS* 28 (1982): 327–28.
5. W. Wuellner, "Paul's Rhetoric of Argumentation," in *The Romans Debate,* ed. K. Donfried (2d ed.: Peabody, Mass.: Hendrickson, 1991), 128–46.
6. R. Jewett, "Romans as an Ambassadorial Letter," *Int* 36 (1982): 5–20.
7. D. Aune, "Romans as a *Logos Protreptikos* in the Context of Ancient Religions and Philosophical Propaganda," in *Paulus und das antique Judentum* (WUNT 58; eds. M. Hengel and U. Heckel; Tubingen: Mohr, 1991), 91–121.
8. M. L. Stirewalt Jr., "The Form and Function of the Greek Letter-Essay," in *The Romans Debate,* 147–71.
9. James D. G. Dunn, *Romans 1–8* (WBC; Waco, Tex.: Word, 1988), lix.
10. See esp. R. Bultmann, *Der Stil der paulinischen Predigt und die kynisch-stoische Diatribe* (FRLANT 13; Gottingen: Vandenhoeck & Ruprecht, 1910).
11. S. K. Stowers, *The Diatribe and Paul's Letter to the Romans* (SBLDS 57; Chico, Calif.: Scholars, 1981).
12. The language comes from the Priene inscription; see W. Dittenberger, *Orientis Graeci Inscriptiones,* II, no. 458.
13. See Peter T. O'Brien, *Introductory Thanksgivings in the Letters of Paul* (NovTSup 49; Leiden: Brill, 1977).
14. See Douglas J. Moo, *The Epistle to the Romans* (NICNT; Grand Rapids: Eerdmans, 1996), 70–76, 79–90.
15. See, e.g., C. E. B. Cranfield, *A Critical and Exegetical Commentary on the Epistle to the Romans* (2 vols.; ICC; Edinburgh: T. & T. Clark, 1975, 1979), 1.155–57.

16. See, e.g., Epictetus, *Diss.* 2.19–20; 3:7, 17. On the diatribe style, see esp. Stowers, *Diatribe.*
17. See *Pss. Sol.* 8:11–13; *T. Levi* 14:5.
18. See 2 Macc. 13:6; Acts 19:37; Philo, *Decalogue* 133.
19. See esp. D. B. Garlington, "ΙΕΡΟΣΥΛΕΙΝ and the Idolatry of Israel (Romans 2.22)," *NTS* 36 (1990): 142–51.
20. Josephus, *Ant.* 20.2.1–4 §§17–48.
21. George Foot Moore, *Judaism in the First Centuries of the Christian Era* (repr.; 2 vols.; New York: Schocken, 1971), 1.323–35.
22. See, e.g., L. E. Keck, "The Function of Rom. 3, 10–18: Observations and Suggestions," in *God's Christ and His People: Studies in Honor of Nils Alstrup Dahl*, eds. J. Jervell and W. A. Meeks (Oslo: Universitetsforlaget, 1977), 141–57.
23. For this view, see esp. J. D. G. Dunn, *Romans 1–8* (WBC; Waco, Tex.: Word, 1988), 153–55; also his essay "Echoes of Intra-Jewish Polemic in Paul's Letter to the Galatians," *JBL* 112 (1993): 465–67.
24. See also *4 Macc.* 18:10; Matt. 11:13; Luke 16:16; John 1:45; Acts 13:15; 24:14; 28:23.
25. See David Hill, *Greek Words with Hebrew Meanings* (SNTSMS 5; Cambridge: Cambridge Univ. Press, 1967), 58–80.
26. See Leon Morris, *The Apostolic Preaching of the Cross* (Grand Rapids: Eerdmans, 1955), 9–26.
27. See ibid., 136–56.
28. D. Flusser and S. Safira, "Who Sanctified the Beloved in the Womb," *Immanuel* 11 (1980): 46–55.
29. G. Fitzer, "σφραγίς," *TDNT*, 7.949.
30. See also *Jub.* 32:19; Sir. 44:21; *2 Apoc. Bar.* 14:13; 51:3.
31. See, e.g., Philo, *Spec. Laws* 2.242; *Dreams* 2.123; Josephus, *Ant.* 3.8.9 §218; 8.4.6 §129; 18.8.2 §263; 18.8.8 §304; 19.6.3 §302.
32. For this interpretation, see esp. H. Moxnes, *Theology in Conflict: Studies in Paul's Understanding of God in Romans* (NovTSup 53; Leiden: Brill, 1980), 241–50.
33. See, e.g., E. Brandenburger, *Adam und Christus: Exegetisch-religionsgeschichtliche Untersuchungen zu Röm. 5:12–21 (1 Kor 15)* (WMANT 7; Neukirchen/Vluyn: Neukirchener, 1962), esp. 157, 175–78.
34. P. Ryl. 2.243, as cited in MM, 204.
35. See esp. J. Jeremias, "πολλοί," *TDNT*, 6:536–41.
36. See esp. Stowers, *Diatribe.*
37. A. J. M. Wedderburn, *Baptism and Resurrection: Studies in Pauline Theology Against Its Graeco-Roman Background* (WUNT 44; Tübingen: Mohr, 1987). Note also G. Wagner, *Pauline Baptism and the Pagan Mysteries* (London: Oliver & Boyd, 1967).
38. J. R. W. Stott, *Men Made New: An Exposition of Romans 5–8* (London: InterVarsity, 1966), 45.
39. Cf. Str-B, 3:232.
40. See esp. H. N. Ridderbos, *Paul: An Outline of His Theology* (Grand Rapids: Eerdmans, 1974), 57–62.
41. Keith Bradley, *Slavery and Society at Rome* (Key Themes in Ancient History; Cambridge: Cambridge Univ. Press, 1994), 29–30. See also A. Rupprecht, "Slave, Slavery," in *DPL*, 880.
42. See, e.g., W. A. Meeks, *The First Urban Christians: The Social World of the Apostle Paul* (New Haven: Yale Univ. Press, 1983), 20–23.
43. See also *b. Šabb.* 151b.
44. Cf. Lev. 22:12; Deut. 24:2; Hos. 3:3.
45. *b. Šabb.* 145b–146a.
46. *Pesiq. Rab.* 21 (107a).
47. See *Life of Adam and Eve* 19; Philo, *Spec. Laws* 4.84–94.
48. Philo, *Decalogue* 142–43, 173; *4 Macc.* 2:6.
49. See, e.g., R. H. Gundry, "The Moral Frustration of Paul Before His Conversion: Sexual Lust in Romans 7:7–25," in *Pauline Studies: Essays Presented to Professor F. F. Bruce on His 70th Birthday*, eds. D. A. Hagner and M. J. Harris (Grand Rapids: Eerdmans, 1980), 80–94.
50. S. Safrai, "Home and Family," in *The Jewish People in the First Century*, eds. S. Safrai and M. Stern (CRINT 1; Philadelphia: Fortress, 1976), 2:771.
51. See also Sir. 17:11; *m. ʾAbot* 6:7; *Pss. Sol.* 14:2; Bar. 3:9. See the discussion in E. E. Urbach, *The Sages: Their Concepts and Beliefs* (Jerusalem: Magnes, 1979), 1:424–26.
52. Rom. 16:18; 1 Cor. 3:18; 2 Thess. 2:3.
53. For elaboration, see Moo, *The Epistle to the Romans*, 442–51.
54. Ovid, *Metamorphoses* 7.21; see also Epictetus, *Diss.* 2.26.4.
55. See also Jer. 15:8; 20:8; 51:56; Joel 1:15; Amos 5:9; Mic. 2:4; Zeph. 1:15.
56. E.g., Deut. 4:1; 5:1; Ps. 119 (29x); Luke 1:6; Rom. 2:26; Heb. 9:1, 10.
57. See also Ex. 4:22; Jer. 3:19; 31:9; *4 Ezra* 6:58.
58. See also Hos. 2:1 [LXX]; Wisd. Sol. 5:5; *T. Mos.* 10:3; *2 Apoc. Bar.* 13:9.
59. See especially J. M. Scott, *Adoption as Sons of God: An Exegetical Investigation into the Background of ΥΙΟΘΕΣΙΑ in the Pauline Corpus* (WUNT 2.48; Tübingen: Mohr, 1992), 3–57.
60. On this institution, see esp. F. Lyall, *Slaves, Citizens, Sons: Legal Metaphors in the Epistles* (Grand Rapids: Zondervan, 1984), 67–99.
61. See MM, 610.
62. See, e.g., Lyall, *Slaves, Citizens, Sons*, 102–3.

63. See also Gen. 15:7; 17:8; Deut. 30:5; Isa. 60:21; Ezek. 36:8–12 (the verbs in these verses mean "to inherit").
64. See also *1 En.* 40:9; *4 Macc.* 18:3.
65. See also *1 En.* 45:5; 72:1; *2 Apoc. Bar.* 29; 32:6; 44:12; 57:2; *Jub.* 1:29; 4:26.
66. E.g., Num. 5:9; Deut. 18:4; 2 Chron. 31:5–6.
67. 2 Thess. 2:13; James 1:18; Rev. 14:4; 1 Cor. 15:20, 23; cf. Rom. 11:16.
68. See also Judg. 2:18; Ps. 6:6; 12:5; 31:10; 38:9; 79:11; 102:20.
69. See Ex. 18:22; Num. 11:17; Ps. 89:21; Luke 10:40.
70. See esp. E. A. Obeng, "The Origins of the Spirit Intercession Motif in Romans 8:26," *NTS* 32 (1986): 621–32.
71. See also Ps. 7:9; 17:3; cf. Acts 1:24; 15:8; Rev. 2:23.
72. Isa. 32:15, 20; 52:7; Jer. 8:15; cf. Sir. 39:25, 27.
73. Clearly in Acts 2:23; Rom. 11:2; 1 Peter 1:20; debated is 1 Peter 1:2; in Acts 26:5, it refers to mental knowledge.
74. Str-B, 3.259–60.
75. For "height" in this sense, see, e.g., Plutarch, *Moralia* 149a; Vettius Valens 241.26. "Depth" (*bathos*) less frequently has such a connotation; but BAGD cite a magical papyrus, *PGM* 4.575.
76. On the Greek view of "conscience," see C. Maurer, "συνείδησις," *TDNT*, 9:902–4; H.-J. Eckstein, *Der Begriff Syneidesis bei Paulus: Ein neutestamentlich-exegetische Untersuchung zum Gewissensbegriff* (Tübingen: Mohr-Siebeck, 1983).
77. E.g., Lev. 27:28; Judg. 16:19; cf. Luke 21:5; Acts 23:14.
78. Josh. 6:17, 18; 7:1, 11–13; 22:20; 1 Chron. 2:7.
79. Str-B, 3.260.
80. See also Isa. 63:16; 64:8; Jer. 31:9; Hos. 11:1; Mal. 1:6; 2:10.
81. See also Ex. 24:16; 40:34–35; Lev. 9:6; 1 Kings 8:11; Ezek. 1:28.
82. *m. ʾAbot* 1:2.
83. N. T. Wright, *The Climax of the Covenant* (Minneapolis: Fortress, 1992), 238.
84. See also Gen. 17:1–8, 15–16, 19–21; 18:18–19; 22:17–18.
85. See Lev. 15:16–17, 32; 18:20; 22:4; Num. 5:20.
86. Philo, *Alleg. Interp.* 3.88.
87. See esp. John Piper, *The Justification of God: An Exegetical and Theological Study of Romans 9:1–23* (Grand Rapids: Baker, 1983).
88. 1 Cor. 9:24, 26; cf. Gal. 2:2; 5:7; Phil. 2:16; 2 Tim. 2:5.
89. See also Ex. 8:15; 9:12, 35; 10:1, 20, 27; 11:10; 14:4, 8, 17; other verbs for the same idea occur in 7:13, 14; 8:15, 32; 9:7, 34.
90. E.g., Job 10:9; 38:14; Isa. 29:16; 45:9–10; Jer. 18:1–6.
91. See also *4 Ezra* 7:72–74; *Pss. Sol.* 13; 1QH 15:14–20.
92. See also Jer. 23:14; 49:18; 50:40; Lam. 4:6; Ezek. 16:46–56; Amos 4:11; Zeph. 2:9; Matt. 10:15; 11:23, 24; Luke 10:12; 17:29; 2 Peter 2:6; Jude 7; Rev. 11:8.
93. See also Deut. 19:6; Josh. 2:5; 1 Sam. 30:8; 2 Kings 25:5; Ps. 7:5; Lam. 1:3.
94. The classic case for the "testimony book" hypothesis was made by J. Rendell Harris, *Testimonies* (2 vols.; Cambridge: Cambridge Univ. Press, 1916, 1920).
95. Cf. John 2:17; Acts 22:3; 2 Cor. 11:2; Phil. 3:6.
96. See also Neh. 9:29; CD 3:14–16; *b. Sanh.* 59b; note also Paul's quotation of Lev. 18:5 in Gal. 3:12.
97. E.g., Joseph Fitzmyer, *Romans* (AB; Garden City, N.Y.: Doubleday, 1993), 591.
98. E.g., M. J. Suggs, "'The Word Is Near You': Romans 10:6–10 Within the Purpose of the Letter," in *Christian History and Interpretation: Studies Presented to John Knox* (ed. W. R. Farmer, et al.; Cambridge: Cambridge Univ. Press, 1967), 289–312.
99. See Ps. 139:8; Prov. 30:4; Isa. 14:13; Amos 9:2.
100. The translation is from M. McNamara, *The New Testament and the Palestinian Targum to the Pentateuch* (AnBib 27; Rome: Pontifical Biblical Institute, 1966), 370–78.
101. E.g., Deut. 33:29; Isa. 45:22; 2 Macc. 3:22; Judith 16:2.
102. Acts 9:14, 21; 22:16; 1 Cor. 1:2; 2 Tim. 2:22; 1 Peter 1:17.
103. See esp. J. Fitzmyer, "The Semitic Background of the New Testament *kyrios* Title," in *A Wandering Aramean: Collected Aramaic Essays* (SBLDS 25; Missoula, Mont.: Scholars, 1979), 115–42.
104. *Mek. Exod.* 14:22 (37b).
105. See also Mark 6:52; 8:17; John 12:40; 2 Cor. 3:14; the noun form, *pōrōsis*, occurs in Mark 3:5; Rom. 11:25; Eph. 4:18.
106. See, e.g., Aristotle, *History of Animals* 3.19; Marcus Aurelius, *Meditations* 9.36.
107. 1 Kings 14:22; Ps. 78:58; 1 Cor. 10:22; Ps. 37:1, 7, 8; Sir. 30:3.
108. See, e.g., *T. Sim.* 6:2–7; *2 Apoc. Bar.* 78:6–7; *4 Ezra* 4:38–43; cf. also Acts 3:19–20.
109. Cf. also *1 En.* 93:5, 8; *Jub.* 21:24.
110. See also *1 En.* 10:16; 93:2, 5, 8, 10; *Jub.* 16:26; 21:4; *Pss. Sol.* 14:3–4; 1QS 8:5; 11:8; 1QH 6:15–16; 8:5–7, 9–10.

111. W. M. Ramsay, "The Olive-Tree and the Wild Olive," in *Paul and Other Studies in Early Christian History* (London: Hodder and Stoughton, 1908), 219–50. Ramsay cites Columella, *De re rustica* 5.9.16, and Palladius, *De insitione* 53–54.

112. See also *4 Ezra* 10:38; 12:36–38; 14:5; *1 Enoch* 9:6; 103:2; *2 Apoc. Bar.* 48:3; 81:4.

113. See, e.g., 1QS 3:23; 4:18; 9:18; 11:3, 5, 19; 1QH 1:21; 2:13; 4:27–28; 7:27; 11:10; 12:13; 1QpHab 7:5, 8, 14.

114. An oft-quoted parallel to Rom. 11:26 is *m. Sanh.* 10:1: "All Israelites have a share in the world to come," since the text goes on to list several kinds of exceptions to this promise. But (1) this text uses the plural "all Israelites" rather than the singular "all Israel," and (2) there are no explicit exceptions in Romans 11.

115. See Ps. 19:9; 36:6; 119:75; Sir. 17:12.

116. *2 Apoc. Bar.* 14:8–9.

117. Marcus Aurelius, *Meditations* 4.23.

118. See, e.g., Philo, *Spec. Laws* 1.208.

119. See esp. C. J. Bjerkelund, *Parakalo: Form, Function und Sinn der parakalo-Sätze in den paulinischen Briefen* (Bibliotheca Theologica Norvegica 1; Oslo: Universitetsforlaget, 1967).

120. E.g., Ps. 50:14, 23; 51:16–17; 141:2; Sir. 35:1; Tobit 4:10–11; 12:12; 2 Macc. 12:43–44.

121. Epictetus, *Disc.* 1.16.20–21.

122. Philo, *Spec. Laws* 1.277.

123. Livy, 2.32; cf. Epictetus, *Disc.* 2.10.4–5.

124. Josephus, *Ant.* 15.11.3 §396; cf. also Philo, *Virtues* 95.

125. See 2 Cor. 11:3; Eph. 6:5; Col. 3:22.

126. Martin Dibelius, *James*, ed. by H. Greeven (Hermeneia; Philadelphia: Fortress, 1976), 3.

127. See also *T. Iss.* 7:5; *T. Zeb.* 7:4; *T. Jos.* 17:7.

128. See also Ps. 34:18; Isa. 14:32; 49:13; Zeph. 2:3; cf. James 4:6.

129. See 2 Sam. 22:9, 13; Ps. 18:8, 12; 140:10; Isa. 5:24.

130. See esp. John Piper, *Love Your Enemies: Jesus' Love Command in the Synoptic Gospels and in the Early Christian Paraenesis* (SNTSMS 38; Cambridge: Cambridge Univ. Press, 1979), 115–18.

131. See S. Morenz, "Feurige Kohlen auf dem Haupt," in *Religion und Geschichte der alter Agypten. Gesammelte Aufsätze* (Weimar: Hermann Böhlaus, 1975), 433–44.

132. Eph. 3:10; 6:12; Col. 1:16; 2:15; cf. 1 Peter 3:22; see also the singular in Eph. 1:21; Col. 2:10.

133. See esp. Karl Barth, *Church and State* (London: SCM, 1939), 23–36; Oscar Cullmann, *The State in the New Testament* (New York: Harper & Row, 1956), 55–70.

134. See also Titus 3:1; 1 Cor. 16:16; Eph. 5:21.

135. Titus 2:9; 1 Cor. 14:32, 34; Eph. 5:24; Col. 3:18; Titus 2:5.

136. See also 1 Sam. 12:8; Prov. 8:15–16; Isa. 41:2–4; 45:1–7; Jer. 2:7, 10; 27:5–6; Dan. 4:25, 32; 5:21.

137. See esp. Bruce W. Winter, "The Public Honouring of Christian Benefactors: Romans 13.3–4 and 1 Peter 2.14–15," *JSNT* 34 (1988): 87–103.

138. See, e.g., in the LXX, Est. 1:10; 2:2; 6:3; Jer. 25:9; cf. also Wis. So. 6:4.

139. Plutarch, *Princip. inerud.* 5.13.22–14.2.

140. Cf. Tacitus, *Histories* 3.68.

141. A. N. Sherwin-White, *Roman Society and Roman Law in the New Testament* (Oxford: Clarendon, 1963), 8–11.

142. Philo, *Spec. Laws* 2.92–95; 3.159–63.

143. See also Acts 13:2; 2 Cor. 9:12; Phil. 2:17, 25; Heb. 1:7, 14; 8:2, 6; 9:21; 10:11; Num. 4:37, 41; 1 Sam. 2:18; Luke 1:23; Rom. 15:16, 27.

144. Cf. 2 Sam. 13:18; 1 Kings 10:5; 2 Chron. 9:4.

145. See, e.g., Luke 18:20; James 2:11; Philo, *Decalogue* 24, 36, 51, 121–37, 167–71; Clement of Alexandria, *Stromateis* 6.16.

146. See Deut. 10:4; Philo, *Heir* 168; *Decalogue* 32; Josephus *Ant.* 3.6.5 §138.

147. Matt. 22:34–40; cf. Mark 12:28–34; Luke 10:25–28; John 13:34–35.

148. See the Targum and *Sifra* on Lev. 19:18.

149. See *T. Zeb.* 5:1; *T. Ash.* 5:7; *T. Naph.* 5:2.

150. See, e.g., Philo, *Migration* 222; *Dreams* 1.117.

151. E.g., Isa. 27; Jer. 30:8–9; Joel 2:32; 3:18; Obad. 15–17.

152. See also Acts 27:35; 1 Cor. 11:24; 1 Tim. 4:3; *Did.* 10:1–6.

153. See esp. Deut. 8:10; cf. Mark 8:6; 14:23; John 6:11, 23.

154. 1 Cor. 15:3–4; cf. also Rom. 8:34; 1 Thess. 4:14.

155. See Matt. 27:19; John 19:13; Acts 12:21; 18:12, 16, 17; 25:6, 10, 17.

156. See Rom. 9:32, 33; 1 Cor. 8:9; 1 Peter 2:8.

157. See 1 Macc. 1:47, 62; Josephus, *Ant.* 12.2.14 §112; 131.1.1 §4.

158. See Rom. 16:10; 1 Cor. 11:19; 2 Cor. 10:18; 13:7; 2 Tim. 2:15; James 1:12.

159. See Philo, *Creation* 128; *Joseph* 201; Josephus, *Ag. Ap.* 1.3 §18.

160. See also Lev. 4:12; 6:11; 7:19; Ezra 6:20; Mal. 1:11; in the New Testament see also Luke 11:41; John 13:10, 11; Acts 18:6; 20:26.

161. Matt. 27:34, 48; Mark 15:35–36; Luke 23:36; John 15:25; 19:28–29; cf. also John 2:17; Acts 1:20; Rom. 11:9.

162. Deut. 32:43 in 15:10; Isa. 11:10 in 15:12; Ps. 18:49 in 15:9b; 117:1 in 15:11.

163. See also Sir. 47:22; 4QFlor 1:11; 4QPat 3–4; Rev. 5:5; 22:16.

164. See S. N. Olson, "Pauline Expressions of Confidence in his Addressees," *CBQ* 47 (1985): 282–95.

165. See Isa. 61:6; 2 Esd. 20:36 (=Neh. 10:39); Sir. 7:30; *Let. Aris.* 95; *T. Levi* 2:10; 4:2; 8:3–10; 9:3; Philo, *Moses* 2.94, 149; *Spec. Laws* 1.249; 4.191; *Alleg. Interp.* 3.175; *Posterity* 184.

166. Cf. Strabo 7.7.4.

167. See esp. W. P. Bowers, "Jewish Communities in Spain at the Time of Paul the Apostle," *JTS* 26 (1975): 395–402.

168. See Roger Aus, "Paul's Travel Plans to Spain and the 'Full Number of the Gentiles,' Romans XI 25," *NovT* 21 (1979): 242–46.

169. Cf. Acts 15:3; 20:38; 21:5; 1 Cor. 16:6, 11; 2 Cor. 1:16; Titus 3:13; 3 John 6.

170. See also 1 Cor. 16:1–2; 2 Cor. 8–9.

171. See MM.

172. E.g., Philo, *Husbandry* 112, 119; in *4 Macc.*, the word describes the struggles of the martyrs.

173. See esp. C.-H. Kim, *Form and Structure of the Familiar Greek Letter of Recommendation* (SBLDS 4; Missoula, Mont.: Scholars, 1972).

174. See D. Madvig, "Corinth," *ISBE*, 1:772.

175. Cf. also 1 Cor. 3:5; 2 Cor. 3:6; 6:4; Eph. 3:7; 6:21; Col. 1:7, 23, 25; 4:7; 1 Tim. 4:6.

176. Cf. *Apost. Const.* 8.19, 20, 28; the feminine *diakonissa* is used.

177. See *New Docs.*, 2:193–94; 4:239–41.

178. See esp. E. Judge, "Cultural Conformity and Innovation in Paul: Some Clues from Contemporary Documents," *TynBul* 35 (1984): 20–21.

179. See esp. Peter Lampe, "The Roman Christians of Romans 16," in *The Romans Debate*, 218; building on his major work, *Die Stadtrömischen Christen in den ersten beiden Jahrhunderten: Untersuchungen zur Socialgeschicthe* (2d ed.; WUNT 2.18; Tubingen: Mohr, 1989).

180. See esp. E. E. Elis, "Paul and His Co-Workers," in *DPL*, 186; cf. Acts 14:4; 1 Cor. 9:5–6; 15:7; Gal. 2:9; *Did.* 11:4; *Herm. Vis.* 3.5.1; *Sim.* 9.15.4; 16.5; 25:2.

181. Josephus, *Ant.* 18.8.4 §§273–76; *J.W.* 2.11.6 §221.

182. Tacitus, *Ann.* 31.1; Cassius Dio, *Rom. Hist.* 60.34.

183. S. Benko, *Pagan Rome and the Early Christians* (Bloomington, Ind.: Indiana Univ. Press, 1984), 79–102.

184. 1 Cor. 16:20; 2 Cor. 13:12; 1 Thess. 5:26; 1 Peter 5:14; cf. Justin, *Apol.* 1.65.

185. *Jub.* 23:29; *T. Mos.* 10:1; *T. Levi* 18:37; *T. Sim.* 6:6.

186. See the discussion in A. D. Clarke, "Another Corinthian Erastus Inscription," *TynBul* 42 (1991):146–51.

Sidebar and Chart Notes

A-1. On the date, see esp. E. M. Smallwood, *The Jews Under Roman Rule* (SJLA 20; Leiden: Brill, 1976), 210–16.

A-2. See esp. W. Wiefel, "The Jewish Community in Ancient Rome and the Origins of Roman Christianity," in *The Romans Debate*, 92–101.

A-3. On rhetoric, see esp. Michael Bullmore, *Saint Paul's Theology of Rhetorical Style: An Examination of I Corinthians 2:1–5 in Light of First-Century Greco-Roman Rhetorical Culture* (New York: International Scholars Press, 1995); Duane Litfin, *Saint Paul's Theology of Proclamation: 1 Corinthians 1–4 and Greco-Roman Rhetoric* (Cambridge: Cambridge Univ. Press, 1994).

A-4. For other examples, see Demosthenes, *Kata Philippou* 3.9.17; Ps.-Xenophon, *Re Publica Athen.* 1.11 and 2.11; Epictetus, *Diss.* 1.10.7; 1.29.9–10; 3.26.29; 4.7.26–31.

A-5. See also Jer. 10:19–20; Lam. 1:9–22; 2:20–22; *Pss. of Sol.* 1:1–2, 6.

A-6. See, e.g., J. Barr, " 'Abba, Father' and the Familiarity of Jesus' Speech," *Theology* 91 (1988): 173–79.

A-7. Josephus, *Ant.* 13.5.9 §§171–73; see also *J.W.* 2.8.2–14 §§119–66.

A-8. See E. Käsemann, *Romans* (Grand Rapids: Eerdmans, 1980), 350.

A-9. Tacitus, *Ann.* 13.50ff.

A-10. See, e.g., Diogenes Laertius 8.38; Philostratus, *Vita Apollonii* 1.8. See J. Behm, "ἐσθίω," *TDNT*, 2:690.

A-11. See also Dan. 10:3; Tobit 1:10–12; Judith 12:2; Rest of Est. 14:17; *Jos. Asen.* 7:1; 8:5; Josephus, *Life* 3 §14; *m. ʾAbot* 3:3.

A-12. See Dan. 1:3–16; *T. Reu.* 1:10; *T. Jud.* 15:4; *m. ʿAbod. Zar.* 2:3.

A-13. Philo, *Contempl. Life* 37.

A-14. See esp. Col. 2:16, 21; 1 Tim. 4:3; 5:23.

A-15. Eusebius, *Eccl. Hist.* 2.23.5.

GALATIANS

by Ralph P. Martin and Julie L. Wu

Introduction

The letter to the Galatians is one of the key documents of the New Testament and the Christian faith. It is written in polemical style and tone, yet with a clear rhetorical structure[1] and deep pastoral concern for the readers, to enforce the twin themes of *faith* and *freedom*. Pivotal verses are, therefore, 2:16: "we, too, have put our faith in Christ Jesus that we may be justified by faith in Christ and not by observing the law," and 5:1: "It is for freedom that Christ has set us free. Stand firm, then, and do not let yourselves be burdened again by a yoke of slavery" (cf. 5:13).

In Christian history this letter has played a significant role as we recall its influence on such leaders as Luther and John Wesley. We may appreciate the richness of its teaching if we set the letter in its context. To do so, we need to ask three questions—two of which may be treated summarily, while the third requires more extended treatment.

PISIDIAN ANTIOCH

Remains of a Byzantine church built on the site of the first-century Jewish synagogue.

▶ **Galatians**
IMPORTANT FACTS:

- ■ **AUTHOR:** Paul.
- ■ **DATE:** 48–49 (if from Antioch).
- ■ **OCCASION:**
  - • To counter the threat to the Galatian churches.
  - • To defend Paul's apostleship.
  - • To set forth the basis of the law-free gospel of grace.
  - • To remind the readers of the obligations of Christian living.
- ■ **KEY THEMES:**
  1. Faith and freedom centered in Christ.
  2. The centrality of the cross for salvation and the life of believers.
  3. The role of the Holy Spirit.
  4. The Old Testament example of Abraham points forward to Christ and his people.

Who Were the Galatian Readers?

This is not easy to answer, since the region called Galatia covered a wide area of Asia Minor, embracing a large portion of the modern country of Turkey. The term Galatia, as used in Acts 16:6; 18:23, refers to the southern part of this territory and included such cities as Antioch in Pisidia and Iconium, where Paul preached during his first missionary journey and formed churches (see Acts 13–14).

But other ancient sources tell us that the Galatians inhabited the region to the north and east of this territory, and from the second century A.D. the area of Lycaonia Galatia became detached from Galatia proper. Thus, patristic writers read 1:2 in a sense familiar to them and considered "Galatia" as the northern parts of the Asian province. This identification was championed, in classic fashion, by J. B. Lightfoot in 1865[2] and has been supported by many modern scholars, of whom J. Murphy-O'Connor gives the latest set of arguments to link the readers' home with the area of the river San-garius (see map)[3], around Pessinus (modern Balahissar).

The work of William M. Ramsay,[4] however, also in the late nineteenth century, broke new ground in defense of the southern Galatia identification on the basis of a study of epigraphy, classical literature, and a personal survey he made of the terrain of Asia Minor and its archaeological significance. In particular he appealed to the data of historical geography and to Paul's missionary strategy of concentrating on main trade routes and centers like Pisidian Antioch.

The tide of scholarly opinion has begun to flow in the direction of this identification proposed by Ramsay, thanks to the support given by commentators like F. F. Bruce[5] and R. N. Longenecker.[6] The former comments, "The burden of proof lies on those who understand Galativa and Galavtai [Galatia/Galatians]. . . in other than the provincial sense" (i.e., as referring to the districts covered in Paul's journeys of Acts 13–14). The letter is taken, then, to refer to these places and congregations because "we have important historical, geographical, literary and epigraphic data which

THE SITE OF PISIDIAN ANTIOCH

provide material for [the letter's] better understanding." Recent epigraphists like S. Mitchell concur that only the South Galatia setting will hold up.[7]

When Was the Letter Written?

How we answer the question of Galatians' identity in part affects our fixing a date for the letter. If we assume the Southern Galatia destination, covering the area of Paul's first mission tour, it becomes possible to suggest a date as soon as possible after that journey and so before the apostolic conference of Acts 15 (c. A.D. 49). The alternate proposal, on the view that the events of Galatians 2 are the same as those recorded in Acts 15, is that the letter must be dated later in Paul's ministry. The usually accepted view, on the ground of common ideas and terminology, is to put Galatians in the period of 2 Corinthians and link it with the composition of Romans, that is, during Paul's Ephesian ministry, Macedonian visit, and sojourn in Corinth (Acts 19:1–20:2).

Later in the commentary we suggest that the first visit to Jerusalem (spoken of in Gal. 1:18) is that of Acts 9:26 and the consultation of Galatians 2:1–10 is to be equated with Paul's visit in Acts 11:30; this proposal makes the mention of his coming to Jerusalem in response to a "revelation" (Gal. 2:2) to agree with Agabus's prophecy in Acts 11:28. If so, then the churches referred to in 1:2 were founded on Paul's mission of Acts 13:14–14:21. His second visit to the area is that of Acts 14:21b–23, and the mention of a preaching of the gospel at "first" or on a former occasion (Gal. 4:13) looks back to the initial evangelism of Acts 13–14:21.

The letter is thus early in terms of Paul's letters, likely the first one he wrote that has survived, and is to be dated prior to the Jerusalem council of A.D. 49, perhaps sent from Antioch in Syria.

Who Were the Agitators in 5:12?

Obviously all was not well within the Galatian congregations. Paul writes to address problems caused by someone "who is throwing you into confusion" (5:10) by trying to pervert the gospel of Christ as brought to the Galatians by Paul; thus, they are branded as "agitators" (5:12; cf. 1:7). But who are these teachers and what are they seeking to do?

H.-D. Betz has correctly seen this as the main issue. "How [was it] possible for the anti-Pauline forces to get a foothold among the Galatian Christians?"[8] Again, no easy answers are possible, and only a mirror-reading of the text will give us the data we need to construct a profile of them. Yet even that characterization is how Paul views them. We have no independent evidence of what they stand for nor a statement of their arguments in their own words. Clearly Paul perceives

ASIA MINOR

The map shows the cities of southern Galatia where Paul planted the churches: Antioch, Iconium, Lystra, and Derbe.

▼

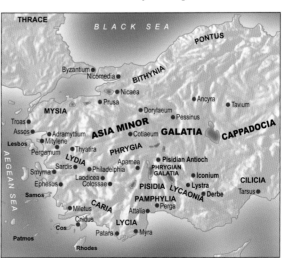

these teachers to be a serious threat to his gospel (1:6–10) since what they have introduced poses a rival message—one the Galatians are in danger of embracing to their eternal peril (5:2–6). Their presence in Galatia may be inferred, even if their number is small (5:9–10); nonetheless it is destructive and requires from Paul serious attention and sustained refutation.

Among the variety of possibilities as to their identity, one designation stands out as eminently reasonable. These agitators are Jewish-Christian emissaries (possibly from Jerusalem, 2:12) who insist that Paul's gospel for the Gentiles by faith alone and without the identity badge of circumcision is insufficient for salvation and living the Christian life. They seem to imply that after his initial evangelization, Paul left behind only "half Christians," who lacked full status within God's covenant people derived from Abraham, a proselyte whom God called to be the founder of a new, elect race with circumcision as their marker (Gen. 17:1–14).

Alongside this doctrinal controversy vitally related to becoming members of the elect people and staying in as his own people in the world—and indeed as part of it—they are conducting a smear campaign against Paul, alleging that he is no true apostle, and is dependent on (and so inferior to) the Twelve, especially the outstanding trio (called "pillar" apostles, 2:9), Peter, James the Lord's brother, and John. Moreover, Paul speaks (they insinuate) with a double voice over circumcision, not requiring it in Galatia but permitting it on occasion because he wants to make it easy for non-Jewish males to enter the church; they will thus owe allegiance to him as a leader sent out from Antioch, not to the mother church in Jerusalem (see 1:10; 5:11; 6:12–16).

A historical sidelight[9] should be noted at this point in the reconstruction of the Judaizers' pitch. Evidence from Jewish-Roman political tensions in Judea in the 40s suggests this was a time of nationalist unrest and a mounting desire to throw off Roman rule in the province. Thus, Jewish Christians may well have been

▶

LYSTRA

The tel of the ancient city (center right).

reacting to the pressure to show themselves as true Jews, faithful to Abraham and such covenant heroes as Moses, Phinehas, and Judith, all of whom were "jealous" for the ancestral faith. Paul seemed, in this light, to be renegade, verging on apostate. There is a rumbling of this accusation of his disloyalty over non-circumcision in Acts 21:20–21.

In any case, Paul's response to these insinuations is to champion the cause of *faith* as the sole gateway of becoming a Christian and *freedom* as the hallmark of staying in the covenant community. Both slogans, however, need to be set in the context of some control, articulated in 5:6, "faith expressing itself through love," which is not a ticket to license (5:13), since the Holy Spirit who leads believers to faith (4:6–7) also works to yield a moral harvest of good social and personal behavior (5:16, 22–26).

With some indignation at the ready welcome given to the false teachers' appeal (1:6; 4:15–16; 5:7), Paul rebuts all charges of dependence on human authority (1:1, 11–12) and presses home the need of justification—that is, acceptance into God's favor and family as the covenant community of the new Israel (6:16). One receives this gift by trusting God's promise ratified in Christ, who came (4:4), died (3:13), and sent the Spirit to make salvation available to all who follow Abraham's faith (3:14). The cross of Jesus is the sign of that promise (1:4; 3:13), and any bid to add to its saving value destroys it (2:21; 5:2–6; 6:14).

Thus, "the law" with its external code and practice of circumcision only leads to a false hope. It yields either frustration (since no one can fully comply, 3:10) or self-confidence as a reliance on the "flesh," a badge of identity in which religious claims become a source of pride

(3:21). The "law" leads us to Christ; when it does so, its function is completed (3:23–25). What the law sought to achieve—love of God and one's neighbor—is made possible in the new age of Messiah's salvation by the Holy Spirit, who provides moral energy to empower human conduct (3:14; 5:16–26). In this way, "the law of Christ" (6:2) is fulfilled.

The sufficiency of Christ and his saving grace in addition to the dynamic of the Spirit—these are the leading themes of the letter, and they give it a timeless (and timely) relevance needed in every age.

Greeting and Address (1:1–5)

Paul, an apostle (1:1). At the outset Paul states his credentials and his case to address the Galatian problems. His commission is directly from both Jesus Christ and God the Father. "Apostle" means one sent by the risen Lord to be his representative and messenger (as the Galatians acknowledged when Paul first came to evangelize, 4:14).

Grace and peace (1:3). This is a greeting that unites the two cultural and linguistic worlds of early churches. "Grace" is a Greek word denoting charm, beauty, goodwill, benefit, and gratitude. Attractive speech and the beauty of the human form are typical examples. Such ideas are virtually absent from the New Testament (but cf. Luke 4:22; Col. 4:6). The Graces are the virgin daughters of Zeus, who hand out feminine charm; occasionally "charm" is linked with magical amulets.[10] Here, however, the term is christianized to describe God's favor and condescension to rescue sinners (Gal. 1:4). "Peace" reflects the outcome in God's plan to restore men and women to wholeness

(Heb. *shalom*) of living. Thus, both Greco-Roman culture and Old Testament-Judaic motifs merge in this common Pauline greeting.

Present evil age (1:4). The evil age from which believers are delivered is one where astrological powers hold sway in Hellenistic society. Life was uncertain and held in a tyrannical grip of cosmic forces, called the "elemental spirits" (cf. 4:3, 9).

Paul Defends His Gospel (1:6–10)

I am astonished that you are so quickly deserting the one who called you (1:6). Paul expresses here in moving terms the issues at stake as he views the situation in the Galatian churches. The central problem is the inroad of a teaching of which he strongly disapproves, branding it a "different gospel."

A different gospel—which is really no gospel at all (1:6–7). Paul uses two words to denote the gospel: One is the gospel he preached, the other what the Judaizers offered. In Hellenistic Greek *allos* and *heteros* are not always distinguished, but here they must be: "a different (*heteros*) gospel—which is really no gospel (*allos*) at all"—is how the NIV makes the point. The opponents' message is not an alternative to Paul's gospel, but a rival to it and a substitute for it.

Some people are throwing you into confusion (1:7). These troublemakers are more than mischievous, and they do more than preach the gospel in a way that irritates Paul (cf. Phil. 1:15–19). Rather, they are opponents who profess to be gospel preachers, but their message is so at variance with the apostolic preaching the Galatians have received and by which they were both saved and given the Holy Spirit (Gal. 3:1–5) that they are self-condemned (see 2 Cor. 11:4, 13–15) as *anathema* (see comments on 1:8).

But even if we . . . should preach a gospel other than the one we preached (1:8). If Paul were to forsake the apostolic message and resort to an insistence on circumcision as necessary for Gentile converts to enjoy a place in God's covenant, then he too would be under divine judgment (see 5:11). The sole sufficiency of the cross as God's power for new life is the issue at stake.[11] See 6:14 for Paul's settled determination, though the price he is willing to pay is a heavy one (6:17).

Let him be eternally condemned (1:8). The Greek *anathema* (NIV "eternally condemned" in 1:8, 9) is the usual translation in the LXX for the Hebrew *ḥerem*, "ban, outside the covenant," a sentence meted out to Achan (Josh. 7:1–26). Perhaps Paul implies a disciplinary action here, excommunicating the teachers from the church and consigning them to Satan's realm.

Divine Revelation (1:11–12)

The gospel I preached (1:11). The reason for Paul's claim to be a herald of the only gospel (i.e., the good news of God) stems, in part, from the following facts: He did not invent his gospel, he is not indebted to any human source for its substance, nor did he get it by instruction from others (namely, the apostles before him, 1:17).

I received it by revelation from Jesus Christ (1:12). The gospel came from God as an act of special revelation from or about Jesus Christ. "Revelation" (Gk. *apokalypsis*) stresses the divine initiative in God's unfolding plan, which is otherwise shrouded in mystery.

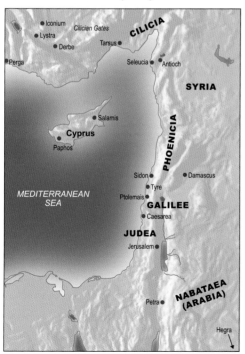

Paul calls this "revelation" God's choice "to reveal his Son in [or to] me" (1:16). Yet this phrase equally implies a commission to proclaim this good news, since the expression can also mean "through me." This defines the nature of the uniqueness Paul claims for his gospel. What came to him in his conversion/call experience on the Damascus road was God's plan *for the Gentiles*. At the same time, he received the shared traditions about Jesus from his Jewish-Christian predecessors (1 Cor. 15:3–8), while the new understanding of God's inclusion of the non-Jews was God's special gift in making him "the apostle to the Gentiles" (see Rom. 15:17).

Paul's Early Life (1:13–14)

My previous way of life in Judaism (1:13). "Judaism" here connotes the practice of living as a Jew, adopting Jewish customs as national badges and identity markers. This definition plays a significant role in Paul's later argument in refusing to grant salvific or covenantal status to such practices as circumcision, regarded by him when imposed on Gentile believers as "works of the law" (2:16; NIV, "observing the law").

To repel the charge that his credentials as a Jew are defective, Paul rehearses the attested claims of his preconversion life. Those claims (amplified in Phil. 3:4–6) are marked by his thorough knowledge of Jewish traditions, learned at the school of rabbi Gamaliel (Acts 22:3; 26:5), and his zeal in rooting out all who compromised the distinctiveness of the ancestral faith and practice.

Extremely zealous for the traditions of my fathers (1:14). "Zealous" (1:14) is another key term, summing up the

◀ *left*

ARABIA (NABATAEA)

earnestness, courage, and devotion of Jewish women like Judith and men like Phinehas, Elijah, and the Maccabean freedom fighters, in opposing the inroads of pagan, immoral influences that would have destroyed the distinctive faith of Judaism ("the traditions of my fathers").[12] In particular, Paul dedicated his zeal, like these Jewish exemplars, to opposing the church of the Hellenists (Hellenistic Jewish Christians, who had begun to catch the vision of Stephen as his followers, see Acts 11:19–21).

His Apostolic Call and Sequel (1:15–17)

The turning point for Paul came in what is usually called his conversion, narrated in graphic detail three times in Acts (9:1–19; 22:3–21; 26:1–23). The autobiography gives the reader the *theological* dimension, spelled out in terms of God's prenatal choice and summons to be his prophet to the nations. Yet it was more than a prophetic calling to which he responded on the road to Damascus. He entered into a personal union with the living Lord, of which he writes movingly in Galatians 2:20 (cf. also Phil. 3:12).[13]

REFLECTIONS

LUKE RECORDS PAUL'S DRAMATIC ENCOUNTER WITH the risen Lord three times in the book of Acts. As Paul tells his own story here in Galatians, he is concerned to pinpoint the *theological* significance of his new life in Christ. His reflection centers on God's sovereign act of choice in claiming him as his servant, and the redirecting of his zeal in the cause of Christ, his new inspiration and goal in living (see also Phil. 1:21; 3:7–14). What we call his conversion, happening in a moment, led to a change of direction; and this, we may say, is the test of genuine experience of Christ today.

Nor did I go up to Jerusalem . . . but I went immediately into Arabia (1:17). Once transformed and turned in a new (opposite) direction, Paul did not seek approval of human authorities, not even from the leaders in Jerusalem, but went off to preach in "Arabia" (i.e., Nabatea, ruled by King Aretas IV, alluded to in 2 Cor. 11:32–33). After that, Paul returned to Damascus.

Aretas reigned at Petra from 9 B.C. to A.D. 39/40. He was father-in-law of Herod Antipas, who divorced Aretas's daughter to marry Herodias (Mark 6:17–18), a move that enraged Aretas. Thus it is not surprising that in A.D. 36 Aretas defeated Herod's army and thereafter, with Emperor Tiberius's connivance, took control of Damascus until the early years of Caligula's reign, the next Roman emperor. Most modern historians date Aretas's control of Damascus from A.D. 37 until his death in 39/40; thus, Paul's experiences in that city fall within this two- to three-year time span.[14]

Paul's escape is prior to Aretas's death (see 2 Cor. 11:32–33), but his chronology is silent as to exactly when it occurred; hence the "after three years" of Galatians 1:18 is presumably to be reckoned from this flight, variously dated from between 31 to 37 (though the "three years" may be dated from his conversion[15]; see comments on 1:18).

Encounter with Jerusalem Leaders (1:18–20)

Then . . . I went up to Jerusalem (1:18). After three years following his conversion (around A.D. 34) Paul visited Jerusalem to make the acquaintance of Peter, with whom he lodged for only a two-week period. Notice that he had already begun his preaching and apostolic ministry, and his time with Peter was brief. No implication that he received his gospel from this apostolic source is possible.

Paul admits to no other contact with the apostles, with the exception of James, the brother of the Lord, to whom the risen Jesus appeared (1 Cor. 15:7).[16] This mention is important since it appears that the emissaries to Galatia may have claimed the authority of James when they came to Antioch to challenge Peter (Gal. 2:12). Paul wishes to head off any idea that he is indebted to or in disagreement with James, the head of the Jerusalem church (Acts 12:17; 15:13).

James (1:19). James, the Lord's brother, played a significant role in early Christianity, much more than the fleeting allusions to him in Acts suggest.[17] Paul only occasionally mentions him, but at crucial points in his letters (e.g., 1 Cor. 15:7; Gal. 1:18; 2:12).[18]

Mission in Syria, Cilicia (1:20–24)

Later I went to Syria and Cilicia (1:21). This is obviously a compressed account of Paul's early ministry, to be filled out by what is contained in Acts 9:19–25 as well as his own autobiographical story in 2 Corinthians 11:32–33.

Titus Was Not Circumcised When He Went to Jerusalem (2:1–5)

Paul is continuing his story of relations with the church at Jerusalem. He now recalls his second visit to Jerusalem "fourteen years later." His actions and interactions with the Jewish Christian leaders there provided additional powerful messages reinforcing the kind of gospel (i.e.,

justification by faith alone) he had been preaching in the Gentile communities.

Fourteen years later I went up again to Jerusalem (2:1). Two questions are involved here: (1) Which visit to Jerusalem in the book of Acts matches the description given here? (2) When Paul counts "fourteen years," what is his starting point? "Fourteen years later" than when?

The view taken here is that Paul is referring to the visit of Acts 11:29–30, and that he reckons from the time of his conversion-call, which probably occurred in A.D. 33–34. This would bring the date to A.D. 47–48 for the second Jerusalem visit. While these are fascinating and complicated matters, they are incidental to the chief point Paul is wishing to establish, namely, that his two short visits to the Jerusalem apostles could hardly have meant that he was going "hat in hand" to gain their approval for his ministry. The geographical note in 1:21–22 suggests that Paul had already gained considerable experience as an evangelist in Syria and Cilicia, especially at Antioch (a city that will play a significant role in his discussion at 2:11). This tallies with

TARSUS

A view of the Taurus mountains from the city of Tarsus (looking in the direction of the Cilician gates).

the descriptions in Acts (9:30; 11:25) of Paul's ministry in his own city of Tarsus in Cilicia.

With Barnabas (2:1). Barnabas was Paul's mentor when Paul first returned to Jerusalem after his conversion (Acts 9:27). But he was also Paul's colleague (11:24–26, 30; 12:25) at the time of the mission to Galatia (chs. 13–14).

I took Titus along (2:1). Who was Titus?[19] In the New Testament, his name is only mentioned by Paul.[20] Apparently, Titus was a Gentile who resided in Antioch and became a Christian through Paul's evangelistic activities there. When Paul and Barnabas brought the famine relief fund to Jerusalem (Acts 11:30), they took Titus along as a test case.

A revelation (2:2). The biblical word "revelation" (*apokalypsis*)[21] connotes an unveiling of supernatural origin. A revelation may come to a person directly (cf. Gal. 1:12), through a group of church leaders (cf. Acts 13:2), or through a prophet such as Agabus (cf. 11:28; 21:10–11). Paul clearly states that his second visit to Jerusalem was not due to the Jerusalem leaders' invitation or his own ambition to have a direct confrontation with them concerning his Gentile mission.

Set before them the gospel (2:2). "Set before" literally connotes the idea of "laying something before for one's own interest or purpose." After fourteen years of evangelistic activities among the Gentiles in the Syria and Cilicia regions, Paul realizes that the advancement of this mission invites the recognition or endorsement (not approval) of the Jewish Christian leaders in Jerusalem (see 2:9 for the outcome).

To those who seemed to be leaders (2:2). This phrase refers to James, Peter, and John (2:9), who were the influential persons in the Christian community in Jerusalem. The first was a member of the family of Jesus; the latter two were part of the original apostolic band.

That I was running or had run my race in vain (2:2). Paul often uses athletic imagery (see Phil. 3:12–14 for his picture of the Christian life as a race; cf. 2 Tim. 4:7). Here "running" describes his apostolic service (cf. Phil. 2:16), though he will return to the race image in Galatians 5:7 in his gentle rebuke of his readers as in danger of being deflected from their loyalty to Christ.[22]

Yet not even Titus . . . was compelled to be circumcised (2:3). Titus's presence clearly sharpened the issues that lay at the heart of the debate: Ought Gentile Christians to be received into the church's fellowship on equal terms with Jewish Christians without insisting on the rite of circumcision? Paul preaches a message that answers that question with a strong yes (2:2), but he is aware that

TARSUS

The recently excavated Roman road (*cardo*) in Tarsus.

▼

this practice is open to criticism from "false brothers" (2:4; see 2 Cor. 11:13–15 for a strong condemnation of these intruders) who dog Paul's footsteps and challenge his apostolic work. Although under pressure, Paul stood firm and refused to concede the need for Titus's circumcision.

Because some Greek manuscripts from the Western tradition (e.g., codex D) omit the word "not" before "Titus," we face an obvious ambiguity: Was Titus circumcised under pressure or not? If he was, the wording is at least clear that the surgical operation, practiced to admit Gentile converts to Judaism as a "rite of passage," was not carried out as a result of "giving in" (2:5) or capitulating to Paul's opponents. Rather, it was done out of deference to the tender feelings and convictions of Jewish Christian leaders in the capital city (1 Cor. 9:19–23 is often appealed to for Paul's willingness to be accommodating). The conclusion, however, that Titus was not circumcised is to be preferred.

False brothers had infiltrated our ranks (2:4). The expression "false brothers" here refers to some Jewish Christians who are treated as insincere people. They have gate-crashed into what was a private meeting between Paul and the Jewish Christian leaders (2:2). Their motives were to challenge Paul's gospel of freedom in Christ and to introduce "bondage" in its place (see 5:1 for the exact wording) so that they might undermine Paul's adherence to the "truth of the gospel" he had brought to Galatia (2:5).

To spy on our freedom . . . and to make us slaves (2:4). Slavery was a common practice in the Greco-Roman world during Paul's lifetime.[23] By law slaves were considered "human tools" (Aristotle). In the first century some slaves wished to be manumitted and became freed persons (cf. 1 Cor. 7:20–24). Paul uses this slavery concept to illustrate the harm these false teachers were doing in trying to impose their ideas on him and Barnabas and especially the Galatians. If Gentile believers must also be circumcised in order to be saved, then Paul and Barnabas themselves have become slaves to Jewish ways, a setback to the gospel message they presented in the Gentile communities.

We did not give in . . . for a moment (2:5). Paul was under extreme pressure to give in to the false brothers' persuasion (see also the use of "compelled" in 2:3), but he held firm to his conviction.

The truth of the gospel (2:5). In this letter, the truth of the gospel refers to the conviction that justification is founded on God's grace (2:21) through faith in Christ Jesus (2:16) apart from circumcision (5:2–3) or the observance of the Mosaic law (2:16; 5:4).

Paul's Ministry Was Acknowledged by the Key Leaders in Jerusalem (2:6–10)

Though facing tremendous pressure before the Jewish Christian leaders in Jerusalem fourteen years after his conversion (possibly because of pro-Zealot pressure in Judea that made conforming to Jewish customs a clear signal of the loyalty of Jewish messianic believers to the ancestral faith), Paul boldly declared that his Gentile mission was of equal footing with Peter's Jewish mission (both men had been commissioned by God and were apostles, 2:7–8). Most significant, the chief leaders of the Jewish-Christian communities unanimously acknowledged his work.

Makes no difference to me (2:6). In the Greco-Roman world, networking and partnership were commonly done through letters of recommendation (cf. Rom. 16:1; 1 Cor. 16:10–11).[24] Itinerant teachers usually acquired these letters of recommendation from conspicuous figures to establish their credentials in order to pave their ways to foreign communities. Paul did not rely on this device (cf. 2 Cor. 3:1; see Acts 18:27 for illustration).

Peter . . . to the Jews (2:7). According to Luke's account in Acts, when Paul and Barnabas were in Jerusalem for the famine relief (11:30), Peter had already evangelized Cornelius (a Gentile) and his household (ch. 10). But that was a unique occasion,[25] which the Jewish Christians willingly accepted after Peter's explanation (see Acts 11:18). Overall, Peter's evangelistic activities were aimed at the Jews.

Pillars (2:9). "Pillars" (*styloi*) was a metaphor commonly used by the Jews in speaking of the great teachers of the law.[26] The church is here regarded as the house or temple of God held up and supported by pillars, that is, these key apostolic leaders (James, Peter, and John).

Right hand of fellowship (2:9). It may be equivalent to the modern greeting. But the use of "fellowship" (*koinōnia*) connotes more than just a friendly handshake. Paul was eager to inform his readers that there was an expression of partnership[27] in this Gentile mission when James, Peter, and John shook hands with him and Barnabas in Jerusalem.

To remember (2:10). This is also an expression of actual actions involved (cf. Phil. 1:3).[28]

The poor (2:10). Why were the Jerusalem saints (1 Cor. 16:1) stricken by poverty? Famine was only one of the factors, though a key one.[29] Other factors also contributed: (1) Many new believers had liquidated their assets by selling their properties to form a common fund for communal life after their conversion (Acts 2–4); (2) there was an increasing number of widows (Acts 6) living in Jerusalem; (3) believers were persecuted following Stephen's martyrdom (Acts 8:1–2).[30]

The very thing I was eager to do (2:10). Paul had already started this famine relief with Barnabas in Antioch. The reasons are clear: (1) Paul, a man of compassion, was always willing to help needy people. (2) He understood that this project could strategically help to cement the relationship between the Jerusalem Christians and the Gentile churches and to promote their unity. (3) He saw that this was an eschatological fulfillment of Isaiah's

"PILLARS"

Columns from the temple of Apollo at Corinth.

▶ Antioch

The place of Antioch in early Christianity is important. It was a bastion of Hellenism in the Syrian lands, the inevitable meeting point of the two worlds. In the time of the Maccabees many of the Jews of Jerusalem showed their adoption of Greek ways by becoming honorary citizens of Antioch. It is easy to imagine, then, how a liberal, tolerant spirit prevailed there. Peter (called here by his Aramaic name Cephas) at first fell in with the practice of sharing a common table with Christian Gentiles.[A-1]

prophecy that Gentiles would bring gifts to the holy mountain in the last days (Isa. 66:20).

Peter's Action Was Rebuked (2:11–13)

In order to demonstrate further the independent authenticity of the message he proclaimed, Paul recalls an unpleasant encounter he had with Peter occurring not long ago before the writing of this letter. He gives an account of Peter's action, the reason behind it, and its impact on other Jewish Christians. His purpose, evidently, is not to expose Peter's weakness. Rather, he wants to show his readers how he went beyond his safety zone to defend the authenticity of this gospel of grace. No one, including Peter, can cause him to yield or compromise (cf. 1:10) when truth is being undermined. This is true in spite of Paul's acknowledgment that Peter is one of the pillars of the Jerusalem church, whom he once made an effort to get acquainted with (1:18) and who had extended the right hand of fellowship not long ago (2:9).

When Peter came to Antioch (2:11). The time of Peter's visit possibly took place after Paul and Barnabas completed their first missionary journey in A.D. 48.[31] Peter came to Antioch to learn about as well as to show support to this unprecedented Gentile outreach program launched by the Gentile-Christian church. "Came to Antioch" may suggest that Paul was at

ANTIOCH
▼

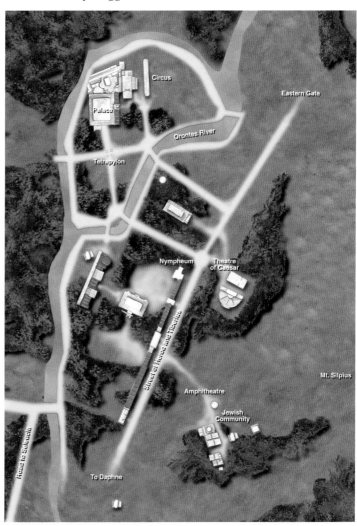

Antioch at the time of his writing of Galatians.

I opposed him to his face (2:11). There was a face-to-face confrontation between Paul and Peter. "I opposed" suggests that Paul is reacting to Peter, who initiates this conflict by his improper behavior toward the Gentile Christians.

Certain men came from James (2:12). These people are evidently not the "false brothers" of 2:4. They were commissioned by James or at least claimed his authorization. They were of the circumcision group (2:13) and possibly came with a special assignment to learn about Paul and Barnabas's Gentile mission (as Peter did). James, we will remember, is the Lord's brother, who became the leader of the Jerusalem church[32] after Peter took on a wider ministry base (Acts 9:32).

He began to . . . separate himself (2:12). Literally, "he cut himself off"—a possible pun, meaning "he played the Pharisee" ("Pharisee" is built on a Semitic root meaning "to separate"). These Jewish leaders were self-styled "separated ones," anxious to preserve their ritual purity and ethnic distinctiveness as elites within God's covenant people.

He was afraid (2:12). Why? Having been commissioned by God to evangelize Cornelius (a Gentile, Acts 10:20) and having witnessed God's saving mercy among the Gentiles (11:4–17), Peter takes an action that is perplexing and betrays his vacillating character. Presumably Peter is trying to avoid another direct conflict with these Jewish brothers. In 11:2–3 he was once criticized[33] by the circumcision group in Jerusalem for eating with uncircumcised people.

The other Jews joined him in his hypocrisy (2:13). Peter's giving in may be due to an unpleasant experience in the past. But the others' behavior, standing up in the midst of a meal and walking away, is intolerable to Paul. Labeling Peter with the word "hypocrisy" (*hypokrisis*) associates him with the Pharisees. According to Paul, Peter not only "played the Pharisee" (see 2:12); he actually behaved "like the Pharisee" in this matter. *Hypokrisis*, however, may have more serious overtones here since the LXX uses it to refer to Israel's enemies as "ungodly people."

Even Barnabas (2:13). Barnabas is mentioned by name because the Galatians know him personally (Acts 13–14). But instead of protecting Barnabas's reputation, Paul chooses to reveal the details so that the readers can appreciate his own integrity. When Paul says he does not please people (Gal. 1:10) for the sake of the gospel, he means it. Barnabas's giving in to the situation reflects the reality of peer pressure in daily life.

ANTIOCH

The ruins of the temple of Augustus at Pisidian Antioch.

▼

Peter's Reasoning Challenged (2:14–17)

Paul carefully rehearses his conversation with Peter to explain to his readers the reason for his harsh attitude toward Peter. At the same time, he endeavors to persuade them about the uselessness of seeking justification by means of observing the law.

I said to Peter (2:14). Paul follows Peter the moment he sees him and other Jewish Christians leave their seats (cf. 2:5, "did not give in to them for a moment"). Instead of lecturing to the crowd, he directly talks to Peter, the leader as well as the initiator of this misconduct. Paul is using a rhetorical device here since his real "audience" is the Judaizers and/or the Galatians influenced by them.

You are a Jew . . . live like a Gentile and not like a Jew (2:14). Peter, being a Jew by nationality, has been able to liberate himself from the restrictive Jewish dietary regulations (cf. Lev. 11). He has learned his freedom as a Christian based on the teaching of Jesus in Mark 7:1–21 and lived like a Gentile, enjoying table fellowship with the Gentile Christians.

[To] force Gentiles to follow Jewish customs (2:14). The verb used here, *ioudaizō* (lit., "to judaize"; NIV, "to follow Jewish customs"), occurs only here in the New Testament. According to Josephus, it means "to live like a Jew" or "to adopt Jewish customs."[34] In this context, Jewish customs specifically refer to the areas of circumcision and strict observance of the Mosaic law. When Peter was eating with them, his action communicated a strong sense of acceptance and fellowship. Paul considers Peter's inconsistent behavior as an indirect way of forcing Gentiles to follow Jewish customs. The harm this might bring to these new Gentile Christians is immeasurable. This explains Paul's fierce reaction in challenging Peter.

Gentile sinners (2:15). This is a general attitude of the Jews toward the Gentiles.[35]

To be justified in Christ . . . we ourselves are sinners (2:17). This may be a charge raised by the false brothers according to their way of reasoning. They claim Paul is teaching that to be justified in Christ, it is necessary to abandon the law (cf. 2:16), and to abandon the law is to become a sinner. That means, in effect, that Christ promotes sin (lit., Christ is the minister or agent of sin). Paul refutes this argument.

In Conclusion: A Personal Note (2:18–21)

Notice a change of pronoun from "we" (2:15–17) to "I" (2:18–21). Before closing this section, Paul adds a personal note, sharing his own spiritual experience in this new relationship to Christ after breaking off from the Jewish way of salvation, which he used to treasure as a Pharisee.

A lawbreaker (2:18). Literally, "a transgressor," that is, one who goes beyond or violates the rules established. In this incident, perhaps Peter should be the speaker who fell short by turning completely under pressure from the presence of James' representatives. Paul, however, may also intend to justify his own actions in not circumcising Titus even under extreme pressure and in rebuking Peter. If he had given in at these crucial points, he would have proved himself to be "a lawbreaker."

Through the law I died to the law (2:19). "To die to the law" means "to break off from a relationship."[36] Through his own legalistic efforts Paul has realized that no one can be justified by observing the law (cf. Rom. 7:7–11). Therefore, he must break off from it for salvation. It is only through faith in Christ that a person can be justified and liberated to a true relationship with God. This is exactly what Paul experienced on the road to Damascus, where he gave up all hope of self-justification and came to a new understanding of the way God saves people.

I have been crucified with Christ (2:20). The verb here is perfect tense, denoting a past action with a continuing effect. The old life of self-effort has been condemned and put on the cross. By using the cross imagery, Paul gives testimony to his new relationship with Christ and his new purpose in living. Now by faith he lives (present tense, denoting a moment-by-moment fellowship) in union with a living Lord, who henceforth controls him and lives out his resurrection life in him.

By faith in the Son of God (2:20). This critical and controversial expression may mean (1) by my trust in Christ, or (2) by Christ's faithfulness to me.

The grace of God (2:21). Above all, it is God's grace that makes it possible for sinners to be justified. It is unthinkable for anyone to set aside what God has already provided and to return to the old ways. Doing so would devalue the cross as the center of our hope (6:14). No wonder in the following statement (3:1), Paul began with an outburst, "you foolish Galatians!"

Paul Confronts His Readers (3:1–5)

Paul's discussion now turns from the past episode at Antioch to the present situation in Galatia. The closing part of his rehearsal of the earlier incident is clear in stating that (1) there is no hope or value in seeking acceptance with God by observing the law (2:21), and (2) in any case, God has himself made full provision for human, specifically Gentile, need in the cross of Jesus, who did not die "for nothing." These twin affirmations are the grounds for Paul's impassioned appeal (3:1).

You foolish Galatians! Who has bewitched you? (3:1). This direct address is unusual for Paul and marks his emotional appeal. He charges that his Galatian friends are under the spell of an "evil eye," a Greek expression to denote the placing of a curse on someone, as

---

R E F L E C T I O N S

IN WRITING GALATIANS 2:19–20, PAUL OPENS UP HIS inner soul in a way he does only rarely. Sometimes this is called "the mysticism" of Paul (as in Albert Schweitzer's well-known title), but it is doubtful if this description is accurate. Rather, it is a revelation of Paul's Christ-centered life, based on a death-to-self reality but issuing in newness that he attributes to "Christ living in me." Commentators note how the pronoun "I" (typical of the old life of striving to please God in one's own strength) has been inflected to "me" to whom God's blessing came as a grateful recipient of grace (2:21). The person Paul knows as his life-changing power is none other than "the Son of God, who loved me and gave himself up for me." Have you opened up your life to the same person who poured his love and grace into the apostle Paul's life?

illustrated in contemporary execration texts and amulets.[37] One such text illustrates the ostensible magical power of the curse known as the "evil eye": "Above all, I pray that you may be in health unharmed by the evil eye and faring prosperously."

Jesus Christ was clearly portrayed as crucified (3:1). Paul harks back to his earlier amazement (1:6) that his readers have succumbed to this spell. He is especially puzzled when he recalls how clearly the picture of the crucified Lord has been presented to them, presumably by his vivid preaching of the cross. "Portrayed" literally means to post a notice in public, like a modern bulletin board—the ancient method of giving out notices of a political or social event.[38]

Paul continues to press home his appeal by a series of questions, each of which concerns the Christian experience of the Galatians. How did they become believers at the beginning? How do they hope to make progress and come to their final salvation (3:3)? How do they explain God's manifest presence and power among them (3:5)?

Give you his Spirit (3:5). The Greek word for "give" here is *epichorēgeō*, from which *chorēgia* ("supply") played an important role in Attic Greek drama. The verb means "to provide for the chorus," whose narration carried the story line for the audience in Greek plays. It thus came to refer to patriotic and generous citizens in Athens who gave contributions to aid the state. One classicist notes: "The importance of the choral element is shown by the fact that the main responsibility of each of the financial sponsors (*chorēgoi*) was the recruiting and maintenance, costuming and training of the chorus."[39]

Because you observe the law, or because you believe what you heard? (3:5). This is the stark alternative, leading to only one conclusion (as Paul's logic insists).

Abraham as Model Believer (3:6–9)

The Jewish teachers who had unsettled the Galatians (1:7; 5:12) are the real persons addressed. They evidently made much of Abraham in their approach, offering a seemingly plausible argument: You Gentiles wish to inherit the blessing of righteousness that our ancestor Abraham received (a common belief found in Philo and the rabbinic sources;[40] for Abraham as an example for future generations, see Sir. 44:19–21); why then do you hesitate to follow his example and get circumcised, as he was told to do (Gen. 17:9–14)?

Abraham, Paul retorts, did indeed receive divine approval, and God put him "in the right" (called justification) with himself. But on what basis? The patriarch was, above all, a person of "faith" (3:6, appealing to Gen. 15:6 and a promise that *precedes* the command to circumcise all Abraham's family). Romans 4:9–12 makes this even clearer.

All nations will be blessed through you (3:8). A second Scripture citation is needed to oppose the Judaizers' argument and their appeal to Abraham. Earlier still in the Genesis story of Israel's ancestors God had given a first promise to Abraham (Gen. 12:3, repeated in 18:18) that he was to be ancestor, not of Jewish people only but of "all nations," a wide inclusion quoted by Paul in Galatians 3:8. The word for "nations" in the Greek Bible can also mean "Gentiles"; here it refers to the Galatians. How then can the Judaizing teachers claim that the Galatians must become Jews in order to be complete Christians? Paul's logic is clear and leads to 3:9—those who believe are blessed in the same way as Abraham the believer.

The Law Cannot Bring Salvation (3:10–14)

One further argument will lead to the same conclusion—stated in 3:14 with even sharper focus on the readers as former pagans (4:8–10).

The law is not based on faith (3:12). The gist of Paul's argument is that religion based on law, so far from being required to gain salvation/justification, lies under judgment. The only exception to this verdict would be if a person could be found who perfectly kept the law. But that possibility is excluded by the sinful human nature, called "flesh" (in 6:13) and is endorsed by the verdict of Deuteronomy 27:26 (quoted in Gal. 3:10). Later on, Paul will develop the way nomistic religion (i.e., "law-oriented" religion), based on an observance for Gentiles of circumcision in order to gain a place in God's covenant, is really a no-win situation, since nomism leads either to frustration and condemnation when we fail (as here), or to pride when we succeed (Phil.

3:6). Either way, it leads to a false hope and a bitter result, as is clear (cf. "clearly" in Gal. 3:11).

Christ redeemed us from the curse of the law (3:13). Yet there is hope once we renounce all attempts to be our own savior, and it centers in the cross of Christ, where he bore our judgment by dying the sinner's death.

Law Versus Promise (3:15–22)

Paul here faces an objection. To be sure, so his opponents argued, God gave Abraham a promise that included his family (3:16)—but we know this refers to the Jewish people by the fact that some centuries later God made a covenant (agreement) with Israel. So, they reasoned, the

REFLECTIONS

ONE OF THE CLEAREST STATEMENTS Paul gives for the basis of our salvation is in Galatians 3:13. Christ has set us free from all vain attempts to win our redemption; he has paid the cost by his death on the cross (2:20–21)—where he assumed our curse as sinners and died as our vicarious Redeemer. We now live with him in freedom, dead to sin's curse.

▶ **Redemption**

"Redeemed" is the terminology used for the way slaves gained their freedom in Greco-Roman society as well as for Israel's deliverance from bondage in Egypt (Ex. 15:13; Ps. 77:15) and servitude in Babylon (Isa. 42:1). The former worldview was exceedingly common in the ancient world. For example, at Delphi the names of former slaves set free by payment of their savings and deposited in the temple of Apollo as by a fiction (since the owners received the money in payment) are recorded on several temple walls. In Roman society slaves' redemption and gaining of freedom was common. The freed slave was also promised Roman citizenship.[A-2]

law of Moses supersedes the Abrahamic covenant.

Paul gives a firm "No" to this conclusion in a series of counterarguments: (1) The allusion to Abraham's "seed' (i.e., offspring) turns on the fact that the word is singular in number (in Gen. 12:7; 13:15–16; 17:8; 24:7) and so must be understood in a collective sense (Gal. 3:16), meaning the Messiah and his people, including both Gentiles and Jews (cf. 1 Cor. 12:12). (See comments below on Gal. 3:16.)

(2) The giving of the law at a *later* period does not invalidate the earlier promise made to Abraham (3:17), any more than a codicil added to a human will destroys the terms of the original document once it has been ratified (3:15). Paul is familiar with the making of wills in Greco-Roman society and uses a technical term (in 3:17: "does not set aside"), evidenced in the papyri for "void by illegality."[41] Yet his understanding of family inheritance based on the principle of primogeniture (the right of the eldest son to inherit) is not the same as Athenian law provided, where the inheritance of property (a person's *klēros* or lot) was divided equally by lot between surviving sons.[42] God's "promise" (a word found eight times in 3:14–19) to Abraham is what the Gentile believers have inherited, thereby bypassing the law's requirement (here circumcision).

(3) The Mosaic law, though coming later in time than the promise to Abraham, has all the marks of inferiority: It was given to define human sin without giving the power to overcome it (3:21), and it came by various intermediaries since it was handed down from God via Moses via the angels to the people.[43] By contrast, the promise to Abraham was given directly from God himself (Gal. 3:20).

The Scripture does not say "and to seeds," meaning many people, but "and to your seed," meaning one person, who is Christ (3:16). Paul's line of reasoning, beginning with the fact that "seed" is singular, has precedent in rabbinic interpretation.[44] It is his extension of this interpretation as messianic and individual that is unusual, since "seed" does not normally refer to one person. Morris observes that it points to the one person as outstanding (not like Isaac over against Ishmael, a discussion to come later in 4:21–31). "It is not one descendant among many but *the* descendant." So, Paul concludes, what is vital is not that "Abraham's descendants became a nation . . . but that . . . God's chosen one, the Christ, appeared in due course and that the covenant God made centres on him."[45]

Added because of transgressions (3:19). This unexplained addendum may be Paul's way of saying that the law gave definition and focus to sin (as in Rom. 3:20; 4:15), as the REB takes it, "to make wrongdoing a legal offence" or simply to point to human need of pardon and atonement that the law was powerless to meet (as 2 Cor. 3:6 may imply, and is seen in Paul's conclusion at Gal. 3:21). Above all, the law is propaedeutic and prophetic, both preparing people for the gospel message (Gal. 3:8) and pointing them to Christ as the promised Redeemer (3:22).

By a mediator (3:19). Literally, "in the hand of a mediator." This phrase evidently refers to Moses since it was by Moses that the Torah was given.[46] Some think the allusion to Moses' hand relates to the tables of the law placed into his hands at Sinai (Ex. 32:19). The function of Moses the lawgiver as a human intermediary is a sign of the law's inferiority in contrast to the direct giving of the promise to Abraham.

Is the law, therefore, opposed to the promises of God? (3:21). It seems the answer must be yes; but Paul replies, "Absolutely not!" The law did have a role to play, such as providing a definition of sin as transgression, i.e., stepping across the line of God's will.

Why the Law? (3:23–29)

The law was put in charge (3:24). The law was temporary, like a custodian, keeping people in check as a disciplinarian (3:23–24). The Greek word is *paidagōgos*, describing a slave in Hellenistic society who acted as tutor and guardian to children as well as imposing discipline. The slave also led the children to the school, "helped to bring up the child and at school must have been a helpful overseer." [47] Hence, the *paidagōgos* was a trusted member of the family

▶

"BAPTISMAL" POOL

A traditional Jewish purification bath (*miqveh*) discovered in the southern wall excavations at Jerusalem just south of the Temple Mount.

and even sometimes had charge of "home-schooling" before group schooling became accepted. [48]

In any case that job lasted only until the children reached the age of maturity. Then his responsibility was at an end. Now, Paul insists, "faith came" and brought our time with the law to an end, since it pointed to Christ, who alone can set us right with God (3:24) and place us in God's family as his adult children (3:26).

You are all sons of God (3:26). Mention of family life leads Paul to rehearse the benefits of belonging to God's new order by various steps. (1) The first step was believing in Christ Jesus (3:26). (2) Then came baptism into him as an act of identification when candidates stripped off old clothes and were given new garments. This was a picture of putting on Christ's character (3:27); (3) In this new family life of believers all the age-old barriers of race, social position, and gender are overcome in Christ, who unites believers as "one" in him. This does away with the pride that thanks God (as in Jewish prayers[49]) that male Jews are not created as Gentiles, slaves, or women (3:28). (4) As a triumphant conclusion, Paul addresses his Gentile audience as Christ's people and so as the family of Abraham and inheritors of God's promise to him (3:29).

God's Children—Not Slaves (4:1–7)

This section shows what inheritance means. The contrast is a direct one between "slaves" and "sons" (4:7), and so what believers are as inheritors. Roman society—with its institution of slavery and its family life, where children had no rights or little significance until they grew up to adulthood—is reflected here. Paul uses this framework to argue for spiritual applications, which we may tabulate: (1) Childhood is a time under control (4:2); (2) it is akin to slavery (4:3); (3) yet it holds the promise of reaching adulthood, just as some slaves hoped to be set free by manumission (see earlier on 3:13).

"Abba, Father" (4:6). *Abba* is Jesus' familiar name for God as "dear father"(Mark 14:32–39; Luke 11:2–4).

No longer a slave, but a son (4:7). (1) Slavery induces fear and can represent the human condition under the power of bad religion, called "the basic principles of the world" (4:3). Here, however, it is more likely a reference to star worship. The cosmic "elements" were thought to control human beings and to lead to uncertainty about human fate, as 4:8–9 makes clear. (2) Slavery pictures men and women in bondage to sin and needing to be "redeemed." This has happened in Christ's coming and death (1:4; 3:13). (3) The outcome is a new life of "sonship," enjoying our full inheritance (4:1, 5) and freedom as God's children who know intimately the smile of their Parent.

Paul's Expression of Concern (4:8–20)

Slaves to those who by nature are not gods (4:8). This is a clear indication that the Galatians were pagan before entering God's family in Christ. Paul marvels (as he does at 1:6) that they should wish to revert to the slavery brought on by fear of cosmic powers—such as the star deities that once ruled their lives—by imposing a regime of observing "special days" when good luck may be expected for an enterprise (a typical sentiment of Greco-Roman religion with its recourse to magic, omens, and horoscope predictions). Their interest was in what "days" were good for business or travel or marriage and which "seasons" were favored by the gods to produce fertile ground or harvest yield.

Because of an illness that I first [or, on a former occasion] preached the gospel to you (4:13). Paul's first visit to Galatia (in Acts 13–14) is the background here. He was evidently a sick person at that time and suffered a disfiguring or debilitating illness that could have made the Galatians reject him as the opposite of a divine messenger. Instead, they welcomed him as a

---

▶ **Elements**

The use of the Greek word *stoicheia* in this context is much discussed. Its basic meaning is what stands in a line, like a row of peas or the characters of the alphabet. Hence it comes to mean rudimentary "elements" or the ABCs in educational theory among Greco-Roman teachers. This is sometimes thought to link it with the reference to *paidagōgos* in Galatians 3:23–24.

Yet the way Paul proceeds in 4:8 to associate these *stoicheia* with pagan religion from which the Galatians have been delivered suggests that he has in mind the cosmic powers, thought to be expressed in the stars, which in turn control human destiny. Diogenes Laertius speaks of "twelve immortal stoicheia," meaning the signs of the zodiac; he refers to human fear of uncertainty in the astrological-magical realm when human life is held in the grip of these planetary powers (see comments on Gal. 4:8).[A-3]

HERMES

person sent from God (like Hermes/Mercury in Acts 14:12) and obeyed the gospel call as if Christ himself were speaking.

You welcomed me as if I were an angel of God (4:14). The surnaming of Paul as a "messenger [*angelos*] of God" combines the two cultural ideas of (1) Jewish representatives (Heb. *seluḥim*) of the synagogues of the Dispersion, charged to carry funds to Jerusalem, and (2) the Hellenistic depiction of a messenger of the gods, notably Hermes in the Homeric pantheon.[50] A son of Zeus and the nymph Maia, Hermes played many roles, notably as a guide for divine children, leading them to safety, and as a *psychopōpos*, i.e., one who escorts souls to the underworld of Hades. But he is best known as a messenger god who is obedient to the king of the gods, Zeus, and executes his orders.

Torn out your eyes (4:15). Some take this to mean that Paul's sickness was ophthalmic—possibly a migraine headache that affected his vision; this is why, perhaps, he had to write in large letters (6:11).

My dear children, for whom I am again in the pains of childbirth until Christ is formed in you (4:19). This sentence is a remarkable window into Paul's pastoral care for his converts. He likens his role as a birth-mother undergoing labor to deliver her child. His goal as an apostle is to see people reflect the likeness of Christ (2 Cor. 3:18). Children were regarded in low esteem in Greco-Roman society.[51] Paul's more positive attitude is given in Colossians 3:18–4:1.

Two Women—Two Covenants (4:21–31)

Paul reverts to an argument from scriptural exegesis, employing an allegorical method familiar in Philo. In Abraham's household two women lived uneasily together: Hagar (Gen. 16:5) and Sarah (21:2). Paul's chief interest is with them as mothers of two children, Ishmael and

---

R E F L E C T I O N S

SOMETIMES PAUL IS VIEWED AS RATHER AUSTERE and aloof from his readers, too authoritarian and browbeating the opposition in severe tones and with a temper. True, he can be harsh in this letter (e.g., 1:6–10; 5:12), but his stern face is usually directed to the teachers who were undermining the Christian faith and experience of his congregation. Toward his converts, he is tender and solicitous; and never more so than at 4:12–20 (esp. 4:19). His role as a mother, caring for her young children and desiring only their best interests, is vividly portrayed. It is one of several places where Paul appears in this light comparing himself to a mother's love for her child.[A-4] This word to pastors and church leaders is especially relevant in any age.[A-5]

Slavery	Freedom
• Hagar was a slave woman	• Sarah was a "free" wife
• Ishmael, born of the flesh, a trademark of the Judaizers (6:13-14)	• Isaac, born through promise (4:23) and the Spirit (4:29)
• Mount Sinai, Jerusalem of the Judaizers (4:25), is a symbol of slavery	• Mount Zion (4:26; Heb. 12:22) stands for joyous freedom (based on Isa. 54:1)
• "Ishmael" is in slavery and opposes his brother	• "Isaac" (Paul and his converts) suffers persecution (Gal. 6:12-13)
• But the Judaizers are to be refused since Ishmael did not gain an inheritance (4:30)	• Rather, Paul's gospel connects believers with the "free woman" and the promise of liberty (4:31)

Isaac. He develops two lines of descent and connects them to a spiritual/figurative meaning. This interpretation is based on his desire to show that only one son was "born as the result of a promise" (4:23) and that this line leads to freedom, not slavery (4:31). That is the key to Paul's thought. We may note that he uses the term "covenant" to include both lines of development from Ishmael as well as Isaac, whereas in 3:15–16 he kept "covenant" to relate to promise, not law.

The table above may help set out the issues as Paul sees them:[52]

Recent study of these verses has helped our understanding of Paul's argument in introducing this extended allegory or illustration of Hagar and Sarah.[53] The Jewish scribes used this story from Genesis to praise the line from Abra-ham/Sarah to Israel,[54] but Paul's purpose is different. The climax comes at 4:30, where he cites Genesis 21:10. The citation in this verse shapes his conclusion in answer to the question, "Are you not aware of what the law says?" (4:21).

The examples given of Hagar and Ishmael (who represent slavery and the life of servitude "under the law") and Sarah and Isaac (who stand for the covenant of grace and freedom) are targeted at the Judaizers, who sought to impose legalism on Paul's Gentile converts. Yet the conclusion in 4:30—"get rid of the slave woman and her son"—is not directed at Judaizers or Jews, but at the covenant of

MOUNT SINAI

▼

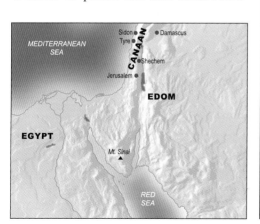

Sinai. The old covenant leads to bondage since it is based on "flesh" and not the Spirit. It belongs to the old order, not the new age of messianic salvation brought by Christ and endorsed by the Spirit.

Paul will develop this line of reasoning at length later when he writes 2 Corinthians 3:1–18. There the same conclusion is reached as in Galatians 4:31: "We are . . . children . . . of the free [one]," Christ Jesus, and we have a spiritual parentage, "the Jerusalem that is above [which] is free" (4:26), the mother of both believing Jews and Gentiles. Paul's use of the figure of the holy city of Jerusalem to relate to a spiritual home, the church of God's new creation, not any geographical or ethnic location, is to be noted, and is parallel with Hebrews 12:22 and Revelation 21:1–5.

Conclusion (5:1)

It is for freedom that Christ has set us free. Stand firm . . . and do not let yourselves be burdened again by a yoke of slavery (5:1). Here Paul concludes his theological argument by driving home the issue of freedom that many of his readers understand well from their own experiences as slaves (cf. 1 Cor. 1:26; 7:21). They are well aware of the essential differences between them and their free masters, who have the freedom to own property, to schedule their own daily activities, to earn as well as to spend their own living in ways they like, and to live wherever they wish. No one would tolerate the reversion to become a slave again, once redeemed and set free. A person's spiritual condition is similar (cf. Gal. 4:8–9), Paul argues. Christ has paid a high price in redeeming sinners and setting them free (1:4; 3:13). No one should therefore return to the state of slavery, whether to be under the yoke of

the law (as the Jews) or under the bondage of the *stoicheia* of this world (as the pagans, 4:8–10).

Freedom in Christ: What It Implies (5:2–12)

Apparently, the matter of circumcision (mentioned five times in 5:2, 3, 6, 11) is at stake here. It is the first time in this letter Paul directly addresses this topic to his readers. Paul emphatically declares (5:2) that freedom in Christ *excludes* the requirement of circumcision (5:6).[55]

If you let yourselves be circumcised, Christ will be of no value to you at all (5:2). Paul makes it clear that circumcision and Christ are incompatible with one another. If there is any saving value in religious ordinances (e.g., circumcision) apart from the cross of Christ, then Christ's death has been in vain (cf. 2:21).

Every man who lets himself be circumcised . . . is obligated to obey the whole law (5:3). Circumcision and keeping the law are two integral components of Judaism. No one can observe one requirement and dismiss the other. Many have argued that Paul's statement about obeying the whole law reflects only his own Christian understanding of Torah. There are, however, many evidences both from rabbinic literature and other literature showing that the conviction of keeping the whole law was adopted prior to and after Paul's time.[56]

For example, a Gentile proselyte was required to offer a gift, to be baptized, to vow to observe the Mosaic law, and to be circumcised (for male proselytes). At the same time, no amount of law-keeping or conformity to Jewish ways mattered in the eyes of stricter Jews unless circumcision had been accepted.[57] Thus, to be circumcised implies an obligation to obey the whole law.

You who are trying to be justified by law have been alienated from Christ (5:4). This is the logical conclusion to which Paul intends to lead the Galatians. If they seek justification by obeying the whole law, they are actually alienated (*katergēthēte*, lit., "you are made impotent," see 3:17; 5:11; 1 Cor. 1:28; 2 Tim. 1:10) from Christ. In other words, their relation with him as the Redeemer is severed.

You have fallen away from grace (5:4). "Fallen away" (*ekpiptō*) originally refers to the falling out of a flower. Later, it also means to be loosened from something. This phrase further illustrates the serious consequence of those who seek justification by keeping the law and allow themselves to be circumcised. Paul emphatically warns his readers not to let go of something too good to be loosed from (i.e., Christ and his grace) for something (i.e., circumcision and law-keeping) that is unable to help them gain acceptance before God (2:15–16; 3:11).

But by faith we eagerly await . . . righteousness (5:5). This refers to the hope of a favorable verdict in the last judgment (cf. Rom. 2:5–16). It marks the key difference between Paul and the Judaizers. Paul has already moved from the entrance of salvation onto the future hope while the Judaizers were still trying to teach people how to get into the door of salvation.

For in Christ Jesus neither circumcision nor uncircumcision has any value (5:6). This is a bold statement guaranteed to evoke an offense in the Judaizers. Paul, who once was a serious Jew (circumcised and striving to observe the whole law, 1:14; Phil. 3:5–6; cf. Acts 26:4–5) is most qualified to testify from his own experiences the fruitlessness of these religious practices (Rom. 7:18–24; cf. Phil 3:7–8).

The only thing that counts is faith expressing itself through love (5:6). Faith is the *only* criterion for justification—a theme emphasized repeatedly in this first canonical letter of Paul (2:16; 3:3, 8, 14, 24; 5:5). His strong conviction on this subject matter first came from a revelation (Gal. 1:11–12).[58] Yet Paul makes it clear that the faith that leads to justification is not merely a cognitive recognition or a matter of mental exercise. It entails actions that stem out of love. Saving faith is, in essence, a practical faith— a message shared by the three pillars (James, Peter, and John, 2:9) of the Jerusalem church (James 2:14–26; 1 Peter 1:22; 1 John 3:18–19).

You were running a good race (5:7). The use of an athletic metaphor in describing the Christian life is frequently found in Paul's writing.[59] It reflects (1) the popularity of athletic sports in the Greco-Roman world that most people would have had no difficulty in understanding; and (2) the strenuous quality of Christian service and life as likened to a race. The Galatians are commended for their beginning steps in the Christian race (see Gal. 4:13–15; cf. 3:2–3).

Who cut in on you and kept you from obeying the truth? (5:7). "To cut in" (*enkoptō*) suggests a breaking into or obstruction of the Galatian Christians in their course of following the truth. The picture is that of a runner who has allowed his or her progress to be blocked or who is still running but on the wrong course.[60] In the track race of the Greek festivals there were rules against tripping or cutting in on an opponent.[61] In the case of the Galatians, they have allowed the Judaizers to come in and distract them.

That kind of persuasion does not come from the one who calls you (5:8). The word persuasion (*peismonē*, found only here in the New Testament) opens a window to the method of the Judaizers in approaching the Galatians, that is, by a form of "contrived persuasiveness."[62] In the Greco-Roman world, politicians, religious leaders, or philosophers were known for their rhetorical speech, which was used to impress as well as to attract the hearers.[63] Paul, however, intends to distinguish himself from the common practice of his time in his apostolic ministry.[64]

Perhaps these Judaizers have tried to allure the Galatians (just as the false teachers did the Corinthians, 2 Cor. 11:3,

▶

CYBELE

The "Great Mother" goddess of Asia Minor.

13–15) to receive circumcision because it is not only necessary for a complete salvation, it is also commendable in that Christ himself was circumcised (see Luke 2:21). Paul's identifying himself with Christ's crucifixion (Gal. 2:20; cf. 6:14) may suggest a correction to the Galatians' desire to identify with Christ's circumcision as something they can boast of (cf. 6:13b).

A little yeast works through the whole batch of dough (5:9). Jewish people saw yeast as a symbol of evil and sin after the Passover event when their ancestors were commanded to eat only unleavened bread (Ex. 12:15, 17–20; Deut. 16:3–8). Paul applies this analogy to the Judaizers, whose influence on the Galatians is considered both evil and corrupting.[65]

The one who is throwing you into confusion (5:10). There was perhaps one person leading this group of agitators (1:7; 5:12) in persuading Gentile believers to be circumcised.[66] He will most surely be punished by God.

The offense of the cross has been abolished (5:11). "Offense" (*skandalon*) literally refers to the arm or stick on which bait was fixed in a trap,[67] that which trips one up, a cause of stumbling.[68] During Paul's apostolic ministry, he repeatedly confronted the same difficulty in winning the Jews to Christ. For in the mind of Jewish people, Christ's death on the cross symbolized his being under a curse.[69] The cross was thus an offense to them. Paul insists, however, that to preach circumcision as a means for salvation is to validate the keeping of the law for justification (5:4). It will in effect nullify the preaching of Christ crucified.

As for those agitators, I wish they would go the whole way and emasculate themselves (5:12). Did Paul borrow from the residents of the southern Galatia region a crude expression to express a challenge to the agitators to cut themselves off from the church, the body of Christ on the basis of the fact that emasculation is prohibited by the Mosaic law[70] (Deut. 23:1)? Yet in fact, sacral castration or emasculation was commonly known in the ancient world. It was frequently practiced by pagan priests in the cult of Cybele, which was prominent in Asia. Here Paul is possibly making a sarcastic challenge[71] to his opponents, who are so eager in persuading the Galatians to be circumcised. They should actually mutilate themselves like priests of Cybele.

Freedom in Christ: What It Means (5:13–26)

Having stated the implication of freedom in Christ, Paul moves on to define the meaning of this freedom. There are two aspects. On the negative side, it is not the freedom to indulge one's sinful nature; positively, it is the freedom to serve one another in love (5:13). But how can Christians do that? In the following statements (5:16–23), Paul provides his readers a way to reach this goal, that is, to live by the Spirit (5:16a). He is confident that when people live by the Spirit, they will not gratify the desires of the "sinful nature" (i.e., "flesh," *sarx*; 5:16b). They will, on the contrary, be able to "serve [*douleuō*, performing the duties of a slave] one another in love" (5:13), because love is part of the fruit or harvest of the Holy Spirit (5:22). The use of a singular noun "fruit" (*karpos*) in 5:22 to include nine virtuous elements of conduct is better considered "a harvest" that

includes various kinds of produce. A list of personality traits or activities are spelled out to further help readers identify the characteristics of the sinful nature (5:19–21) and the harvest of the Spirit (5:22–23). A logical exhortation leads to the conclusion: "Since we live by the Spirit [cf. 3:3], let us keep in step with the Spirit" (5:25).

You ... were called to be free ... do not use your freedom to indulge the sinful nature (5:13). This statement reconnects to the earlier statement in 5:1 on Christian freedom. Paul began with an encouragement to stand firm (5:1); now he voices a warning against indulgence. "Sinful nature" translates the Greek word *sarx*, which may simply refer to a person's physical body, just like the Hebrew word *basar*.[72] Paul, however, also uses it in an ethical sense, referring to a person's "desires and passions" (Gal. 5:16–17, 24; cf. 1 Cor. 3:3) that is essentially self-centered.[73]

The entire law is summed up in ... "Love your neighbor as yourself" (5:14). Being well aware of the Judaizers' emphasis on the law, Paul also makes a reference to the Mosaic law in Leviticus 19:18b (a command to love one's neighbor) as the background of his call to serve one another in love (Gal. 5:13). The emphasis on love as the *summary* of all law was first introduced by Jesus himself.[74] It was later reinforced by Paul[75] as well as the three pillars of the Jerusalem church[76] as a primary Christian virtue and a hallmark of Christian identity.

If you keep on biting and devouring each other (5:15). The two verbs "to bite" (*daknō*) and "to eat up" (*katesthiō*) usually refer to fighting among wild animals.[77] Coupled with the warning given in 5:26, "let us not become conceited, provoking and envying each other," we have a glimpse of the internal situation within the Galatian churches. Ramsay has observed that there was a close connection between the lifestyle of the South Galatian cities and the new converts. He points out, owing to (1) the national religion, (2) their position in a municipality, and (3) the customs of society in Hellenistic cities, these new converts are liable to be led astray by habits and ways of thought known to them.[78] Therefore, this unpleasant picture of "biting" and "eating up" may indeed explain Paul's choice of conduct listed as the acts of the sinful nature in 5:19–21.

The sinful nature (5:17). The literal translation of the Greek word is "flesh" (*sarx*). The rabbinic background and terminology of the two "impulses" (denoted in Paul by "flesh" and "Spirit") are well-attested (W. D. Davies has the seminal discussion of the rabbinic texts[79]). Yet more recently there is a move to locate Paul's dichotomy in the world of apocalyptic dualism.[80] On this reading Paul is contrasting not simply the good and evil parts of human nature ("higher"/"lower," as in NEB), but more

profoundly the contrasted setting of sinful humankind in the domain of moral and cosmic evil (and expressed as opposition to God) and the Christian released to new life in Christ by the Spirit.

Contrary to the Spirit. . . . They are in conflict with each other (5:17). These statements may be derived from rabbinic teaching. The rabbis contended that every human being has two desires, the *yetser tob* (good impulse) and the *yetser ra*ᶜ (bad impulse). These desires are in conflict with each other.[81] As a Pharisee, Paul could testify from his own experience about the constant struggle between the good and the bad impulses within himself (cf. Rom. 7:7–24).

The acts of the sinful nature (5:19–21). In order to clarify what he means, Paul provides a list of behaviors classified as stemming from the sinful nature. These behaviors may be divided into four categories: (1) irregular sexual practices (5:19, "sexual immorality, impurity and debauchery"); (2) perverted religion (5:20, "idolatry and witchcraft"); (3) antisocial behavior (5:20, "hatred, discord, jealousy, fits of rage, selfish ambition, dissensions, factions"); and (4) personal lapses (v. 21, "envy; drunkenness, orgies, and the like").

The fruit [harvest] of the Spirit (5:22–23). The Holy Spirit's transforming power in a person's life, on the other hand, produces a harvest of ethical characteristics that cover a threefold relationship: (1) with God (love, joy, peace); (2) with fellow believers (patience, kindness, goodness); and (3) with oneself (faithfulness, gentleness, self-control).

The acts of the sinful nature are essentially self-centered, gratifying a person's

MAENAD WITH TWO SATYRS

The Bacchic (Dionysiac) rituals embodied many features of Paul's list of the acts of the sinful nature.

▼

THE ITEMS PAUL MENTIONS IN Galatians 5:19–23 may also be employed as a "spiritual thermometer" for measuring one's own spiritual health: "How am I doing as a Christian? Am I living according to my sinful nature (*sarx*) or walking according to the Spirit? How can I tell?" A chart of comparison may help to identify the contrasts between the two ways of life:

physical and emotional desires. They are destructive of community life. The fruit of the Spirit, on the other hand, is a list of actions that promote community life.[82] As mentioned above, some of the Galatians were beset by severe conflict and competition (cf. 5:15, 26). Thus Paul's teaching here can be understood as directly addressing the problems and needs of these new Christian communities.[83]

Freedom in Christ: How It Works (6:1–10)

After mentioning the meaning of freedom in Christ (5:13) and spelling out the qualities of the harvest of the Spirit (5:22–23), Paul adds several practical instructions as ways of applying these principles to the Galatians' daily life as well as church life.[84]

Restore him gently (6:1). The word "restore" (*katartizō*) is a medical term for setting a fractured bone. Those who are spiritual (i.e., who live by the Spirit, 5:16, 25) are those who care enough to help other members when they fall and who are able to deal with it with *gentleness* (5:23). By this kind of mutual helping (carrying each other's burdens) for spiritual restoration, believers are fulfilling (in action) the law of Christ, which is the law of *love* (5:22; cf. 5:14).[85]

Each one should carry his own load (6:5). Spiritual people are able to be responsible for their own needs. The word "burden" here (*phortion*) is different from the burden in 6:2 (*barē*). *Phortion* is a common term for a soldier's pack.[86] Bearing one's own burden is a traditional maxim. Paul adopted this idea to exhort the Galatians to see themselves as soldiers of Christ, setting out on their march and discharging their own obligations (i.e., *faithfulness*, 5:22) rather than taking pride in their current achievements through comparison or competition (6:4, which is an act of sinful desire such as *selfish ambition*, 5:20). Ultimately at the final judgment, each believer is responsible for his or her "pack" (life and service) before God.[87]

Share all good things with his instructor (6:6). By using *koinōneō*, Paul perceives the relationship between the catechumen (the

Acts of the Sinful Nature	Harvest of the Spirit
• Sexual immorality, impurity & debauchery	• Love, joy, peace
• Idolatry and witchcraft	• Patience, kindness, goodness
• Hatred, discord, jealousy, fits of rage	• Faithfulness, gentleness, self-control
• Selfish ambition, dissensions, factions	
• Envy, drunkenness, orgies, and the like	

learner) and the teacher in a form of partnership,[88] especially in the area of material possessions. Although pagan priests often received fees for their sacrificial services, Paul prefers to train his converts in voluntary liberality as distinguished from payments received from performing sacrificial rites.[89] This is also a concrete manifestation of the fruit of the Spirit in *kindness* and *goodness* (5:22).

Let us do good to all people (6:10). "Doing good" in Paul's mind may be a direct fund-raising drive to the Galatians to participate in the Jerusalem famine relief fund project, which is now under his care (2:9; cf. 2 Cor. 9:6–9).[90] This exhortation is compared to sowing and reaping for the purpose of assuring the Galatians that good results will be guaranteed from kind actions.[91]

Closing Remarks and Final Greeting (6:11–18)

This section not only sums up Paul's letter, but is also important for the interpretation of the letter. "It contains the interpretive clues to the understanding of Paul's major concerns in the letter as a whole and should be employed as the hermeneutical key to the intentions of the Apostle." [92]

Large letters I use as I write to you with my own hand (6:11). Large letters appearing in ancient correspondence are often seen as an indicator calling for special attention.[93] It is like using bold type in modern printing or double underlining in a manuscript. Paul wants his swayed readers to pay special attention to his concluding remarks (6:12–18), which he now pens personally.

To avoid being persecuted for the cross of Christ (6:12). In the first century of the Christian era, Jewish Christians in Jerusalem evidently faced social pressure from the Zealots, the nationalists. They made efforts, therefore, to persuade the Gentile Christians to accept circumcision with the hope of preserving the Jerusalem church and other Christian churches in Judea from falling into the hands of Zealot-minded militants by having connection with uncircumcised Gentiles.[94]

May I never boast except in the cross (6:14). The Greeks and the Romans considered the cross a symbol of shame and unspeakable horror. Death in this way was not mentionable in polite Roman society.[95] Paul, as a Roman citizen, knew well the meaning and implication of the cross. Yet he was able to embrace it as the most worthwhile goal in life with the knowledge of the crucified Christ and boasted in his cross (cf. 2:20; Phil. 3:8–10). For it was at the "cross" where salvation was wrought and it is the "cross" that sets the pattern of self-denial.[96]

Peace . . . to all who follow this rule, even to the Israel of God (6:16). The word "rule" (*kanōn*, lit., a measuring rod) refers to the principle of justification by faith in this letter. Paul pronounces his greeting of peace to all God's people, whether

Jews or Gentiles. As long as they follow the *kanōn* of salvation (i.e., justification by faith on the basis of God's grace), they are the true Israel of God (cf. Heb. 11:17).[97]

For I bear on my body the marks of Jesus (6:17). In the Greco-Roman world, slaves were usually marked with the mark (*stigma*) or name of their master as a sign of ownership.[98] Marks or scars can also be seen as symbols of loyalty. For example, Josephus refers to an incident in which Antipater (Herod's father) strips off his clothes and exhibits his many scars as witnesses to his loyalty to Caesar.[99] Likewise, in contrast to the mark of circumcision, which the Judaizers have insisted on for Gentile converts, Paul asserts that he has marks/scars on his body that were acquired in his service for Christ. He possibly received these when he was in Iconium and Lystra during his first missionary journey (Acts 14:5, 19). They are the true marks of Christian identity, not circumcision.

The grace of our Lord Jesus Christ be with your spirit. . . . Amen (6:18). Paul now follows the epistolary custom of his time by ending his letter with a wish. The mention of "your spirit" instead of "you" may be intended to remind the Galatians, who have been influenced by the Judaizers to put too much attention on the *sarx* (flesh or body), the importance of their spirit, which is to be led by the Holy Spirit.[100]

The insertion of a liturgical "Amen" (from Heb. *ʾmn*, meaning "firmness and certainty" or "so let it be") at the end unquestionably places this letter in a public worship setting, where all believers are given an opportunity to affirm what they have just heard (the truth of the gospel) in unison.

ANNOTATED BIBLIOGRAPHY

Betz, H-D. *Galatians.* Hermeneia. Philadelphia: Fortress, 1979.
> A learned and detailed commentary on Greco-Roman and Jewish backgrounds.

Bruce, F. F. *The Epistle to the Galatians.* NIGTC. Grand Rapids: Eerdmans, 1982.
> An excellent commentary, covering all the exegetical problems and options, but requiring some knowledge of Greek.

Burton, E. *A Critical and Exegetical Commentary on the Epistle to the Galatians.* ICC. Edinburgh: T. & T. Clark, 1921.
> A solid commentary, strong on word studies and historical background.

Dunn, J. D. G. *The Epistle to the Galatians.* Peabody, Mass.: Hendrickson, 1993.
> A highly readable commentary with good insight into the text.

_____. *The Theology of Paul's Letter to the Galatians.* NTT. Cambridge: Cambridge Univ. Press, 1993.
> An excellent survey of the key theological themes in Galatians.

Elliot, Susan M. "Choose Your Mother, Choose Your Master: Galatians 4:21–5:1 in the Shadow of the Anatolian Mother of the Gods." *JBL* 118 (1999): 661–83.
> An article that provides important background information for interpreting the letter.

Hansen, G. W. "Galatians, Letter to" in *Dictionary of Paul and His Letters.* Downers Grove: InterVarsity Press, 1993, 323–34.
> A mine of information on Galatians.

Longenecker, R. N. *Galatians.* WBC. Dallas: Word, 1990.
> A detailed discussion of all the issues and full of scholars' opinions as well as the author's preferences.

Morris, L. *Galatians.* Downers Grove: InterVarsity, 1996.
> This is probably the most serviceable commentary for the general reader with many insights and much helpful comment.

Main Text Notes

1. For an accessible discussion of the rhetorical setting of the letter as deliberative and an example of "the art of persuasion," see B. Witherington III, *The Paul Quest* (Downers Grove, Ill.: InterVarsity, 1998), 119–22.

2. J. B. Lightfoot, *Saint Paul's Epistle to the Galatians* (1865; reprint, Grand Rapids: Zondervan, 1957).

3. J. Murphy-O'Connor, *Paul: A Critical Life* (Oxford: Clarendon, 1996), 160, 187.

4. W. M. Ramsay, *A Historical Commentary on St. Paul's Epistle to the Galatians* (London: Hodder & Stoughton, 1899; reprint, Grand Rapids: Baker, 1979).

5. F. F. Bruce, *The Epistle to the Galatians* (NIGTC; Grand Rapids: Eerdmans, 1982), 15.

6. R. N. Longenecker, *Galatians* (WBC 41; Dallas: Word, 1990).

7. S. Mitchell, "Population and Land in South Galatia," *ANRW* II.7.2 (1980): 1053–81.

8. H.-D. Betz, *Galatians: A Commentary on Paul's Letter to the Churches in Galatia* (Hermeneia; Philadelphia: Fortress, 1979), 8.

9. See R. Jewett, "The Agitators and the Galatian Congregation," *NTS* 17 (1970–1971): 198–212.

10. C. Spicq, *TLNT*, 3.500–506; Pindar, *Ol.* 14.5; cf. Philo, *Migration* 31.

11. J. D. G. Dunn, *The Theology of Paul's Letter to the Galatians* (NTT; Cambridge: Cambridge Univ. Press, 1993) 65.

12. Judith 9:3–4; Num. 25:6–13; Sir. 45:23–24; 1 Macc. 2:54; Sir. 48:2; 1 Macc. 2:58; 1 Macc. 2:15–28.

13. Paul's new life and career have been intensively studied in recent times. See M. Hengel and Anna Maria Schwemer, *Paul Between Damascus and Antioch* (Louisville: John Knox/Westminster, 1997); *The Road from Damascus*, ed. R. N. Longenecker (Grand Rapids: Eerdmans, 1997).

14. See D. F. Graf, "Aretas," *ABD*, 1.373–76.

15. The options are listed in R. P. Martin, *2 Corinthians* (WBC 40: Waco, Tex.: Word, 1986), ad loc.

16. See also the apocryphal *Gospel of the Hebrews* and the gnostic *Gospel of Thomas* 12.

17. See Acts 12:17; 15:13ff.; 21:18ff.

18. These verses and the picture of James in both Jerusalem Christianity and at Antioch are surveyed, along with the developing trajectory that traces the part he played in Jewish-Christian relations and later in gnostic circles, in R. P. Martin, *James* (WBC 48; Waco, Tex.: Word, 1988), Introduction.

19. For a more detailed introduction of Titus, see C. K. Barrett, "Titus" in *Neotestamentica et Semitica*, eds. E. Ellis and M. Wilcox (Edinburgh: T. & T. Clark, 1969), 1–14.

20. In 2 Cor. 2:13; 7:6, 13–15; 8:6, 23; also his letter to Titus.

21. Colin G. Kruse, *Paul, the Law, and Justification* (Peabody, Mass.: Hendrickson, 1996), 59.

22. V. C. Pfitzner, *Paul and the Agon Motif* (Leiden: Brill, 1967).

23. See A. A. Rupprecht, "Slave, Slavery," *DPL*, 881–82; S. S. Bartchy, "Slave, Slavery," *DLNT*, 1098–1102.

24. See C. W. Keyes, "The Greek Letter of Introduction," *AJP* 56 (1935): 28–44.

25. See A. W. F. Blunt, *The Epistle of Paul to the Galatians* (Oxford: Clarendon, 1960), 75 for a different explanation.

26. Cf. *Clem Hom.*18:14, where the patriarchs are called *styloi*. For more detailed explanation of this word, see Ulrich Wilckens, "στύλος," *TDNT*, 7.732–36.

27. See E. de Witt Burton, *Galatians* (ICC; Edinburgh: T. & T. Clark, 1980), 95–96.

28. D. Georgi, *Remembering the Poor* (ET, Nashville: Abingdon, 1992), 40.

29. Acts 11:27–28; see also Josephus, *Ant.* 20.2.5 §§51–53; 20.5.2 §101.

30. Ibid., 43–48.

31. F. F. Bruce, *Paul, Apostle of the Heart Set Free* (Grand Rapids: Eerdmans, 1977), 176.

32. See Acts 12:17; 15:13. In later church tradition, James is known as the bishop of the Jerusalem church (Eusebius, *Eccl. Hist.* 2.1). See also comments on 1:18.

33. Louw and Nida, eds., *Greek-English Lexicon of the New Testament* (New York: United Bible Societies, 1989), 1:435.

34. Josephus, *J.W.* 2.17.10 §454.

35. Burton, *Galatians*, 119.

36. Cf. Rom. 7:1–4, where Paul uses the death of one's spouse to illustrate the breaking off from the law when one is in Christ. See also Burton, *Galatians*, 132.

37. G. Milligan, *Selections from the Greek Papyri*, #14.

38. See *New Documents Illustrating Early Christianity*, vol. 8, *A Review of the Greek Inscription and Papyri*, ed. S. R. Llewelyn (Grand Rapids: Eerdmans, 1998), 23, 62, 64.

39. See "The Greek Tragedy," in *The Oxford Companion to Classical Civilization*, ed. S. Horn-

blower and A. Spawforth (Oxford: Oxford Univ. Press, 1998), 733–39, esp. 736.

40. *Jub. 23:10* describes Abraham as a model Jew, "perfect in all his actions with the Lord." As Dunn (*The Theology of Paul's Letter to the Galatians*, 81) remarks, he is important in Paul's response because he was in effect "the first proselyte and type of true conversion"; Dunn shows this by appealing to Philo, *Abraham* 60–88; Josephus, *Ant.* 1.7.1 §155; *Apoc. Abr.* 1–8. See too Nancy L. Calvert, "Abraham," *DPL*, 1–9.

41. MM, s.v.

42. O. Murray, "Life and Society in Classical Greece," in *Greece and the Hellenistic World*, ed. J. Boardman et al. (Oxford: OUP, 1991 ed.), 249 therefore comments: "This is one important reason for the instability of the Athenian family."

43. Gal. 3:19–20; see Acts 7:38, 53; Heb. 2:2, based on Deut. 33:2.

44. Str-B, 3.553.

45. Morris, *Galatians*, 110.

46. Philo, *Moses* 2.166; *Dreams* 143.

47. OCCC, 245.

48. Xenophon, *Mem.* 2.2.6.

49. See *b. Ber.* 13b for the Jewish prayer, where the male worshiper thanks God he was not made a woman, a slave, or a Gentile.

50. Hermes (in Greek vase motifs) is often portrayed as winged and shod (as befits a messenger).

51. See the evidence, mainly Stoic, in A. J. Malherbe, *Moral Exhortation: A Greco-Roman Sourcebook* (Philadelphia: Westminster, 1986); see also W. A. Strange, *Children in the Early Church* (Carlisle, Eng.: Paternoster, 1996), which covers a wider field.

52. C. K. Barrett's essay, "The Allegory of Abraham, Sarah and Hagar in the Argument of Galatians," in *Essays on Paul* (London: SPCK, 1982), 118–32, has a good discussion. See also A. C. Perriman, "The Rhetorical Strategy of Galatians 4:21–5:1," *EvQ* 65 (1993): 27–42; P. Borgen, "Some Hebrew and Pagan Features in Philo's and Paul's Interpretation of Hagar and Ishmael," in *The New Testament and Hellenistic Judaism*, eds. P. Borgen and S. Giversen (Peabody, Mass.: Hendrickson, 1997), 151–64.

53. Most notably by Perriman, "Rhetorical Strategy," 27–42.

54. See Longenecker, *Galatians*, 200–206.

55. Frank J. Matera points out that chs. 5–6 are the climax of Paul's deliberative argument aimed at persuading the Galatians not to be circumcised. Paul employs the paraenesis of these chapters to support his argument and bring it to its culmination. See "The Culmination of Paul's Argument to the Galatians: Gal. 5:1–6:17," *JSNT* 32 (1988): 79–91.

56. See Bruce, *Galatians*, 230–31; Longenecker, *Galatians*, 227; Kruse, *Paul*, 102, n. 121; e.g., *b. Sanh.* 81a; *Midr. Tehillim* 15.7; Sir. 7:8; *4 Macc.* 5:20–21.

57. Cf. Josephus, *Ant.* 20.2.4 §§44–48.

58. Possibly during his conversion experience on his way to Damascus; see Seyoon Kim, *The Origin of Paul's Gospel* (Grand Rapids: Eerdmans, 1982), for a full discussion about the connection between Paul's gospel and his conversion experience.

59. Acts 20:24; 1 Cor. 9:24–27; Gal. 2:2; Phil. 3:14; cf. 2 Tim. 4:7.

60. See Carl E. De Vries, "Paul's 'Cutting' Remarks About a Race: Galatians 5:1–12," in *Current Issues in Biblical and Patristic Interpretation: Studies in Honor of M. C. Tenney*, ed. G. F. Hawthorne (Grand Rapids: Eerdmans, 1975), 115–20; Rogers & Rogers, *New Linguistic and Exegetical Key to the Greek New Testament* (Grand Rapids: Zondervan, 1998), 430.

61. See E. N. Gardiner, *Greek Athletic Sports and Festivals* (Oxford: Clarendon, 1955), 146.

62. Longenecker, *Galatians*, 230.

63. See *The Oxford History of Greece and the Hellenistic World* and *The Oxford History of the Roman World*, 2 vols., eds. J. Boardman, J. Griffin, and O. Murray (Oxford: Oxford Univ. Press, 1986).

64. 1 Cor. 2:1–5; cf. 2 Cor. 10:10; 1 Thess. 1:5.

65. Cf. 1 Cor. 5:6–8; later *1 Clem.* 5:6; Ignatius, *Mag.* 10.2; and Justin, *Dial.* 14.2.3.

66. See D. C. Arichea Jr. and Eugene A. Nida, *A Translator's Handbook on Paul's Letter to the Galatians* (London: UBC, 1976), 127.

67. Cf. Josh. 23:13 LXX; Ps. 69:22; 141:9; 1 Macc. 5:4.

68. Cf. Judith 5:20; Sir. 7:6; 27:23. See also Michael B. Thompson, "Stumbling Block," *DPL*, 918–19.

69. Deut. 21:22–23; 1 Cor. 1:23; Gal. 3:13.

70. Ramsay, *Galatians*, 437–39; Arichea and Nida, *Galatians*, 129–30.

71. Lightfoot, *Galatians*, 207; Burton, *Galatians*, 289–90; Bruce, *Galatians*, 238; Longenecker, *Galatians*, 234; R. A. Cole, *Galatians* (TNTC; Grand Rapids: Eerdmans, 1989 rev. ed.), 201–2; Dunn, *Galatians*, 1.

72. Gal. 2:20; Phil. 3:4; Gen. 2:21; 40:19; Ex. 21:28; 33:31.

73. F. T. Gench, "Galatians 5:1, 13–25," *Interp* 46 (1992): 294. For a more detailed discussion of *sarx* in the New Testament, see R. Jewett,

Paul's Anthropological Terms (Leiden: Brill, 1971).

74. See Matt. 22:35–40 (cf. 7:12); Mark 12:28–31; Luke 6:27–38; John 13:34–35. See also J. Nissen, "The Distinctive Character of the New Testament Love Command in Relation to Hellenistic Judaism," in *The New Testament and Hellenistic Judaism*, eds. Borgen and Giversen, 123–50.

75. See Rom. 13:8; 1 Cor. 8:1b; 13:13; Gal. 5:14; Col. 3:14; 1 Tim. 1:5.

76. See James 2:8; 1 Peter 4:8; 1 John 3:11, 23; 2 John 5.

77. Arichea and Nida, *Galatians*, 132.

78. Ramsay, *Galatians*, 447. See also John Matthews, "Roman Life and Society," *OHRW*, 380–87.

79. W. D. Davies, *Paul and Rabbinic Judaism* (Philadelphia: Fortress, 1980). A more recent discussion is in R. J. Erickson, "Flesh" in *DPL*, 303–6.

80. E.g., at Qumran and *T. Jud.* 19:4; *T. Zeb.* 9:7.

81. See S. McKnight, "Galatians," *NIVAC* (Grand Rapids: Zondervan, 1995), 264; cf. *T. Ash.* 1:6.

82. Cf. Gench, "Galatians," 294–95.

83. See P. F. Esler, "Group Boundaries and Intergroup Conflict in Galatians: A New Reading of Galatians 5:13–6:10," in *Ethnicity and the Bible*, ed. M. Brett (Leiden: Brill, 1996), 215–40; cf. C. D. Stanley, "'Neither Jew Nor Greek,': Ethnic Conflict in Graeco-Roman Society," *JSNT* 64 (1996):101–24.

84. Longenecker, *Galatians*, 271.

85. Bruce, *Galatians*, 261; Dunn, *Galatians*, 114; Kruse, *Paul*, 106.

86. Xenophon, *Mem.* 3.13.6.

87. David W. Kuck, "'Each Will Bear His Own Burden': Paul's Creative Use of an Apocalyptic Motif," *NTS* 40 (1994): 295–97; see also Betz, *Galatians*, 303–4.

88. Arichea and Nida, *Galatians*, 150.

89. Ramsay, *Galatians*, 459.

90. L. W. Hurtado, "The Jerusalem Collection and the Book of Galatians," *JSNT* 5 (1979): 53; Ramsay, 460–61.

91. The metaphor of sowing and reaping for conduct and its results is a frequent one, e.g., Job 4:8; Prov. 22:8; Hos. 8:7; 10:12; Luke 19:21; 2 Cor. 9:6; Plato, *Phaedr.* 260c; Sir. 7:3; Philo, *Confusion* 21.7. See also J. L. North, "Sowing and Reaping (Gal. 6:7b): More Examples of a Classical Maxim," *JTS* 43 (1992): 523–27, esp. 526; Frank Stagg, "Galatians 6:7–10," *RevExp* 88 (1991): 247–51.

92. Betz, *Galatians*, 313. See also J. A. D. Weima, "Gal. 6:11–18: A Hermeneutical Key to the Galatian Letter," *CTJ* 28 (1993): 90–107.

93. Ramsay, *Galatians*, 466.

94. Josephus, *J.W.* 4.5–7 §§ 305–437 provides some information about the military actions of the Zealots before the Fall of Jerusalem; also R. Jewett, "Agitators," 205.

95. Cicero, *Pro Rabirio* 16.

96. See M. Hengel, *Crucifixion in the Ancient World and the Folly of the Message of the Cross* (Philadelphia: Fortress, 1977); see also Bruce, *Galatians*, 271.

97. Lightfoot, *Galatians*, 225; Longenecker, *Galatians*, 299; Arichea and Nida, *Galatians*, 159.

98. Bruce, *Galatians*, 361; Luther, *Galatians* (Wheaton, Ill.: Crossway, 1998 ed.), 303.

99. Josephus, *J.W.* 1.10.2 §197; W. Klassen, "Galatians 6:17," *ExpTim* 81 (1970): 378.

100. Lightfoot, *Galatians*, 226; Arichea and Nida, *Galatians*, 160.

Sidebar and Chart Notes

A-1. For more information about Antioch, see J. McRay, "Antioch on the Orontes," *DPL*, 23–25.

A-2. See J. Griffin, "Introduction," in *The Roman World*, eds. J. Boardman, J. Griffin and O. Murray (*OHCW*; Oxford: Oxford Univ. Press, 1997), 4.

A-3. Diogenes Laertius 6.102.

A-4. 1 Cor. 4:14–16; 2 Cor. 6:13; 12:15; Phil. 2:22; 1 Thess. 2:7–8.

A-5. See P. Beasley-Murray, "Pastor, Paul as," *DPL*, 654–58; M. J. Wilkins, "Pastoral Theology," *DLNT*, 876–82.

CREDITS FOR PHOTOS AND MAPS

ALSO AVAILABLE

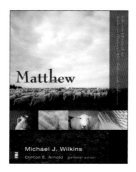

Matthew

Michael J. Wilkins
Clinton E. Arnold general editor

Mark

David E. Garland
Clinton E. Arnold general editor

Luke

Mark L. Strauss
Clinton E. Arnold general editor

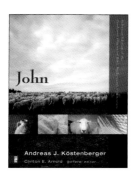

John

Andreas J. Köstenberger
Clinton E. Arnold general editor

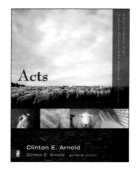

Acts

Clinton E. Arnold
Clinton E. Arnold general editor

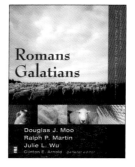

Romans
Galatians

Douglas J. Moo
Ralph P. Martin
Julie L. Wu
Clinton E. Arnold general editor

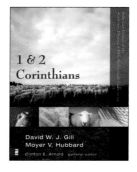

1 & 2
Corinthians

David W. J. Gill
Moyer V. Hubbard
Clinton E. Arnold general editor

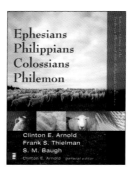

Ephesians
Philippians
Colossians
Philemon

Clinton E. Arnold
Frank S. Thielman
S. M. Baugh
Clinton E. Arnold general editor

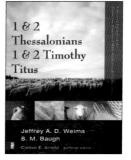

1 & 2
Thessalonians
1 & 2 Timothy
Titus

Jeffrey A. D. Weima
S. M. Baugh
Clinton E. Arnold general editor

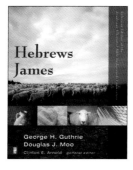

Hebrews
James

George H. Guthrie
Douglas J. Moo
Clinton E. Arnold general editor

1 & 2 Peter
1, 2, & 3 John
Jude

Peter H. Davids
Douglas J. Moo
Robert W. Yarbrough
Clinton E. Arnold general editor

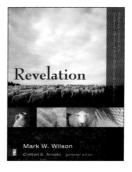

Revelation

Mark W. Wilson
Clinton E. Arnold general editor

We want to hear from you. Please send your comments about this book to us in care of zreview@zondervan.com. Thank you.

ZONDERVAN.com/
AUTHORTRACKER
follow your favorite authors